CBT
SUPERVISION

Praise for the Book

'This terrific book is comprehensive, evidence-based, and practical. Geared toward both supervisors and supervisees, it provides a number of important learning exercises to encourage active reflection. The case studies help the reader transfer what they are learning to real-life situations. I highly recommend this book to trainees, therapists who need to improve their skills in self-reflection, and to supervisors.'

Judith S. Beck, PhD, President, Beck Institute for Cognitive Behavior Therapy; Clinical Associate Professor of Psychology in Psychiatry, University of Pennsylvania

'Ever wanted some well-organised supervision for your supervision? Would you welcome some guidance in your role as a supervisee? Then this exceptionally clear and systematic book is for you! What's more, it tackles the core tasks of CBT supervision from a well-developed understanding of the nature of CBT, continuing the reflexive tradition. For example, the reader is expected to reflect carefully on the central questions raised, while the realistic and engaging case studies are used to pose dilemmas and prompt procedural thinking. Feedback is effectively provided in the form of the authors' responses to the dilemmas.

This is a highly practical "nuts and bolts" guide to CBT supervision, optimistic and empowering. Unlike many competitors, *CBT Supervision* keeps theory and research details to an absolute minimum, sticking firmly to established supervision practices and sensible recommendations (for both supervisors and supervisees), based on the authors' extensive supervisory experience. It is written with exceptional clarity and systematically covers all the bases. In sum, this is a highly informative, soundly based, exceptionally practical guide to CBT supervision. It is all the more welcome given the pressing need to tackle CBT supervision in a professional manner.'

Derek Milne, PhD, retired Director of the Newcastle University Doctorate in Clinical Psychology and author of Evidence-Based Clinical Supervision

'Corrie and Lane's *CBT Supervision* is a well-researched, well-organized, thorough, practical workbook that will be a valuable resource for clinical CBT supervisors at all levels of experience. This volume's supervisory case studies, chapter-by-chapter learning activities, and "tips for supervisees" make this volume ideal for a graduate seminar in learning to become a CBT supervisor. More experienced supervisors will benefit greatly from the authors' wise suggestions in handling challenges and dilemmas in supervision, and from their emphasis on supervisor self-reflection, self-care, and lifelong professional and personal growth. *CBT Supervision* is at once a great asset to the field.'

Cory F. Newman, PhD, Director, Center for Cognitive Therapy and Professor of Psychology in Psychiatry, University of Pennsylvania

'The authors have produced something new, fresh and original. For the first time a book that focuses on how to effectively practise cognitive behavioural supervision. This text is an essential practice and professional development aid for both new and experienced cognitive behavioural supervisors. Each chapter takes the reader through how to prepare, undertake, refine and enhance their supervision, illustrated with examples and reflective activities – is there any other CBT supervision book that makes understandable the complexity of supervision? This book won't just be on my book shelf it will be on my desk as I will be turning to it time and time again as a supervisor of clinicians and other supervisors and as academic responsible for the delivery of supervision workshops.'

Michael Townend, PhD, Reader in CBT, University of Derby

CBT
Sarah Corrie
David A Lane
SUPERVISION

Los Angeles | London | New Delhi
Singapore | Washington DC

Los Angeles | London | New Delhi
Singapore | Washington DC

SAGE Publications Ltd
1 Oliver's Yard
55 City Road
London EC1Y 1SP

SAGE Publications Inc.
2455 Teller Road
Thousand Oaks, California 91320

SAGE Publications India Pvt Ltd
B 1/I 1 Mohan Cooperative Industrial Area
Mathura Road
New Delhi 110 044

SAGE Publications Asia-Pacific Pte Ltd
3 Church Street
#10-04 Samsung Hub
Singapore 049483

Editor: Susannah Trefgarne
Assistant editor: Laura Walmsley
Production editor: Rachel Burrows
Copyeditor: Sarah Bury
Proofreader: Derek Markham
Indexer: David Rudeforth
Marketing manager: Camille Richmond
Typeset by: C&M Digitals (P) Ltd, Chennai, India
Printed and bound by:
CPI Group (UK) Ltd, Croydon, CR0 4YY

MIX
Paper from
responsible sources
FSC
www.fsc.org   FSC® C013604

© Sarah Corrie and David A. Lane 2015

First published 2015

Apart from any fair dealing for the purposes of
research or private study, or criticism or review, as
permitted under the Copyright, Designs and Patents
Act, 1988, this publication may be reproduced,
stored or transmitted in any form, or by any means,
only with the prior permission in writing of the
publishers, or in the case of reprographic
reproduction, in accordance with the terms of
licences issued by the Copyright Licensing Agency.
Enquiries concerning reproduction outside those
terms should be sent to the publishers.

Library of Congress Control Number: 2014948595

British Library Cataloguing in Publication data

A catalogue record for this book is available from the
British Library

ISBN 978-1-4462-6638-0
ISBN 978-1-4462-6639-7 (pbk)

At SAGE we take sustainability seriously. Most of our products are printed in the UK using FSC papers and boards.
When we print overseas we ensure sustainable papers are used as measured by the Egmont grading system.
We undertake an annual audit to monitor our sustainability.

Contents

List of Learning Activities, Figures and Tables

Learning Activities

Figures

Tables

About the Authors

Professor Sarah Corrie is a Consultant Clinical Psychologist, Chartered Psychologist and Visiting Professor at Middlesex University. She received her undergraduate degree in Psychology and Counselling Psychology from the University of Surrey. Recipient of the Professors Newstead and Gale Prize in recognition of 'an exceptionally high standard of attainment in examination and course work', she went on to obtain her doctorate in clinical psychology with Canterbury Christchurch College and completed her post-qualification training in cognitive-behavioural therapy at the University of Oxford.

Among her roles for The Central London CBT Centre, Sarah is Programme Director of the Postgraduate Diploma & MSc in Cognitive Behavioural Psychotherapy offered by Central and North West London NHS Foundation Trust in conjunction with Royal Holloway, University of London; Programme Director of the Certificate in CBT Skills and joint Programme Director of the Post-Qualification Certificate in CBT Supervision. She has extensive experience in supervising, training and lecturing practitioners in the fields of psychology, psychiatry and counselling, and is an accredited therapist, supervisor and trainer with the British Association for Behavioural & Cognitive Psychotherapies (BABCP).

Sarah was Chair of the British Psychological Society's Special Group in Coaching Psychology from 2012 to 2014, is a faculty member of the Professional Development Foundation, Membership Officer for the International Association for Professional Practice Doctorates and a member of the Course Accreditation Committee of the BABCP.

Professor David Lane has been providing services within CBT since the early 1970s. He established the first behaviour support service operating in the UK to support children and schools in 1975 for the Schools Psychological Service of the Inner London Education Authority (ILEA). Prior to this he worked directly within the school system. As part of this, programme supervision was offered to both staff at the service and to other professionals. David worked with Vic Meyer and Ted Chesser at Middlesex Hospital under their supervision for work with adults to expand his understanding of the field. He provided training in case formulation to students on the Middlesex Programme for more than 20 years. He has acted as a supervisor for almost 40 years.

David was part of the group that created Counselling Psychology within the British Psychological Society and served on the governing committee of the Association for Behavioural Approaches with Children. He has been a member of BABCP for more than 30 years. He was Chair of the British Psychological Society Register of Psychologists Specialising in Psychotherapy, and has served on committees of the British Psychological Society (BPS), the Chartered Institute of Personnel and Development (CIPD) and European Mentoring and Coaching Council (EMCC). He convened the Psychotherapy Group of the European Federation of Psychologists Associations.

His contributions to counselling psychology led to the senior award of the BPS for 'Outstanding Scientific Contribution'. In 2009 he was honoured by the British Psychological Society for 'Distinguished Contribution to Professional Psychology'.

Sarah and David's previous co-authored publications include: *The Modern Scientist-Practitioner: A Guide to Practice in Psychology* (Routledge); *Constructing Stories, Telling Tales: A Guide to Formulation in Applied Psychology* (Karnac), and *Making Successful Decisions in Counselling and Psychotherapy: A Practical Guide* (Open University Press).

Acknowledgements

There are a number of people who have contributed to the development of this book and whose interest, encouragement and support we wish to acknowledge.

First, we would like to thank Kate Wharton, Susannah Trefgarne and Laura Walmsley, our editorial team at Sage, who have been such a solid source of support throughout the process. We are grateful to them for their guidance on the many issues encountered along the way. Our thanks also to Rachel Burrows, her colleagues in the production team, and everyone at Sage who has worked with us to bring this project to completion.

Special thanks to Rita Woo for providing the material for the 'Tips for Supervisees' sections of each chapter, as well as our primary readers Anna-Maria Smit and Simon Dupont. All three provided feedback on the fledgling chapters and remained steadfast and wise guides as the manuscript gradually took shape. We are grateful also to Derek Farrell for reviewing the manuscript and for his interest in and enthusiasm for the project.

There are a number of people and organizations who have generously given permission for us to draw upon, and in certain cases reproduce, material. We wish to acknowledge and thank the following: James Bennett-Levy for his interest in the project and for access to his materials and forthcoming publications; the British Association for Behavioural & Cognitive Psychotherapies for permission to reproduce the 'Duties as a Member of BABCP' from the Standards of Conduct, Performance and Ethics; Kenneth Gordon and Cambridge University Press for permission to reproduce the 'Ten Steps for Supervision', and Peter Hawkins for permission to reproduce the 'Helping Roles' table. We thank Christine Padesky for permission to reproduce the Supervision Options Grid, Anthony Roth and Stephen Pilling for permission to reproduce the outline model of the CBT Competence Framework, and Noreen Tehrani for permission to use and adapt her work on 'Daily Rituals to Support Self-Care'.

Beyond those directly connected with this project, we are deeply grateful to all those who, over the years, have shaped our understanding of both cognitive-behavioural therapy and supervision. A particular mention goes to the many supervisors with whom we have had the good fortune to work and from whom we have learned so much. Our gratitude also goes to our colleagues at the Professional Development Foundation, Middlesex

University, and our students and clients who have influenced our thinking in profound ways.

Sarah Corrie wishes to acknowledge the talented team of supervisors, trainers and students at The Central London CBT Centre, who have provided the inspiration for many of the ideas presented in this book. It has been a privilege to work with all those who have chosen to study with us over the years and who courageously share their practice in an attempt to master this complex activity called CBT. Particular thanks go to Michael Worrell for permission to reproduce the Supervisor Evaluation Scale, for our many discussions about supervision over a ten-year period, and in conversation with whom the idea of writing this book was born. In developing my knowledge and skills as a supervisor and trainer, special thanks must also go to Don Baucom, whose approach to training others has been an inspiration.

David Lane wishes to acknowledge colleagues at University College Hospital, particularly the late Ted Chesser and Vic Meyer for their inspiration and Mary Watts and Michael Bruch. Colleagues at the Islington Educational Guidance Centre and other Behaviour Support Teams throughout the UK have supported him through their active participation as he explored various approaches to supervision.

Finally, special thanks go to Peter Hoy for proof-reading the manuscript and to Ian Lacey for his encouragement, critique and unfailing belief in the project and its authors.

Confidentiality

The case scenarios and case material included in this book have been inspired by dilemmas encountered in the context of either providing CBT supervision or providing consultation to those who are providing supervision. However, care has been taken to ensure anonymity and the supervisors and therapists in all of the case scenarios provided are fictitious.

Introduction

What makes an effective supervisor? What is good CBT supervision? How can CBT supervisors best facilitate the development of those they supervise, and how can qualified CBT therapists learn to become good CBT supervisors? These are some of the questions we seek to address in this book.

In our work as CBT trainers, one of the first questions we ask those who approach us for supervision is not only what they are seeking from us, but also what they believe makes a good CBT supervisor. Working with many practitioners over many years, we have been struck by the similarities in the responses received, which express a belief that a CBT supervisor will ideally:

1. Convey human qualities of relating, such as warmth, curiosity and appropriate humour, that are likely to enhance a sense of safety and trust.
2. Demonstrate a genuine interest in the clinical work of the supervisee.
3. Communicate an authentic interest in, and commitment to, the development of those they supervise.
4. Be enthusiastic about CBT and how this can facilitate change in people's lives.
5. Be a solid, reliable and consistent presence during the supervisee's learning experience, who both supports and challenges in order to foster therapist development.

6. Be appropriately transparent in motivation for the use of specific interventions.
7. Provide regular feedback.
8. Possess subject matter expertise, and make explicit use of the knowledge- and evidence-bases of CBT in the service of supervisee development.
9. Foster self-reflection.
10. Be an effective trainer.

Although there may be other criteria you would include, this confection of ideal qualities highlights two critically important points about CBT supervision: namely, that it is a complex undertaking characterized by multiple roles and activities, and that providing consistently high-quality CBT supervision is likely to be a challenge!

What do we know about CBT supervision?

Supervision is widely regarded as playing a vital role in the quality control of psychotherapies, referring to, '...a formal, independent process of reflection and review which enables practitioners to increase individual self-awareness, develop their competence and critique their work' (Lane and Corrie, 2006: 192).

Within CBT, supervision is deemed to be an essential component of therapist development and, more broadly, has been described as the 'signature pedagogy' of the mental health professions (Barnett et al., 2007). However, while elevated to the heart of effective and ethical practice, our actual knowledge of what represents 'optimal' CBT supervision, the range of competences and skills needed to supervise effectively and how to adapt the style and approach of supervision to meet the needs of individual supervisees remains limited. There is currently little substantive guidance on what competent CBT supervision entails and how best to deliver CBT supervision, and a paucity of information on how supervisors should go about developing the prerequisite knowledge and skills to become effective in this domain of professional practice.

This lack of clear guidance is not specific to CBT. Reviewing the supervision literature as a whole, Bernard and Goodyear (2014) note that while there is a well-established body of knowledge concerning the development of those receiving supervision, far less attention has been given to the development of those providing it. The professional practice literature has not kept pace with the widespread official endorsement of supervision as a primary vehicle for therapist development and, as argued by Milne and James (2002), the field of CBT now needs to address this.

Developing a thorough understanding of the requisite competences, knowledge and skills underpinning CBT supervision is critically important for a variety of reasons. These include:

1. As the lead professional body for the practice and theory of CBT in the UK, the British Association for Behavioural & Cognitive Psychotherapies (BABCP) will only accredit therapists who can demonstrate that they receive regular CBT-focused supervision.

2. The increasingly diverse clinical populations for whom CBT is recommended, as well as the extension of cognitive and behavioural principles into different but related areas of professional activity (for example, the emergent field of coaching psychology), has resulted in a proliferation of concepts, models, procedures and techniques that practitioners must learn to navigate effectively. High-quality CBT supervision across this expanding body of knowledge is critical to ensuring that practitioners can remain abreast of the knowledge and skills they need to offer their clients an optimal service.

3. The advent of the UK Government's initiative Improving Access to Psychological Therapies (IAPT; Department of Health, 2008) has resulted in closer scrutiny of the supervision arrangements that need to underpin the development of CBT competences. As a national initiative that aimed to support Primary Care Trusts in implementing National Institute for Health and Clinical Excellence (NICE) guidelines for people suffering from depression and anxiety disorders, IAPT has trained a new workforce of cognitive-behavioural therapists, all of whom require supervision to deliver CBT-focused interventions to offer patients a 'realistic and routine first-line treatment'. Central to the Government's mental health strategy set out in the White Paper, *No Health without Mental Health* (Department of Health, 2011), was completing the nationwide roll-out of IAPT with further investment to extend access to empirically-supported psychological therapies to children and young people, older people, and those with long-term physical or mental health conditions. Supervision has remained central to the governance of CBT in this context.

4. There is a growing recognition that professional 'survival' is tied to our commitment to remain informed and justify our practice (Guest, 2000). Increased public expectations of what psychological interventions can offer, coupled with a challenge to the traditional notion of the professional as the sole source of expert knowledge, has resulted in an increased emphasis on credentialing and state regulation of the psychological professions (Lane and Corrie, 2006). Supervision has a critical role to play in enabling practitioners to justify the services they deliver and reassuring the public that appropriate quality assurance mechanisms are in place.

5. One of the most significant contributions of CBT to the field of psychotherapy has been its allegiance to the scientist-practitioner model (see Lane and Corrie, 2006, for a contemporary interpretation of this) in which CBT research and practice have mutually shaped the development of knowledge and its translation into the clinical practice setting. The historical dearth of investigative interest in CBT supervision – in terms of theories and research that can support the systematic development of this area of professional practice – is at odds with the values

underpinning CBT itself and is unsustainable in a current professional climate that places a strong emphasis on empirically-supported interventions (Reiser and Milne, 2012).

These, among other, developments have led the competences and skills required to deliver CBT supervision to become an increasing focus of both clinical services and training providers. This has been evidenced by the development of a Supervision Competences Framework (Roth and Pilling, 2008a), as well as the option to pursue Supervisor Accreditation through the BABCP. However, there remains a lack of formal guidance on how supervisors can develop the required competences and a virtual absence of standardized methods of assessment for providing supervisors with accurate and meaningful feedback on their work. The gulf between what is expected and the knowledge that is available poses a significant challenge to those practitioners seeking to provide (or indeed receive) high-quality CBT supervision, as well as for services wishing to commission and organize effective CBT supervision for their clinical staff.

Who is this book for?

This book seeks to meet the needs of an increasing number of practitioners who are required to provide CBT supervision in a wide range of contexts, for therapists who are working with an increasingly diverse range of clients and clinical presentations. It is intended for those who, through choice or of necessity, find themselves providing CBT supervision and who wish to add to their armoury frameworks, models, tools and strategies to enhance their effectiveness.

Our primary aim is to meet the learning and development needs of CBT supervisors operating in 'real world' contexts where the evaluation of supervisee (and supervisor) competence may increasingly serve multiple and potentially conflicting agendas. We hope, therefore, that the book will be useful for a wide range of professional groups, including:

- Those starting out in their supervisory careers, who are trying to assist therapists in learning particular CBT approaches and who are in effect operating within an 'expert–apprentice' role.
- Experienced CBT practitioners offering supervision to other experienced clinicians who seek to refine their professional practice.
- Those who are working with colleagues as peer supervisors in dyad or team contexts.
- CBT supervisors who are increasingly asked to work with non-CBT practitioners and who are, therefore, having to function outside their comfort zone in order to present new perspectives on clients' needs.

This book is also intended for those in higher education settings who are providing substantive trainings or workshops on how to deliver CBT supervision and who want some guiding principles for the development of course materials. Finally, we have sought to give a voice to those receiving CBT supervision and who want to learn how to capitalize on the learning opportunities provided, as well as discover the criteria that will be guiding their supervisors' thinking and actions.

Consistent with our primary aim we do not attempt to provide an exhaustive review of the supervision or CBT literatures. Rather, we draw selectively on ideas that appear to have direct practical relevance in order to provide a means through which CBT supervisors can, independently, work towards honing their craft. We do, however, assume that readers will have a good working knowledge of the concepts, theories and techniques of cognitive and behavioural therapies. Believing that the field provides a sound basis for learning and development, we also assume that the principles and methods that underpin CBT are also relevant for CBT supervision. For this reason, we often draw parallels between the two activities and use cognitive and behavioural concepts to elucidate aspects of the supervisory process.

An overview of the book: Introducing the PURE Supervision Flower

A function of this book is helping you decide where you wish to direct your energy at this point in your supervisory career. Supervision, like therapy, is a complex, multifaceted intervention that defies simplistic categorizations and definitive formulae. There are multiple tasks that a supervisor undertakes and many ways in which the process can unfold – some intended, some unintended – as a function of the type of CBT being practised and the context in which supervision takes place. How, then, can a book such as this do justice to the multiple forms of CBT supervision that exist while equipping you with ideas and methods that you can readily 'import' into your practice without elaborate instruction or training?

Our response to this challenge has been to develop an organizing framework to help you navigate the different sections of this book and the individual chapters therein. We term this organizing framework the 'PURE Supervision Flower' which is illustrated in Figure 1.

The PURE Supervision Flower is not offered as a distinct model of CBT supervision. Rather, it is a visual heuristic for assisting supervisors (and those who train them) in identifying specific areas of skill that may need to be a focus of attention or refinement.

We have chosen the concept of the flower as a basis for our heuristic as this is commonplace in CBT as a means of illustrating maladaptive ('vicious flower') and adaptive ('virtuous flower') maintenance cycles and so is likely to be familiar to all CBT practitioners.

Figure 1 illustrates that the PURE Supervision Flower has 12 petals. Each 'petal' is concerned with an area of practice that, in our experience,

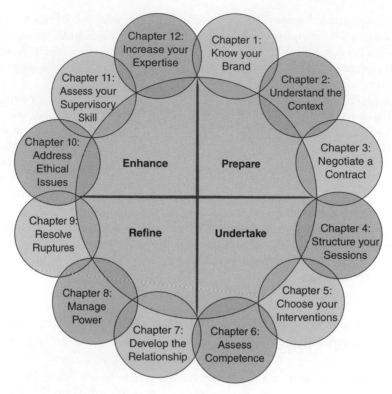

Figure 1   The PURE Supervision Flower

tends to emerge as a source of reflection, dilemma or concern, and for which CBT supervisors typically seek guidance and support. Thus, each 'petal' denotes a specific domain of activity which the CBT supervisor needs to master in order to provide an optimal learning experience. These 12 domains of activity can be grouped into four classes of activity, indicated by the acronym 'PURE':

Prepare (for CBT supervision: Part I, Chapters 1–3)

Undertake (CBT supervision: Part II, Chapters 4–6)

Refine (your CBT supervision: Part III, Chapters 7–9)

Enhance (your approach to CBT supervision: Part IV, Chapters 10–12)

The content of the book is organized around the PURE Supervision Flower as follows:

Part I focuses on preparing for supervision (the Prepare component of the PURE Supervision Flower) in which we identify what needs to be in place in order to establish an appropriate, effective and ethical basis for

CBT supervision. Part I comprises three chapters that enable you to identify and work with those factors that provide the foundations of any supervision arrangement.

Chapter 1 enables you to reflect on the personal and professional values that shape your beliefs about, and approach to, supervision. CBT is
now widely regarded as comprising a broad range of scientifically
grounded approaches, rather than a single school, theory or method. There
are ongoing debates and developments within the family of CBT
approaches, which have implications for the practice of CBT supervision
as both practitioners and supervisors need to 'situate' themselves within
the range of approaches available. This chapter will help you reflect upon
this diversity, consider where you locate yourself within this conceptual
landscape and identify some of the factors that have shaped your position.

Having established the values that underpin your approach, **Chapter 2**
supports you in thinking about the context in which supervision is provided. CBT supervision is provided in a range of settings that span primary
care, secondary mental health care and specialist health care settings as
well as a wide range of private and public sector services. Additionally,
supervision is increasingly organizationally mandated and embedded, and
supports methods of service delivery that are themselves evolving. This
chapter helps you develop a clearer understanding of the current and
emerging contexts in which CBT supervision is delivered, and offers ideas
on how best to manage the opportunities and pressures to which these
contexts can give rise.

Drawing on the material of chapters 1 and 2, **Chapter 3** examines how
to develop a supervision contract for the work that is to take place. The
importance of establishing appropriate objectives, selecting an appropriate
supervision 'methodology' and clarifying the methods of evaluating practice
to be used are discussed. We also identify some of the common pitfalls in the
contracting phase of supervision and offer guidance on how to avoid them.

Part II examines the delivery of CBT supervision (the Undertake component of the PURE Supervision Flower). In Part II, we examine the specific
content and tasks of CBT supervision. This includes how a supervisor's
values and theory of supervision are expressed in what is actually delivered.
Part II comprises three chapters that enable you to identify and work with
those factors that facilitate the development of those whom you supervise.

In **Chapter 4** we take forward the frequently endorsed position that
the practice of CBT supervision should in many respects mirror the practice of CBT itself. We focus on how CBT supervisors can usefully structure
their sessions and develop a supervisory style which is an expression of the
CBT approach employed.

Chapter 5 considers the range of possible supervisory interventions
that can be drawn upon to provide effective CBT supervision and that
attend to the development needs of supervisees. A clear implication of the
notion that good CBT supervision should mirror the practice of CBT itself

(whichever version of CBT is being embraced) is that a broad range of supervisory methods should be used, taking into account the strengths and needs, developmental level and learning style of the supervisee. We consider what some of these methods might be in the context of an increasing focus on supervision as a vehicle for the development of specific competences.

Chapter 6 examines the central issue of how to assess supervisee competence and deliver feedback based on your evaluations. We offer some ways of undertaking this often challenging task, identify common obstacles to the effective delivery of feedback and provide recommendations on how to hone your approach.

Focusing on the content of supervision must be balanced with managing the process of supervision. Supervisors typically have to act as 'gate keepers' as well as educators and mentors and, as such, are required to meet the needs of multiple stakeholders. This introduces a 'policing' function that can create tensions in the supervisory relationship.

Part III focuses on managing the supervision process (the Refine component of the PURE Supervision Flower) where we consider some of the process issues that can arise and which need addressing to ensure that supervision remains a productive learning environment. Part III comprises three chapters as follows:

In **Chapter 7**, we consider the role of the supervisory relationship in facilitating therapist development. We examine ways in which the relationship can be conceptualized in order to better balance the managerial, educational and mentoring functions of supervision, and provide recommendations on how to refine your relationship building in this context.

Chapter 8 explores the important issue of power in supervision, which unfolds in complex ways as our work is applied to increasingly diverse populations. We suggest that cognitive-behavioural supervisors need to be aware of the relevance of power in the practice of CBT and possess competence in working with power issues as they arise in supervision.

Chapter 9 explores some of the more potentially uncomfortable aspects of CBT supervision – namely, when the process does not go as planned. Like CBT itself, various 'resistances' to the supervisor's interventions, and ruptures occurring within the working alliance, are common. This chapter examines a range of factors that have the potential to undermine the supervisory process and how you might approach addressing these.

Finally, in **Part IV** the book explores how you can hone your competence as a CBT supervisor (the Enhance component of the PURE Supervision Flower) in the context of the complex issues that can arise. In the final three chapters, we consider ethical issues and also explore what makes a good supervisor. Additionally, we provide a means through which you can assess your own level of competence and compile a professional development plan for enhancing knowledge and skill in key areas.

Chapter 10 extends the topics covered in Chapters 8 and 9 to examine some of the ethical challenges that can occur. Supervision, like therapy, always exists within an ethical and legal context and cognitive-behavioural supervisors need to develop skills in the identification and resolution of potentially complex dilemmas. We provide three approaches to considering and resolving such dilemmas: thinking about ethics within the context of an external framework, developing your own ethical maturity and developing a shared ethical understanding with supervisees as issues arise in supervision.

Chapter 11 introduces current thinking about the supervisor competences that are central to effective CBT supervision. Building on ideas discussed in previous sections, this chapter examines a recent supervision competence framework and enables supervisors to undertake a personal audit of their supervisory strengths and needs. This chapter will help you decide how to assess your own competence and any areas you may need to develop.

Finally, in **Chapter 12**, we look at how you can increase your expertise as a CBT supervisor in the longer term. Specifically, we consider pathways for continued professional development as well as the critical importance of self-care in a world of professional practice that is rapidly changing and increasingly uncertain.

Learning features

Because the aim is to retain a strong, practical focus, all theoretical material is grounded in a range of learning activities. In particular, the book capitalizes on two principal types of learning activity: (1) tools to analyse your practice and (2) questions, offered as reflective 'prompts', to engage you in personalizing the content to your own practice.

An additional learning feature is the inclusion of case material. This takes the form of specific supervision dilemmas in which you, the reader, are asked to act as 'supervisory consultant' to two CBT supervisors – Patrick and Nina. These supervisors are fictitious individuals but the challenges that they encounter are common. By asking you to visit the world of CBT supervision through the eyes of Patrick and Nina, we seek to provide a narrative into which the specific themes of the chapters can be embedded. We take this opportunity now, to introduce you to each of them:

Introducing Patrick

Patrick qualified as a CBT therapist three years ago. His core profession is mental health nursing but, following his accreditation as a CBT therapist, he has worked exclusively as a CBT therapist for a large Mental Health Trust in an inner-city area. He currently has a split post working two days each week in a child and adolescent mental health service and three days in an adult primary care (IAPT) service. He is well regarded by his colleagues and line managers in both services. Patrick is new to providing CBT supervision and enjoys the experience but sees this as forming part of his role, rather than as a distinct vocation. He has attended a five-day 'Introduction to CBT Supervision' course, which he found useful.

Introducing Nina

Nina qualified as a clinical psychologist over 25 years ago and chose CBT as an area of specialism, based on her commitment to this way of working. She runs a small private practice, holds managerial responsibility for a mental health charity and has a part-time post as a senior lecturer and supervisor on a university-based postgraduate CBT training course. She also offers supervision on a private basis and is an accredited supervisor and trainer with the BABCP. Nina has been involved in the professional development of junior colleagues for more than 20 years and highly values the training environment. Supervision is a distinct domain of professional activity which she sees as part of her vocation.

Finally, each chapter (with the exception of Chapter 12) also includes a boxed section entitled, 'Tips for Supervisees'. These tips offer recommendations to those who are receiving CBT supervision. At the core of supervision lies a relationship to which supervisors and supervisees both contribute. As such, we believe that a text on CBT supervision needs to give space to supervisees' perspectives, even though the principal focus remains the development needs of the supervisor.

How to use this book

Having ideas that you can personalize to your own context is a principle that lies at the heart of the book. A function of the PURE Supervision Flower is that it can enable you to decide where you need to focus your efforts at this particular point in your supervisory career. For example, if you are relatively new to supervision, you may find it advantageous to focus on the Parts I and II of this book (the Prepare and Undertake components of the Supervision Flower). If you are an experienced CBT supervisor and are seeking a conceptual and practical guide to assist you in critiquing and refining your work, you may find it more useful to focus on Parts III and IV (the Refine and Enhance components). Equally, if, on reflection, you recognize that you need to attend to particular aspects of your supervisory practice (it may be, for example, that you are highly effective at CBT skill development, but less confident at managing process issues), you may choose to focus on one particular petal in order to gain fresh perspectives on how to strengthen your practice in this area.

However you choose to use this book, we recommend that you resist the temptation of trying to absorb the contents all at once. Take time to build a relationship with the ideas presented and to consider how they relate to your work as a supervisor (or indeed as a supervisee). As you travel through the book, we invite you to refer back to earlier chapters, so you can explore dilemmas from the perspective of multiple models. It is our wish to support you in compiling a personal portfolio of knowledge that will support you in your work. Our task is to help you navigate the different ideas and approaches presented. Your task is to transform everything you read into a form that makes sense for you and your professional context.

So before you get underway, give some thought to what you might need to support you through the process. We recommend that you invest in a learning journal for recording any insights, thoughts or questions that occur to you. As we will be inviting you to participate in a series of experiential exercises to refine your practice, having a method for recording your results and insights will be important in enabling you to reflect upon your learning.

It is also important to be aware that this book is not intended to be a substitute for supervised practice by an appropriately qualified individual. The material is designed to aid your learning and development but not to replace formal training in CBT supervision. Indeed, you may decide that you need access to additional support when experimenting with some of the exercises provided. We warmly encourage you to discuss your reactions, discoveries and learning with colleagues, peers, supervisors and trainers (and if you are a trainer yourself, your students).

For the purposes of this book, we use the terms 'therapist' and 'supervisee' interchangeably to refer to the person/persons receiving supervision. Those providing CBT supervision are referred to as 'supervisors' or 'CBT supervisors'. For subsequent chapters, the acronym 'CBTS' will be used as a short-hand for CBT supervision.

Learning Activity A   What do you want from this book?

Before you continue, we recommend that you spend a few moments reflecting on your primary learning needs, making a written note of any key points. This will help you plan your learning with us to optimal effect. For example, are you:

1. Just about to start working as a supervisor and want to become clearer about some of the main points to hold in mind as you offer cognitive-behavioural supervision for the first time?
2. Relatively early on in your supervisory career, seeking one specific model of supervision that can help you establish a systematic approach?
3. An experienced cognitive-behavioural supervisor wanting to critique and refine your existing approach, perhaps seeking to 'iron out' any habits that might negatively impact your ability to offer a high-quality service?
4. Encountering difficulties with specific types of supervisee or supervisory issue?
5. A therapist seeking a cognitive-behavioural supervisor and needing to know what types of qualities to look for, and the sorts of questions to ask?
6. A supervisee who wants to understand how their CBT supervisor might approach supervision, and how to get the most out of the process?
7. A practitioner who wants to develop cognitive-behavioural supervision as a distinct area of specialism?

And finally...

Lesser commented that, 'It is important to be aware that the supervisory room is crowded with all sorts of "persons" who create anxieties for both the supervisor and the supervisee' (1983: 126). Although writing from a psychoanalytic perspective, we believe that this observation is equally relevant to CBT supervision. Indeed, we would argue that it is precisely because the supervision setting is 'crowded' with the stories, priorities, wishes and needs of multiple stakeholders that supervision is such a complex, fascinating and potentially transformational vehicle of professional development.

While the journey of supervision may start out as a requirement of your professional role, it can also become a vocation, affording the privilege of supporting the development of a colleague and providing a unique perspective on the complexity of therapeutic work. If, in the pages that follow, we are successful in providing you with some useful ways of facilitating more effectively the extraordinary journey of development that supervision can provide, we will have fulfilled our purpose.

PART I

Preparing for Supervision

In Part I we consider what needs to be in place in order to establish an effective and ethical basis for CBT supervision (CBTS). This is the 'Prepare' phase of the PURE Supervision Flower and focuses on the first three petals, as shown below:

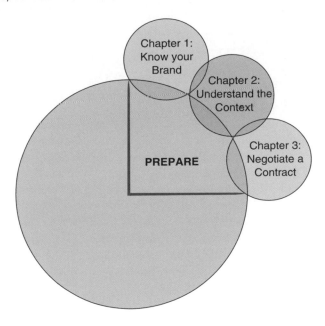

Figure 2   The PURE Supervision Flower: Prepare

Reading this section and working through the various exercises in these first three chapters will enable you to identify, plan for, and work effectively with those factors that provide the foundation for an effective working relationship that will meet your supervisees' learning and development needs.

ONE Know your Brand: Identifying your Position on the CBT Landscape

Learning objectives

After reading this chapter and completing the learning activities provided, you will be able to:

- Better understand the beliefs and values that you bring to CBTS.
- Describe your distinctive 'brand' of CBTS.
- Apply methods for identifying and critiquing the ways in which your beliefs and values shape your delivery of CBTS.

Introduction

Contemporary CBT is not so much a single school of therapy as a broad, emerging landscape of theories, models and interventions that is 'full of controversies' (Westbrook et al., 2012: 1). Because of this, claiming to be a CBT practitioner reveals less about an individual's method and style of working than might initially be assumed. Practitioners need to position themselves within the range of possible CBT approaches in order to provide a theoretically coherent and technically competent service to their clients. The choice a practitioner makes about where they position themselves on that landscape will reflect beliefs about the nature of human distress, assumptions about how therapy facilitates change, and a range of personal and professional values. This is equally the case for CBTS, where the supervisor's beliefs and values provide a foundation for what is offered and permeate the work that unfolds.

The aim of this chapter is to help you clarify, reflect upon and critique what you bring to CBTS in terms of your beliefs and values. As a basis for developing your effectiveness as a supervisor, reading this chapter will help you clarify where you situate yourself within the theoretical and technical landscape of CBT and define your 'brand' of supervision. By becoming clearer about these factors, the aim is to help you gain clarity about the nature of what it is you offer, those supervisees who are most and least likely to benefit from that offer, and the implications of this for the clients whom you seek to serve through your work together.

Identifying your beliefs about CBT

When introducing supervisees to what may seem like an unfamiliar way of working, or perhaps to a new way of being supervised, Liese and J. Beck (1997) propose that it is helpful for CBT supervisors to assess for the presence of any beliefs about CBT that may interfere with (or, we might add, help) therapeutic practice. Friedberg et al. refer to the importance of 'Harvesting open and flexible attitudes' in supervisees (2009: 111). They cite Freiheit and Overholser (1997), who have observed that therapists' preconceived ideas impact their degree of receptiveness to novel information in critical ways. Specifically, attitudinal biases can fuel selective attention such that supervisees may devote more energy to identifying the flaws in an approach rather than learning how to deliver it.

In a similar vein, Liese and J. Beck (1997) highlight that supervisees may adhere to common misconceptions about CBT that have arisen over the course of its history, such as a belief that CBT underplays the importance of emotions or the therapeutic alliance. In our experience, therapists do indeed bring to the practice of CBT a range of cognitions, some of which are more helpful (and more accurate) than others. Reading the list of beliefs about CBT that we often encounter, consider which of these have been prevalent among those whom you supervise (or indeed those you might hold yourself) and how they may have impacted the work that followed:

1. CBT fits clients to models.
2. CBT is evidence-based.
3. CBT aims to reduce negative thinking and increase positive thinking.
4. CBT is concerned with the 'here-and-now' and is less concerned with the client's developmental history.
5. CBT does not work for clients with complex needs.
6. CBT is protocol-driven.
7. CBT is primarily concerned with teaching clients techniques.
8. CBT can obtain symptom relief but is unlikely to produce enduring personality change.

At the start of any supervision engagement we recommend that supervisors talk openly about thoughts, assumptions and beliefs that therapists may be bringing to their CBT practice and also how these might shape their expectations of supervision as a learning environment. For example, if a supervisee believes that the field of CBT offers protocols for every clinical presentation which deliver clear instructions about which intervention should be used and when, this is likely to create an expectation that the supervisor will provide didactic and piecemeal instructions. Alternatively, if a therapist believes that CBT principally comprises the delivery of a series of techniques, this may create an expectation that the supervisor will focus predominantly on the teaching of specific cognitive and behavioural strategies. Confusion may follow when the supervisor insists on devoting time to assessment and formulation, and prevents the therapist from 'leaping' into interventions before sufficient clinical data have been obtained.

The various traditions that now comprise the field of CBT adhere to different beliefs about the nature of human distress and how best to bring about change. For example, the so-called first, second and third generations of CBT (see Hayes, 2004) differ conceptually in their views on the extent to which behaviour or cognition, and acceptance or change methods should be privileged when working to enhance clients' well-being. These differing perspectives provide orienting contexts that have significant implications for the way in which therapist learning and development is undertaken. Thus, how CBTS is delivered in the context of a randomized controlled trial to examine the effectiveness of a specific treatment protocol derived from a second-generation (cognitively focused) approach will look very different from the style and content of supervision provided by a therapist who is offering Acceptance and Commitment Therapy in a drug and alcohol service. It follows, therefore, that as supervisors, it is just as important to work towards uncovering our own beliefs and assumptions about CBT and its relevance to our clients, as it is helping our supervisees uncover theirs.

In Learning Activity 1.1 we invite you to identify those beliefs and assumptions that are relevant to how you approach your work as a CBT supervisor. How do they shape what therapists experience when they receive supervision from you?

Learning Activity 1.1   What type of CBT therapist are you?

Take some time to consider your own beliefs about CBT. To what are you referring when you use the term 'CBT'? On which part of this broad conceptual paradigm are you focusing? Based on this definition:

(Continued)

(Continued)

1. What do you value most about CBT?
2. What do you value least about CBT?
3. If you, or a member of your family needed therapeutic support, would you recommend CBT or not? (If so, why? If not, why not? If you are unsure, what are the factors you would need to take into account in order to reach a decision?)

Then consider:

1. What are your beliefs about the causes and maintenance of human distress?
2. What are your beliefs about therapeutic change? How do you know when it has been achieved? What does it look like?
3. What are your beliefs about pathways to change? By what mechanisms or methods do you believe this occurs?

Having spent some time sifting through your answers, look at the continua below. Place a cross on each one according to your own understanding of CBT when you practise this as a therapist. Notice if there are any discrepancies between the type of CBT you practise and the type of CBT you supervise. Notice also if there are any differences between the kind of CBT you offer (as a therapist) and the kind of CBT you would like to receive if you were a client.

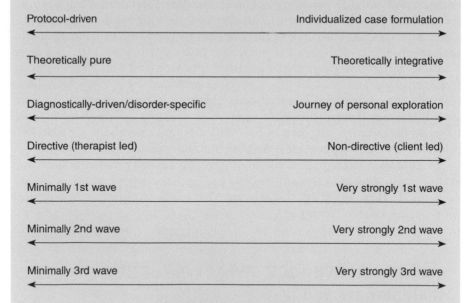

Protocol-driven ← → Individualized case formulation

Theoretically pure ← → Theoretically integrative

Diagnostically-driven/disorder-specific ← → Journey of personal exploration

Directive (therapist led) ← → Non-directive (client led)

Minimally 1st wave ← → Very strongly 1st wave

Minimally 2nd wave ← → Very strongly 2nd wave

Minimally 3rd wave ← → Very strongly 3rd wave

It is important to note that there are no right or wrong responses to this exercise. However, where you and your supervisees position yourselves on these continua will have implications for how supervision unfolds, potentially influencing the ease with which you can use different supervision interventions. Your responses may also provide important information on those whom you may be best and least equipped to supervise.

The role of values in CBT supervision

So far we have made the case that an essential starting point in supervision is to enhance awareness – in ourselves and our supervisees – of the beliefs to which we subscribe when we look at our clients' needs through a CBT lens. However, the approach taken will also be informed by a supervisor's values.

Values are inherent in all helping relationships and are closely associated with our goals for client work and the interventions we employ in the service of client change (McCarthy Veach et al., 2012). Supervision is also a value-laden activity, shaping the learning environment that the supervisor seeks to offer and serving as a filter for the educational and evaluative methods employed (Nadelson and Notman, 1977).

Despite the dearth of studies examining the influence of values on the content and process of supervision (McCarthy Veach et al., 2012), initial investigations point to the importance of supervisor values as a mediating variable on therapist development. Buckman and Barker (2010), for example, found that the philosophical orientation of the supervisor had an influencing effect on the preferred theoretical orientation of trainee therapists. Multicultural models of supervision have also emphasized the mediating impact of values (see Garrett et al. (2001), who recommend that supervisors and supervisees discuss their respective beliefs about human nature, social relationships and human behaviour in order to identify and address areas of conflict that could arise). Abeles and Ettenhofer (2008) also highlight that many models of supervision are based on Western, Eurocentric and biological perspectives, with all the embedded values to which these worldviews give rise. In such a context, there is the potential for supervisors to adversely affect the learning and development of their supervisees (and perhaps also the well-being of their supervisees' clients) by failing to attend to differences in value systems. Without an awareness of the values that permeate our work, supervision runs the risk of being dominated by what Hawkins and Shohet (2012) term our 'shadow motives'.

The empirical neglect of the influence of values in supervision is perhaps unsurprising given that the concept is rarely operationally defined or underpinned by a consistent typology through which specific, testable hypotheses might be generated (Beutler and Bergan, 1991). Indeed, supervisor values are typically referenced indirectly through terminology such as 'personality and working style' (Korinek and Kimball, 2003). However, as Long (2011) observes, many supervisors are instinctively aware that how they practise is closely associated with who they are as human beings. Our values are close to our sense of identity, comprising prized personal beliefs that direct goals and motivate behaviour (Brown and Brooks, 1991), personally or socially-derived ideals about appropriate courses of action (Rokeach, 1973), and criteria that individuals use to select and justify actions and evaluate themselves and others (Schwartz, 1992).

Beutler and Bergan (1991) have defined values as stabilizing rules that provide continuity in both the personal and social domains. The notion of values as 'stabilizing rules' can be seen as consistent with the concept of conditional beliefs in CBT; that is, enduring cognitions that we may not have articulated to ourselves or others but which manifest as rules, attitudes and assumptions about self, others, life and the world that govern both our actions and sense of our choices. Derived from experience (often early in life), the beliefs inherited from significant others (such as parents, peers, teachers) and culture of origin, their purpose is to serve as a guide to behaviour that enables adaptive functioning. Such assumptions also define the parameters of 'good' and 'bad' behaviour, and thus prescribe and proscribe what is acceptable. Examples of such stabilizing (and problematic) rules that are often encountered when working with clients in CBT (and indeed some supervisees) might include: 'If I make an error it means I am incompetent', 'I must always please people to be accepted', and 'In order to be of worth, I must be successful in everything that I do'.

Within the CBT movement, one approach that has elevated work on values to the heart of therapy is Acceptance and Commitment Therapy (ACT) (Hayes et al., 1999). A central aim of ACT is to enable clients to identify, and behave in ways that are consistent with, valued life directions. Within their framework of how to approach change, Ciarrochi and Bailey (2008: 119) conceptualize values as a 'chosen quality of purposive action that can never be obtained as an object but can be put into action from moment to moment'. A detailed review of ACT is beyond the scope of this book (the interested reader is referred to Hayes et al., 1999). For the purposes of this chapter, it is sufficient to note that from an ACT perspective, personally defined values are deemed to provide a stable anchor for selecting meaningful goals and can enable sustained effort in the face of obstacles and uncomfortable internal states (such as anxiety and doubts about self-competence).

Values are pursued for their own sake, are chosen (and thus, personally meaningful) and represent a direction rather than a tangible outcome. As such they operate at a higher level of intention than goals which, in contrast, are pursued in the service of values and can be definitively achieved (Bryant and Kazan, 2013). In CBTS, for example, a supervisor might hold a value of being an empowering educational presence that nurtures the talent of others. This might lead to the goal of listening to recordings of entire CBT sessions on a weekly basis in order to give detailed feedback. The goal (which can be assessed as achieved or not achieved) is meaningful only in that it supports the valued direction for the supervisor of nurturing the talent of others.

Values provide what Hayes et al. (1999) refer to as a 'glue' that can ensure coherence in the ways we approach goal setting and organize activity. There are a number of ways in which excavating the values that supervisors and supervisees bring to CBTS might be useful in supporting the development of an effective working relationship. These include the following:

1. Knowing our values affords a sense of purpose to our actions and is likely to increase the level of satisfaction we experience as we offer supervision.
2. Acknowledging and working within specific value systems can make it easier to address obstacles effectively. Undrill (2012) proposes that a

focus on values can help address 'stuck moments' in therapy, enabling the therapist to consider how a client's behaviour might represent the expression of a particular philosophical stance which is inconsistent with their own worldview. Equally, in supervision, certain frustrations can be understood as the manifestation of diverse worldviews that can be acknowledged, explored and used as examples of how to conceptualize and work with the interpersonal processes that arise.

3. For the field of CBT more widely, the incorporation of values and value conflicts provide what McCarthy Veach et al. (2012: 224) describe as 'a conceptual bridge that may help theorists, researchers, and practitioners investigate and address in a more integrated fashion supervision events that are low frequency but certainly high impact'. An emphasis on values perhaps holds the potential for a CBT-specific framework for exploring factors that influence interpersonal interactions occurring moment-to-moment.

What are your values as a CBT supervisor?

Having presented the rationale for identifying personal and professional values in the context of supervision, and in the absence of extant guidelines from the CBTS literature, we offer an exercise to support you in considering your own values in relation to CBTS and how these might inform your supervisory approach.

Learning Activity 1.2   Uncovering your values as a CBT supervisor

Imagine that you are the recipient of an award that honours your excellence as a CBT supervisor. A number of your supervisees (who nominated you for this award) are interviewed and asked to provide an account of their experience of supervision with you.

What would you most like them to say about you? This might include forms of learning to which you introduced them, the type of working relationship you established, values you instilled in them, methods of working you taught them, your style and clarity, or how you functioned for them as a mentor or guide. In this exercise, have your supervisees state exactly what you would like them to say about you.

Examine your responses in detail and see what stands out for you. You may find it helpful to consider the following questions:

- What do your responses tell you about your values as a supervisor? (For example, is this a role that is central to your professional identity, or an activity that you are required to undertake as part of your job but which does not hold particular meaning for you?)
- How are these values expressed in the way in which you work as a supervisor?
- What opportunities do your values open up for those who are receiving supervision from you?

(Continued)

(Continued)

- What limits or constraints might your values impose upon those who are receiving supervision from you?
- Based on an analysis of your values, what types of CBT are you not best placed to supervise? (Note: this question does not relate to your technical competence but rather those prized personal beliefs that organize your work around the pursuit of specific goals.)
- Thinking about each supervisee to whom you are currently providing CBTS, if you could choose anything, what would you most want them to gain through working with you, and why?

Incorporating a value-based perspective as you prepare for CBTS: Some recommendations

As we have seen, it is important for supervisors to be able to identify their own values as well as being skilled in identifying the values of those whom they supervise. We would concur with McCarthy Veach et al.'s (2012) recommendation that therapy training programmes should include the opportunity for students to clarify their values and anticipate value conflicts that might arise, both in therapy and in supervision. The contexts in which supervision is provided will present dilemmas that reflect the demands of working in increasingly complex environments. The capacity to identify, reflect upon and critique the different assumptions, expectations, beliefs and values that may be operating in such contexts is a task that we believe should precede a consideration of the domains of technical competence that need to be acquired and assessed.

To support you in developing a more systematic approach to identifying, reflecting upon and critiquing the beliefs and values that may have an impact on how supervision is organized and delivered, we offer the following recommendations, presented as a three-stage process, for you to adapt to your professional needs.

Step 1. Identify your own CBT-related beliefs and values

1. Be clear about the values that underpin your own views on therapy generally, and CBT specifically. Be clear also about how you define your own 'brand' of CBTS. (The exercises in this chapter offer a good basis for helping you clarify this.)

Step 2. Help your supervisees identify their CBT-related beliefs and values

4. Spend time getting to know your supervisees' values and beliefs about therapy generally and CBT specifically. How would they define and

describe this method of working? How do they believe that it achieves change? (You might ask them to undertake Learning Activity 1.1 as a homework assignment in order to clarify their beliefs.) By comparing them with your own, is it possible to identify any areas of difference that could lead to potential conflict?

Step 3. Share CBT-relevant beliefs and values as a basis for mutual understanding and contracting

1. Encourage transparency and trust by sharing your own beliefs and values. Discuss why reciprocal understanding is important as a basis for fostering collaborative working relationships, and how awareness of differences can support the management of any challenges that might arise.
2. Discuss how the different values represented in the supervisory relationship, or supervision group, might manifest. How would you know? What would be the signs that a 'clash' of values is occurring? Agree how you might manage this.
3. Discuss what is not negotiable, and the boundary of the approach that you take. For example, a refusal to engage in role-play or other forms of experiential skills practice on the basis that it conflicts with a supervisee's beliefs about how they learn best may not be considered a valid point of negotiation!

Pulling it all together

Having read this chapter and completed the learning activities, we invite you now to adopt the role of supervision consultant for Patrick, one of the fictitious supervisors whom we introduced at the start of this book. You will recall that Patrick is a relatively new CBT supervisor, having completed his post-qualification CBT training three years previously. Your task is to provide consultation on a specific supervision dilemma that he is encountering, drawing on the ideas presented in this chapter. This case study is followed by some recommendations for supervisees on how to approach the issue of beliefs and values in order to gain the most from the supervision experience.

Case Study 1

It was yet another session where Jen looked confused by the feedback that Patrick was giving her and he wondered (not for the first time) whether he was the best supervisor for her.

(Continued)

(Continued)

A new staff member in the IAPT service where Patrick worked, Jen had recently completed a post-graduate training in CBT where she had excelled. Patrick knew that Jen had had a very positive relationship with her former supervisor, who had experience of working as a therapist in research trials. This supervisor emphasized the critical importance of being 'on model'. As a result, Jen had become very well-acquainted with disorder-specific models and, although early in her career, was rapidly becoming a skilled CBT therapist.

It seemed to Patrick that Jen struggled with accepting his supervisory input. This latest client was a good example of how they just didn't seem to be on the same wavelength. Jen said that, to her, it was obvious that the client had a relatively straightforward diagnosis of panic disorder. So she had constructed a detailed, theoretically-informed, formulation of maintaining factors that provided a logical basis for intervention planning. Patrick was concerned that by taking this approach Jen was missing important information about the client's context and needs – in particular his recent diagnosis of hepatitis B and previous use of street drugs. For this reason, he insisted that she first develop a formulation that was grounded in a more thorough developmental history and included a greater consideration of environmental and health-related factors.

Patrick was clear that there were good clinical grounds for proceeding in the way he advocated. However, he had never particularly warmed to the idea of disorder-specific models and, deep down, did not believe that they were sufficient to bring about enduring change. He was aware that Jen's allegiance to this way of working was triggering a negative reaction, but also believed that she still had a great deal to learn about the complexity of clients' needs. Nonetheless, Patrick was worried that unless he took swift action, a rupture in their working alliance could occur.

- How would you encourage Patrick to conceptualize this dilemma?
- What beliefs and values about effective therapy might be operating in this scenario?
- How would you advise Patrick to proceed?

(We provide suggestions on how to approach this dilemma in Appendix 1.)

Tips for Supervisees No. 1

As a supervisee, it is important to remember that CBT is a broad conceptual paradigm and that different supervisors will have different ideas about what 'good' CBT looks like. For this reason:

Ensure that you can have an open discussion with your supervisor about their particular 'brand', of CBT. This will enable you to gain optimally from the experience that is on offer. To support you in this, remember to:

- Ask your supervisor about which forms of CBT they adhere to and practise.
- Identify your supervisor's thoughts about aspects of CBT that work well and those that are less helpful. Are there aspects that are more useful for specific clients or presenting difficulties? Are there aspects that are incompatible with certain clients or clinical presentations?
- Discuss how your supervisor keeps up with developments in CBT. How do they decide which theories to integrate into their practice?
- Ask what lets your supervisor know when they have helped a client or when they think that they have delivered CBT effectively.
- Ask what your supervisor thinks would be useful for you, as a supervisee, to consider so that you can use supervision effectively. How do they understand a supervisee's contribution to the supervisory process?
- (If you feel able) ask your supervisor about some of the factors that may affect the quality of supervision they offer.

To help you get the most out of supervision it might be helpful to share with your supervisor your understanding of:

- What helps you maintain an open and curious stance during supervision and therapy.
- The specific aspects of CBT you like and any with which you struggle.
- The opportunities and constraints of working in a group or a team and how you manage tensions within a group (if group supervision is offered).

Conclusion

Before you are able to harness the potential of supervision, it is first necessary to be clear about the type of CBTS you seek to provide and the values that underpin what you offer. It is also necessary to know whether there is a goodness of fit between your values, beliefs and expectations and those of your supervisees.

In this chapter, we have sought to help you develop a clearer understanding of your distinct 'brand' of CBTS through helping you uncover fundamental beliefs about therapy generally and CBT specifically, which will form the backbone of the supervisory engagement. While we recommend a careful scrutiny of underlying beliefs and values, the circumstances in which we live and work do not always permit an uncomplicated manifestation of these. As Hayes et al. (1999) observe, our values are often controlled by the pervading cultures in which we are embedded. In consequence, it is necessary to ensure that the supervision you provide is congruent with the beliefs and values of any third parties who may be external to the supervisory relationship but who nonetheless exert a key influence on what takes place. In the next chapter we take a closer look at the context in which supervision is provided and consider some of the challenges, pressures and opportunities afforded by delivering CBTS in the current climate.

Chapter summary

✓ There are a number of CBT approaches for which therapists may seek supervision.

✓ As supervisors mature in experience and expertise, they need to be aware of their unique 'brand' of supervision and who is best and least served by this particular brand.

✓ Central to this brand are a supervisor's beliefs and values. These need to be identified and understood as helping to create the context in which supervision will take place, and as a potentially highly influential factor on how supervision unfolds.

✓ The effectiveness of supervision is likely to be enhanced if supervisors are able to elicit their supervisees' values, and are confident in speaking openly about differences in values and how these may influence the course and content of supervision.

TWO   Understand the Context: Identifying your Key Stakeholders

Learning objectives

After reading this chapter and completing the learning activities provided, you will be able to:

- Be more aware of the impact of the wider context in which you are delivering CBTS.
- Better understand how this wider context shapes how you deliver CBTS.
- Identify the key 'stakeholders' whose interests and priorities need to be accommodated within any agreed supervision contract.

Introduction

Having established the values and beliefs that underpin your approach to supervision, we now examine the wider context in which supervision is mandated and delivered. In the past 50 years or so, the ways in which psychological interventions are organized and delivered have changed exponentially (Lunt, 2006). CBT is delivered amidst an increasingly complex array of social forces and in an economic climate characterized by unprecedented levels of uncertainty, unpredictability and change. If CBT supervisors are to provide an effective learning environment for supervisees, they need to understand the climate in which CBT is commissioned and the implications of this for the type of learning that supervision is expected to foster. They must also be well equipped to navigate the sometimes competing pressures to which these social and economic forces give rise.

The aim of this chapter is to enhance your understanding of the current and emerging contexts in which CBTS is delivered and how these contexts impact on your practice. By becoming clearer about the range of stakeholders who shape your approach – both directly and indirectly – you can better understand the nature of your supervision offer and manage expectations about what you can and cannot provide.

Learning Activity 2.1   Understanding the contextual factors that shape your approach

Developing a thorough understanding of the broad spectrum of influences that shape your approach will enable you to decide what represents a judicious application of best practice guidelines and which factors might be a source of tension. Use the following questions to guide you:

- To what extent does the individual, service or organization commissioning supervision understand its purpose and appreciate its role in enhancing therapist effectiveness?
- To what extent are you able to implement your 'brand' of CBTS (the work of Chapter 1)? Do you have the autonomy to determine this or is your brand largely determined for you (e.g. by the service in which you are employed)?
- To whom are you accountable? How does this accountability translate into the 'deliverables' expected of you, as well as the pressures, opportunities and constraints upon you as a supervisor?
- What are the values and expectations of the different parties who have a vested interest in the outcomes of the supervision you provide? Which values and expectations are most and least consistent with your own? Are there any that you find yourself resisting? If so, why and what form does this resistance take?

CBT in context: Implications for supervision

Supervision does not take place in a vacuum. Regardless of any apparent autonomy that supervisor and supervisee have in determining the focus of their work together, environmental factors are always present and will, to a greater or lesser extent, frame the nature of the supervision relationship and the work that follows. It is essential, therefore, that any supervision agreement clarifies whose interests need to be accommodated, and how supervision will address the expectations of relevant stakeholders, such as service managers, commissioners, sponsoring organizations and credentialing bodies. It is also important to consider how the interests of these stakeholders may enable or constrain the work that follows, and the learning and development opportunities provided (Copeland, 1998, 2006).

One significant contextual factor is that in recent years, CBT has undergone a marked increase in popularity. The speed with which CBT has been propelled into the limelight of the therapeutic professions has resulted in a burgeoning CBT community, increased opportunities for training in CBT in the UK and clearer criteria for credentialing. In addition, there is a growth in clients and referrers who are requesting CBT, sometimes without understanding what they are asking for (Corrie, 2003). This exponential increase in demand warrants exploration, and both CBT therapists and those who supervise them need to understand the ideologies and interests that underpin this trend.

In order to enhance awareness of the impact of contextual factors, Drake (2009) has argued that practitioners need to map the needs and values of their stakeholders. Drawing on levels of influence proposed by Mohan (1996), Corrie and Lane (2010; see also Lane and Corrie, 2006, 2012) have proposed that one such way to approach this task is to categorize influences as occurring at the local, national or global level. These levels of influence equip supervisors with values and ideologies that can help or hinder the supervision process, informing beliefs about what constitute acceptable and unacceptable explanations of human behaviour and forms of 'intervening' that are sanctioned and forbidden. As such, they permeate the in-session behaviour of supervisor and supervisee, as well as shaping choice of supervision strategy. So what might be some of the dominant influences at each level and how do they shape what is expected of CBT supervisors?

1. Local level influences

Local level influences refer to the belief systems, priorities and processes operating internally to those institutions that influence or determine a practitioner's work. These include training institutes, employing organizations and professional bodies which confer accreditation or otherwise judge practitioners competent to practise. Local influences shape supervisors' thinking both explicitly (e.g. through a requirement to adhere to codes of conduct) and implicitly (through values, assumptions and ethical principles imparted during core professional training). They impact on the way in which a supervision question is framed (including the belief that a supervision question is required at all), the style and content of the supervision provided, the roles that supervisor and supervisee adopt, and the ways in which supervision is evaluated.

Local level influences inform choice of assessment tool and intervention strategy, such as via the values of the training bodies through which individuals acquired their qualifications. For example, CBT supervisors might draw on the Cognitive Therapy Scale – Revised (CTS-R) (Blackburn et al., 2001), a widely sanctioned and frequently used measure of competence, to track progress, provide feedback and select targets for supervisee development. Influences at the local level also include the requirements of credentialing bodies such as the BABCP (which specifies that supervision must involve live observations of therapists' work) as well as a particular service's view on how supervision is provided (individual, group, weekly, monthly, etc.) and any intended outcomes of the supervisory process. In the case of the IAPT initiative, therapists are offered employment contracts on the basis that they successfully complete a rigorous academic and professional training – an outcome on which their future employment depends. As the training is designed to be completed within a year, this is likely to impact on the balance of supervisory interventions used, with the potential for the supervisor to be more didactic in order to achieve the required outcome in a relatively short time-scale.

The service in which we work has to meet the needs of the community it serves. The nature of that community, including its ethnic and cultural mix, is therefore also an important local influence. How we seek to understand our local community and its needs and preferences for how service is provided will impact on the work we do and, consequently, how we need to offer supervision.

2. National level influences

While local level influences are concerned with the ways in which supervision practice is tied to the priorities of professional bodies and local services, national influences are concerned with the broader, dominant ideologies and policies that shape how we think and operate. National level influences that are dominant currently include the increased scrutiny and greater monitoring of the professions (e.g. through systems of audit and evaluation arising from concerns about the variability in standards of service delivery), emphasis on the use of evidence to inform practice-related decisions (Harper and Chitty, 2005) and achieving cost-containment in an austerity-driven climate. All of these factors have a critical impact on how CBT is delivered and therefore what is expected of supervisors. Additionally, as we discuss later (Chapter 8), as access to psychological therapies has become a UK Government priority, lack of use of services by minority communities has been an issue. Hence, attitudes to provision of services locally will also be influenced by national debates on cultural issues.

The growing popularity of CBT can be understood in part as a response to the growing demand for empirically-supported interventions that has emerged from the need for more objective standards to guide policy. Among the psychological therapies, its commitment to empirical demonstrations of outcome has enabled CBT to secure for itself an advantageous position with government and other funding bodies who seek evidence of effectiveness as a basis for confidence in commissioning (McHugh and Barlow, 2010). As the importance of grounding practice in evidence-based procedures is likely to continue (Department of Health, 2008), CBT is likely to remain a desirable commissioning choice. Indeed, through the IAPT initiative, it has been uniquely placed within the Government's mandate to increase the availability of psychological therapies.

Simultaneously, we are witnessing the development of new models of service delivery. In its operational guidance to the NHS, the Department of

Health (2011) outlined the concepts of Any Qualified Provider (AQP) and Payment by Results (PbR) as a means of extending patient choice and improving service quality and efficiency. This is achieved through the mechanism of competition between providers. The introduction of a market system to service delivery and the contractual arrangements between those who commission and provide services has potentially far-reaching consequences for psychological therapies.

In their analysis of PbR, Griffiths et al. (2013) identify a range of perverse incentives that are creating perverse outcomes for clients. These include how PbR is impacting decisions about whether to accept a referral (low tariffs and PbR mean that some providers are not paid for treating clients who do not recover); the 'mechanistic throughput' of clients; and possibly even financial incentives to misuse measurement scales in order to ensure payment. In CBT, one form this could take is reducing the number of sessions provided (in an attempt to increase service efficiency) at the expense of delivering the full intervention recommended by the National Institute for Health and Care Excellence (NICE). However, even where NICE guidelines are used to underpin decisions about interventions offered, the emphasis on case-based and outcome-oriented supervision has shaped the focus and style of CBTS to one of what Milne (2009: 107) terms 'exceptional efficiency'.

These changes are heralding an evolution in the identity of CBT itself. CBT is no longer solely a therapeutic approach, but has become the foundation of a distinct and emerging workforce trained to deliver evidence-based psychological therapies. Whereas once in the UK CBT training was largely the domain of those choosing to specialize in the approach after completing a core professional training in a recognized mental health field (such as psychology, psychotherapy or mental health nursing), it is now possible to become an accredited CBT therapist by demonstrating equivalent clinical and professional experience evidenced through a 'Knowledge, Skills and Attitudes' portfolio. As such we are witnessing the unprecedented trend of CBT – a model of therapy predicated upon a distinct approach to understanding and working with human distress – becoming an emergent workforce and a basis for service redesign (Lewis, 2012). Thus, it is no longer clear whether CBT is a style of therapy, an occupation, a profession, or an industry.

Determining the identity of CBT within the psychological professions is far from neutral in its implications. The professions are distinct from other occupations in specific ways. As noted by Lane and Corrie (2006), those upon whom the title of 'professional' is conferred are given licence to work with greater degrees of autonomy, and to exercise judgement under conditions of increased uncertainty and complexity, than skilled technicians who work from treatment protocols within carefully prescribed parameters. If CBT emerges as a distinct profession, supervision will, therefore, entail far more than equipping individuals to deliver empirically-supported interventions. It will include ensuring that therapists are highly skilled in identifying, adapting and evaluating a wide variety of information and using this knowledge in an autonomous fashion for the benefit of clients and other stakeholders.

Equally, seeking training in CBT may previously have been seen as a choice. Now it might be regarded as a necessity for certain professional groups who experience the increased number of trained and accredited CBT therapists as a threat to their domain of expertise. Not everyone comes to supervision as a willing participant and supervisors need to be able to recognize this, identify where tensions might arise and be able to address such tensions so that they do not create ruptures in the supervisory relationship.

3. Global level influences

Global level influences include international trends in welfare and the delivery of health and social care, the power of capitalism, the popularization of psychological knowledge (in the form of self-help and personal development initiatives) and concerns facing the global community, such as cost-containment and the growing trend of appealing to science to justify our choices.

Global level influences permeate supervision in subtle and complex ways, having an important function in how professionals come to understand their identities and roles. Of the many global influences in which supervisors, supervisees and their local and national contexts are immersed, two are particularly worthy of note: (1) the medicalization of human distress and (2) the changing status of the professions in society.

In relation to the medicalization of human distress, Martell et al. (2001: 4) draw attention to what they term 'the zeitgeist of internal causation'. In examining the reasons underpinning the appeal of internal causes as explanations of distress (thoughts, emotions, neurotransmitters, etc.), they highlight how depression has increasingly become depicted as an illness and provide a compelling argument as to why this might be the case. One of the factors they identify is the 'culture of blame' in which people live, and in which professionals work, that negatively stereotypes those living with emotional difficulties. Yet if labelled as ill or as suffering from a disorder, individuals are exonerated; it is the illness (rather than the person) that is held responsible for the experience of suffering.

The medicalization of distress opens up pathways into services on the basis that people are 'ill' and require 'treatment'. However, this perspective draws attention away from the contexts in which distress manifests and also opens up possibilities for an increasingly wide range of human experiences and behaviours to be labelled as 'pathological' (see, for example, debates about the inclusion of paraphilias as a diagnostic category in DSM-V; Hinderliter, 2010). As is apparent from the global debates within the Anglican Church, how societies respond to sexuality can create great divisions over whether sexual preferences and behaviour constitute a disorder to be treated, acts to be condemned, or legitimate choices that should be honoured (Lambeth Commission, 2004).

In relation to the changing status of the professions in society, Lane et al. (2010) observe how, in recent decades, the concept of 'the profession' has become fragile. The professions no longer enjoy the same privileged status in society, have the same degree of autonomy in relation to credentialing, licensing and regulation, or possess the monopoly on knowledge that they once did. Further analyses of their status and function (Lo, 2005; Lane and Corrie, 2006) have also highlighted how the professions are carriers of socially sanctioned values of both the state and the market place.

As our customers become increasingly fluent in the language of therapy, we can anticipate that global level influences will shape expectations of those receiving, delivering and commissioning psychological therapies. Specifically, in a knowledge-driven labour market, our explanations need to become customer-focused in a way that differs from previous eras where professionals' role as interpreters of research into practice was largely unquestioned. Defining our core business and being able to articulate what differentiates us in an already crowded professional market is critical to our survival (Drake, 2008).

Mapping the local, national and global level influences that shape your supervision practice

Local, national and global levels of influence are not mutually exclusive; there is overlap, and influences at one level will inevitably permeate others. The value of separating them out lies in enabling supervisors to identify and categorize influences that might be immediately obvious (such as the BABCP requirements about use of live observation in supervision) as well as those that may not (the way in which our thinking has become shaped by disorder-specific models underpinned by the medicalization of difficulties in the context of diagnosis).

In the service of becoming more aware of these sources of influence, we recommend that during the Preparation phase of supervision, you undertake a mapping exercise to become clearer about what is shaping your supervisory offer, as well as your supervisee's response to that offer. Learning Activity 2.2 provides some questions that can form the basis of such an exercise.

Learning Activity 2.2   Mapping the influences on your supervisory offer

Consider your current work setting or settings (if you work across multiple contexts) and the settings of your supervisees (some of their contextual influences may be different from yours).

A. What local level influences permeate the supervision you provide?

What local level influences are currently impacting on your role, style and actions as a CBT supervisor? Consider your responses to the following questions:

(Continued)

(Continued)

1. What assumptions (explicit and implicit), held by the organizations to which you are accountable, govern your approach to CBTS and the interpretation of your role? (If not stated explicitly, clues to these can be found in mission statements and strategy documents; changes taking place in your organization; stated priorities; and the way in which changes are cascaded through the system.)
2. How is supervision viewed by these organizations: As essential? As helpful but secondary to more pressing priorities (such as clinical contact hours)? As something the organization doesn't really value (you find yourself having to defend the time you put aside for supervision, or suspect that this protected space is under threat due to service constraints)?
3. What formats of supervision (including style and content) are considered acceptable by these organizations and why? What forms of supervision would be considered unacceptable and why?
4. How do you think that your approach and effectiveness as a supervisor is enabled and constrained by the culture in which you are working?

Based on your responses to the above questions, consider how the local level influences in which you are immersed shape your approach to supervision for good or ill.

B. What national level influences permeate the supervision you provide?

What national level influences are currently impacting on your role, style and actions as a CBT supervisor? Consider your responses to the following questions:

1. What government-led guidelines or regulations have been introduced relating to the health and well-being of the nation?
2. What are the current, nationwide beliefs about psychological interventions generally and CBT specifically?
3. What is being talked about at CBT conferences and written about in the academic and professional journals and trade magazines relevant to CBT specifically and the organization and delivery of psychological interventions more broadly?
4. What priorities are foremost for the professional and credentialing bodies which regulate or otherwise guide the development and provision of CBT? How might these priorities reflect broader priorities and concerns at a national level?

Based on your responses to the above questions, consider how the national level influences in which you are immersed shape your approach to supervision for good or ill.

C. What global level influences permeate the supervision you provide?

What global level influences are currently impacting on your role, style and actions as a CBT supervisor? Consider your responses to the following questions:

1. In relation to the health and well-being of the global community, what are the most pressing areas of concern that governments need to come together in order to resolve?
2. What are the current global concerns about mental health and human distress and what are some of the international beliefs about the place of psychological interventions in facilitating positive change in people's lives?
3. What shared themes and topics are being talked about at international CBT conferences and written about in the literature across the globe?
4. In the cultures in which you live and work, what assumptions are widely endorsed about human dilemmas, the causes of emotional distress and how to alleviate these?

Based on your responses to the above questions, consider how the global level influences in which you are immersed shape your approach to supervision for good or ill.

Pulling it all together

Having read this chapter and completed the learning activities, spend a few moments sifting through your reactions and any emerging insights. Are there any conversations you need to have, or actions you need to take, in order to prepare for the supervision you are expected to provide? Once you are confident that you have gained what you need from this chapter, we invite you once again to adopt the role of consultant to Patrick. This case study is followed by some tips for supervisees on how to approach the issue of understanding context in order to gain the most from supervision.

Case Study 2

Patrick listened attentively as Ben talked him through his client's latest scores on the weekly measures that the service was required to use. There had been no change for several weeks now and Patrick was starting to feel concerned. He recalled a conversation with his manager the previous week about the importance of raising the profile of the service through evidence of outcomes.

Patrick was all too aware that the data obtained from the measures had important implications for his service – a service with a difficult past, poor staff retention and now managed by a clinical lead keen to transform both the image and the reputation of the organization. He was anxious that the clinical lead would somehow hold him responsible for Ben's difficulties in producing change and with his own appraisal coming up was wondering if he should adopt more stringent measures with Ben in an attempt to enhance performance.

Patrick felt a wave of anxiety mingle with a surge of irritation as Ben began to describe the client as 'resistant' to CBT. Not for the first time, he noticed

(Continued)

(Continued)

himself respond in an overly confrontational manner, barely concealing his irritation and insisting that Ben play an extended section of his audio-recording so they could see where things were going wrong. His awareness of this left him feeling guilty and as though he were failing as a supervisor.

- How would you encourage Patrick to conceptualize this dilemma?
- What factors might be helping to create this dilemma for Patrick?
- How would you advise Patrick to proceed?

(We provide suggestions on how to approach this dilemma in Appendix 2.)

Tips for Supervisees No. 2

Listed below are some points that might be useful to reflect on and discuss with your supervisor to help you gain the most out of supervision.

Be clear about the purpose of supervision:

- How would you define the core purpose of supervision?
- How does your supervisor understand the purpose of supervision?
- How might any similarities or differences in your perspectives facilitate or hinder supervision?

Clarify the contextual influences that have shaped how you have come to work together:

- Supervisees may not have the option of choosing their supervisors (this can occur when receiving CBTS in the context of postgraduate training). If this is the case, what is the context in which you and your supervisor have come to work together and who has had a role in deciding this? How (if at all) does this affect your shared understanding of the purpose of supervision?
- How might you maximize your learning from supervision given the demands of your work setting, the demands of the supervisory process, and any other pressures (e.g. of the training course)? What would be useful for your supervisor to know to help you balance the various demands on your time?
- In relation to the above, it will be helpful for your supervisor to understand your current work context and the priorities of the service, including the expected number of client contacts or clinical hours per week, the number of sessions that you can offer a client and how your service measures outcome.

Clarify the contextual and stakeholder influences on your approach to and use of CBTS:

- Reflect on a positive experience of supervision and think about the context in which this took place (e.g. group or individual supervision, service setting, the values of your supervisor and the similarities between you and your supervisor about the purpose/function of supervision. What factors contributed to making this a useful learning experience for you?

- Reflect on a less positive experience of supervision. What factors contributed to this? From this, can you deduce what might be useful to discuss when contracting for supervision (see Chapter 3)?
- When discussing clinical material, it might be useful to think about the local, national and global level influences shaping the way in which you discuss your clients. How do these influence your assessment and conceptualization of clients' presenting concerns and the type or length of CBT offered?

Conclusion

As Hess, Hess and Hess (2008: 165) observe, as psychotherapists, we are '...conveyers of social values ... embedded within a specific matrix of values'. We face the demand to serve many masters (Drake, 2009). In this chapter we have sought to enhance your understanding of the matrix of values in which your supervision practice is immersed through considering the current context in which CBTS is commissioned and delivered.

Viewing the supervision you provide through the lens of local, national and global levels of influence will enable you:

1. To become clearer about the stakeholders who impact (explicitly or implicitly) on what you provide.
2. To be better able to anticipate and manage any tensions arising from a conflict in individual and system-wide values.
3. To be in a stronger position to construct a supervision contract that is well placed to achieve the outcomes required.

Gray and Jackson (2011: 20) make the point that supervisors need to '...add the systemic and cultural aspects of organisations to their knowledge sets, as well as their understanding of an individual's perspectives. The influences of organisational culture become a significant rather than an incidental factor in the process of supervision'. We would see an awareness of such aspects as a critical foundation for effective CBTS and one that needs to precede the introduction of any method of instruction, intervention or evaluation to ensure that supervision remains both ethically secure and optimally effective. For this reason, we would recommend that time is spent during the earliest stages of supervision engaging in explicit discussion about the different contexts you and your supervisees inhabit, and analysing these in order to identify those factors that might enable and constrain the work you do together. Ultimately, this is no different from the kind of work that might take place with a client in the early stages of therapy and so can be seen as a form of modelling that the supervisor can usefully provide for their supervisees. In the next chapter, we consider the implications or 'outputs' of such an analysis – namely, how an emerging awareness of context can become built into the supervision contract that forms the basis of the work that is to follow.

Chapter summary

✓ CBT has attracted considerable interest in a health care climate that is complex, rapidly changing and in which the concept of 'the profession' has come under scrutiny.

✓ It is important to understand how the approach to CBTS adopted is immersed in a range of local, national and global contexts that influence our practice in complex and often subtle ways.

✓ Any supervision agreement should be couched within an understanding of the expectations and requirements of key stakeholders, such as line and service managers, commissioners of psychological services and credentialing bodies.

✓ It is important to consider how the interests of different stakeholders may contribute enabling and constraining conditions to the work that follows and to discuss these explicitly with supervisees.

THREE   Negotiate a Contract: Preparing the Terms of the Learning Agreement

Learning objectives

After reading this chapter and completing the learning activities provided, you will be able to:

- Appreciate why it is important to negotiate an explicit supervision contract with all those to whom you offer CBTS.
- Construct supervision contracts that are fit for purpose in the context of your service setting and unique supervisory offer.
- Identify and avoid common pitfalls in the contracting process.

Introduction

Once you have clarified your own 'brand' of CBTS (Chapter 1), and established the context in which that brand is delivered (Chapter 2), you are well placed to devise a supervision contract that will frame the work that follows.

Osborn and Davis (1996) describe the development of a supervision contract as a necessary ritual for both supervisor and supervisee. In this chapter we consider why this might be the case. Specifically, we examine the case for establishing a clear, comprehensive and agreed supervision contract, and identify what needs to be in place to achieve this. As a critical but often neglected element of planning the supervision experience, we identify some of the multiple functions that contracting serves, consider important content areas to include and provide guidance on how to devise contracts that are fit for purpose.[1] We also alert you to some of the common pitfalls to avoid.

The role of contracts in CBTS: What are they and why are they necessary?

In general terms, a contract is an agreement between identified parties that defines the terms and conditions, as well as the rights and responsibilities, that each party has in relation to specific objectives. Such agreements can be formal and legally binding or more informal and flexible but whatever form they take, they essentially serve the function of defining the obligations and entitlements of each party entering into some form of conjoint activity or relationship for an identified purpose.

Similarly, within supervision the contract is the principal, tangible means through which the roles, rights and responsibilities of supervisor and supervisee – and the limits of those roles, rights and responsibilities – are explicitly articulated. These terms may also become the basis for an appeal or complaint if a learning agreement is not subsequently honoured.

Ensuring that supervision is underpinned by a clearly defined contract may afford additional benefits. In their guidelines on CBTS, Townend et al. (2002) observe that while there is little empirical substantiation for their use, contracts are typically recommended in both books and supervision manuals for reasons that include:

- Helping both parties prepare for a situation where supervisor and supervisee have differing expectations of supervision that could, if unidentified at the outset, lead to a rupture in the alliance later in the process.
- Supporting effective negotiation around content and process.
- Helping to establish an approach to working that is consistent in structure and style with CBT itself.
- Establishing professional boundaries through identifying the different functions of supervision.
- Creating a foundation for the work that is to follow to ensure that supervisor and supervisee experience the setting as safe and supportive.

These points would echo recommendations across the supervision literature more broadly (e.g. Osborn and Davis, 1996; Freeston et al., 2003; Luepker, 2003; Thomas, 2007) where the rationale for underpinning supervision with a written contract has been cogently argued. The Newcastle

---

[1] This chapter is concerned exclusively with the supervision contract as the principal, tangible means through which the roles and responsibilities of each party are explicitly articulated. Ethical and legal issues are explored in Chapter 10.

Cake Stand Model (Freeston et al., 2003) encourages consideration of a range of issues which can usefully be explored in setting up a contract. Indeed, there is some evidence that having a contract can contribute to overall increased therapist satisfaction with supervision. Specifically in relation to goal setting, Lehrman-Waterman and Ladany (2001) found a strong positive correlation between supervisors engaging in collaborative goal setting with their supervisees and the development of a positive supervisory relationship, and also with overall supervisee satisfaction. This would seem to echo the earlier work of Talen and Schindler (1993), who found that ensuring supervisee-initiated goals were included in any learning agreement paved the way for a more productive working alliance.

Learning Activity 3.1   Your experience of supervision contracts

Think back over the CBTS you have received (rather than provided). How did your different supervisors approach the task of contracting in each case? How formally or informally was this task undertaken? What did you find most and least helpful about the approach adopted and why? Were any areas omitted from your discussions about the contracting process, or indeed from the contract itself, that subsequently left you feeling disadvantaged in your learning?

Now think back over your practice as a supervisor. What types of contract do you attempt to establish with your supervisees? How formally or informally do you approach the contracting aspect and what factors have shaped the way you approach this task? Is there anything about your approach to contracting that you think it might be useful to change at this point? If so, why?

Approaching the task of devising a contract

Arriving at a contract is the first stage in defining and structuring the working alliance between supervisor and supervisee, the aims and objectives that the alliance seeks to achieve, and the methods of education and evaluation through which the supervisee's learning needs will be met and monitored. Establishing an effective supervision contract draws upon the supervisor's skills in two distinct but interrelated domains. The first concerns deciding on the content areas of the contract, which will depend in part on understanding the purpose of supervision, the preferences and needs of the supervisee, and the preferences, knowledge and skills of the supervisor. The second domain concerns facilitating a process of negotiation. This requires an ability for clear, effective communication, managing an interpersonal exchange that enables the elicitation of learning aims and objectives, and ensuring that any contract achieves 'buy in' from relevant stakeholders. As such, we see the task of putting together a supervision contract as entailing both content and process elements, which we examine in turn.

What does a good supervision contract look like? Content areas to consider

First and foremost, the content of any CBTS contract will be informed by the purpose the contract needs to serve. This may seem self-evident, but it is not always immediately obvious or easy to discern, holding in mind the local, national and global level influences examined in Chapter 2. Consider, for example, how the content areas of any contract might vary as a function of context in the following:

1. A CBT-focused placement in a core professional training (such as clinical or counselling psychology) where there is an existing contract 'template' that you are expected to use derived from the service setting in which supervision is to be provided.
2. A learning agreement in which an experienced CBT practitioner seeks to broaden their knowledge and skills within a particular domain of CBT (such as advancing skills in conceptualization and treatment using compassion-focused therapy).
3. 'Remedial' supervision where the aim is to provide a learning experience that addresses sub-optimal performance.
4. Peer supervision between accredited CBT therapists who work in private practice and who meet in order to support their learning in the context of broader career development objectives.

Proctor (1988) has identified three functions of supervision that can assist supervisors in identifying broad domains which need to be considered. These are the normative, formative and restorative functions of supervision.

The *normative function* of supervision refers to those aspects of the supervisory engagement concerned with management and evaluation of performance. Its role within the supervision engagement is to ensure that supervisees follow relevant organizational procedures and that they work safely with clients. Here, supervisors will be holding in mind any service and/or training course requirements, the requirements of professional and credentialing bodes, and ethical and professional codes of conduct. This function translates into supervisor behaviour and specific interventions that are distinctly managerial in focus, monitoring performance as part of a broader quality control agenda and the extent to which the therapist conforms to the guidelines of their professional bodies.

Representing these functions contractually, the content areas on to which the normative function maps are likely to include:

1. The duration of the supervisory engagement.
2. The frequency and duration of individual meetings.
3. The format of supervision sessions (individual, group, face-to-face, telephone or Skype) and any issues arising from this (e.g. how use of Skype might impact on sharing recordings in the context of client confidentiality).
4. Expectations around preparation for supervision.

5. Policies and documents with which the supervisee can expect to be provided and/or should already be familiar.
6. Service expectations concerning professional standards and protocols.
7. Confirmation of the supervisor's relationship with other stakeholders, including with whom, and how, information about the supervisee will be shared.
8. How the boundary of the relationship between different roles will be managed (this is particularly important if the supervisor and line manager are the same person).
9. How confidentiality for both supervisee and client will be preserved (especially where session material is audio- or video-recorded).
10. The sharing, storage and retention of any supervision notes. For example, if a service uses an electronic record-keeping system, it will be important to clarify who has responsibility for entering any clinical decisions made in supervision and the amount of information to be included.
11. The methods by which performance will be evaluated, including how concerns about competence and 'fitness to practice' issues would be identified and addressed.
12. The avenues of support and consultation available to the therapist should concerns about the supervisor's performance or conduct arise.

> How might you expect to see the normative functions of supervision expressed in a CBTS contract? What specific features would you anticipate being included?

The *formative function* of supervision refers to the educational aspects of supervision. Its purpose within the supervision engagement is to ensure that supervisees have the level of knowledge and skill they need to be able to deliver therapy effectively. Here, supervisors will be holding in mind the existing CBT competence framework and any relevant treatment protocols, degree of therapist proficiency relative to stage of professional development and work experience, individual areas of strength and need, and also the supervisor's own strengths and limitations that will influence what can be offered. For example, if a therapist working in a medium secure forensic setting is seeking CBTS and the supervisor has no prior experience of delivering CBT in these environments, the formative needs of the supervisee may not be adequately met.

The formative function translates into supervisor behaviour that is focused on the educational components of supervision and is likely to take the form of teaching, advising, coaching, modelling and providing formative feedback. Representing these functions contractually, the content areas are likely to include:

1. The frequency and duration of individual meetings and how these relate to the educational objectives specified.

2. The format of supervision sessions (individual, group, face-to-face, tele-phone or Skype) and (in the case of group supervision) expectations of supervisee contribution to peer support and learning.
3. Expectations around preparation that is required, as well as bringing 'live' samples of practice through audio- or video-recordings.
4. Specific areas of competence and skill that will be a focus of supervi-sion, incorporating the supervisee's own learning objectives as well as those that the supervisor believes are important for the supervisee and any additional stakeholders.
5. Broader educational objectives associated with a supervisee's participa-tion in any formal programme of study that is underpinned by a national curriculum (as is the case with CBTS in the context of an IAPT training course).
6. The supervision methods that will be used to guide learning and development.
7. The way in which feedback will be delivered and the difference between formative and summative feedback. (It is difficult, for exam-ple, to engage with 'safe to fail' experiments such as role-play if the supervisee is uncertain whether their performance will subsequently provide the basis for a summative evaluation).
8. If relevant, the boundary between the educational experience provided by supervision and that provided by the training body and how, if at all, the supervisor will dovetail their approach with formal teaching pro-vided on a CBT training programme.
9. The ways in which the style and delivery of supervision might mirror the style of therapy being mastered (i.e. how CBTS is similar to, and different from, CBT itself).

> How might you expect to see the formative functions of supervision expressed in a CBTS contract? What specific features would you anticipate being included?

The *restorative function* of supervision refers to the interpersonal climate created by the supervisor and supervisee which enables supervisees to feel respected and valued in their contributions, and safe to express their doubts and needs. In considering this, supervisors need to hold in mind a supervisee's capacity for self-reflection and self-management; the impact of workload and stressors; areas of personal strength and challenge for the therapist; and their stage of professional development. The restor-ative function typically translates into supervisor behaviour that takes the form of support, containment and encouragement, as well as eliciting feedback from the supervisee on their experience of both the therapy they are delivering and the supervision that is provided. It might also involve some psychological problem-solving or cognitive restructuring, particu-larly if a supervisee has automatic thoughts, assumptions or beliefs that are impacting negatively on supervision.

Representing these functions contractually, the content areas are likely to include:

1. The type of contact and support that is offered (e.g. if the supervisee is experiencing difficulties in their personal or professional life, to what extent will the supervisor wish to be kept informed?).
2. The extent to which the identification of personal material will feature in supervision and how this will be managed (e.g. if working with personal material is a feature of supervision, where will the boundary lie between supervision and personal therapy? If personal material is not a feature of the supervisor's offer, where will this need be met?).
3. Discussion around self-management tools (e.g. to what extent would the supervisor expect the therapist to make use of CBT methods for the purposes of personal development and self-support, and assign homework in the service of this?).
4. The extent of the supervisor's availability outside formal sessions and the basis on which any additional contact is agreed.

> How might you expect to see the restorative functions of supervision expressed in a CBTS contract? What specific features would you anticipate being included?

How to go about effective contracting: Managing the process

Proctor's categorization of supervision is one of several available to inform your thinking about the content of a supervision contract, and it should be approached in the spirit of facilitating discussion rather than as a structure to be rigidly applied. The form that these different functions take will vary according to the supervision that you are being commissioned to provide.

From an educational (formative) perspective, establishing a contract achieves more than clarity about the work that is to follow; it also models for supervisees a specific competence that they will be seeking to acquire. Establishing a collaborative and boundaried relationship that supports the accomplishment of identified goals is the therapeutic offer that CBT makes to its clients. Through introducing this in the earliest stages of supervision, therapists discover how contracting can be conducted in an effective and respectful manner that fosters a sense of safety and trust. Equally, through the experience of the supervisor offering a collaborative venture, supervisees can learn that their perspectives are welcomed and that they can exert an influence on the terms and conditions of engagement. This is important because in a study on the relationship between supervisors and supervisees, Carroll (1996: 92) found that supervisees tend to '...have few expectations from which to negotiate with supervisors, and are prepared to "fall in" with the supervisor's ways of setting up and engaging in supervision'. Moreover, supervisees are likely to have many concerns relating to how supervision might develop. Typical cognitions might include:

- Will my supervisor like and understand me?
- Will they be able to meet my needs for learning and support?
- Is it safe to be honest about my practice with this person?
- What is expected of me?
- How will my supervisor evaluate my competence and with what implications?

As these concerns often remain unarticulated, it falls to the supervisor to elicit any cognitions and emotions that could influence how the supervision process unfolds. Use of guided discovery can provide invaluable insight into the supervisee's stage of professional development (see Chapter 4 for a review of developmental stages), prior knowledge and experience, general educational experience and attainment, and learning opportunities afforded by the clinical context. Assessing whether a supervisee can identify appropriate learning targets will also enable a supervisor to gain better understanding of the therapist's capacity for self-awareness. Does the supervisee, for example, come with a relatively accurate sense of their strengths and needs? Or are they less clear about their baseline level of competence and what might represent appropriate learning objectives?

Additionally, the contracting phase provides a context in which the supervisor can discuss explicitly his or her own areas of expertise, helping to foster an atmosphere of trust in which strengths and limitation can be openly acknowledged. Where your thinking is informed by a specific educational framework or CBT approach (e.g. first, second or third generation), we would advocate sharing this with your supervisee in the service of transparency. These 'professional disclosure' statements (Bernard and Goodyear, 2014) can help supervisors be clear about what they have to offer, and enable supervisees to reflect on what they are most likely to gain from that offer.

In facilitating the process of discussion about the main content areas of the contract, a useful starting point can be to engage the therapist in a self-reflective task that demonstrates the supervisor's commitment to learning about the person of the therapist and the range of influences that inform their approach. Chapter 1 provides a range of exercises that might assist supervisor and supervisee in identifying core areas for development, as well as enabling the supervisor to become alert to possible blind spots.

A further option is to ask your supervisee to construct a 'Supervision Résumé'. This can be completed either during a supervision session, or as a homework assignment. Essentially, the Supervision Résumé is a mapping exercise which enables supervisees to produce a summary of past supervision experiences in order to consider, thematically, their history of learning in this environment, as well as any experiences that have proved particularly impactful. (Mead (1990) proposes that some goals may reflect the influence of past experiences in supervision that need 'working through' before new goals can be established.) There are multiple variations of this exercise, which is flexible enough to be adapted according to the preferences of the supervisee (the use of genograms can be a helpful way to approach this task for those who are familiar with this tool for organizing client material). The illustration below provides one example that you can use with those whom you supervise. However, we would also recommend that you complete this exercise for yourself as a means of becoming clearer about the experiences that have shaped your own approach.

Learning Activity 3.2   The Supervision Résumé (for use with supervisees)

The purpose of the Supervision Résumé is to give you an opportunity to reflect on your past experiences of supervision in order to identify helpful and unhelpful sources of influence that may impact on how you approach supervision now. It can be helpful to share your findings with your supervisor as it will enable them to understand more about you, your preferences and needs, and how your supervision may need to be tailored to provide an optimal learning experience. In constructing your Supervision Résumé you want to make a note of:

1. Who provided the supervision.
2. Supervisor characteristics such as gender, age, culture of origin, profession and theoretical/therapeutic orientation.
3. When the supervision took place (the time frame and any factors relevant to your age and stage of life or professional development at that time).
4. What kind of material you covered in supervision.
5. Service setting.
6. Context, such as placement, privately commissioned, separate from or combined with line management supervision.
7. Whether the relationship was helpful/transformational/inspiring or the opposite of this.
8. How much about yourself, your work and your life you chose to share and conceal (and why).
9. How your learning was shaped by each experience.

When you have your Résumé, examine it thematically. What do you notice? You may discover that most of your supervisors have been of one gender, age group or cultural background. Your supervision may have been heavily influenced by one type of format (such as individual or group). Your experiences may have been very positive or more mixed. As you sift through past supervisory relationships, see if you can identify the legacy of these experiences. Based on your thematic analysis, is there anything in your history of receiving supervision that would be important for your new supervisor to know to enable them to support your learning now?

Contracting pitfalls to avoid

Arriving at a contract that is fit for purpose can be simpler to achieve in theory than it is in practice. In this section, we consider some of the pitfalls that can confront a supervisor and supervisee during the contracting phase and offer some recommendations on how to avoid them.

One common pitfall is spending insufficient time on the contracting process, particularly where supervisors have supervised many therapists over an extended period of time. Although it can feel tempting to rush into interventions, supervision can have a negative impact when therapists are not clear about what is expected of them, or how supervision will proceed (Nelson and Friedlander, 2001). Careful attention to establishing an agreed basis for moving forward communicates that the supervisor is sufficiently invested in the therapist's development to want to devote the time to establishing the foundations upon which later work will be based.

Another pitfall is assuming that a contract devised for one supervisee will automatically generalize to other supervisees (as might be the case when a trainee joins a service for the purposes of a placement). Certain elements may well be transferable. However, even where supervision forms part of a formal programme of study that is informed by a specific syllabus, supervision contracts should always incorporate individualized elements (Bernard and Goodyear, 2014).

It is also easy to avoid open discussions about potentially emotive aspects of supervision such as how competence will be evaluated. Kennerley and Clohessy (2010) highlight the importance of providing clear information on how feedback will be given and received. They encourage supervisors to ask themselves questions such as:

- What forms will feedback take?
- What measures will I use to support this?
- How will my supervisee know if I have serious concerns about their level of competence?
- How will I know if my supervisee has concerns about the quality of supervision they are receiving from me?

We examine how to evaluate therapist competence and provide feedback in Chapter 6.

An additional common pitfall is to underestimate the range of agendas that the contract serves. Supervision contracts often mirror the requirements of the service in which supervision is taking place. This creates a template of what Bernard and Goodyear (2014: 143) have described as 'how the supervisee must conform in order to be successful'. Here, the implicit function of the contract is to reduce the legal vulnerability of the service, with the content of the contract organized around a risk management strategy that privileges protection of the agency over the educational and support needs of the supervisee. Considering the normative, formative and restorative aspects of supervision and the relative weighting given to each of these functions can help protect against this. It is important to consider where your responsibilities and liabilities lie. If in doubt, we recommend that you consult your line manager, your own supervisor or your professional body.

Finally, we would recommend that any contract remains open to revision. It can be challenging for supervisors to support supervisees in identifying realistic and meaningful goals at the outset, particularly if no prior working relationship exists. For this reason, it may be preferable to encourage a regular revisiting of the supervision contract generally, or the goals component of the contract in particular, as the need for adjustments come to light.

Pulling it all together

In the current professional climate, it is often challenging for supervisors to retain awareness of all the potential complexities inherent in setting up and providing good quality supervision (Sutter et al., 2002). Supervisors need to be skilled in unearthing unarticulated assumptions and blending the potentially conflicting priorities of multiple stakeholders, including supervisee, line manager and the clinical service. Discrepancies in values and beliefs about supervision can occur and it is important to allow ample time during the contracting phase for identifying and resolving such discrepancies (Mead, 1990).

Having read this chapter and completed the learning activities provided, we invite you to adopt, once again, the role of supervision consultant and consider the following scenario in which Nina would appreciate some assistance. This is followed by hints for supervisees on points to hold in mind during the contracting phase of supervision.

Case Study 3

Nina has been providing CBTS to Jas for eight months and they have established an effective working alliance. Jas approached Nina in a private capacity and pays for supervision himself, as he said he wanted to pursue his professional development in CBT outside his current professional role where he already receives line management and integrative supervision for his therapy practice.

Jas is a counsellor by background, experienced in integrative ways of working with an emphasis on emergent processes in therapy. He is relatively new to delivering CBT interventions. At Nina's recommendation, they spent the first two meetings negotiating a supervision contract which has been formalized in writing and which focuses on the responsibilities and limits of responsibility of both parties. Working in this way is a new experience for Jas.

(Continued)

(Continued)

From Nina's point of view, Jas is a thoughtful practitioner who is committed to becoming an effective CBT therapist. Nonetheless, he tends to equate CBT with teaching the client 'stand-alone' techniques and Nina has been working with Jas to develop a more sophisticated perspective that includes focusing on case conceptualization skills. This is an area where Jas needs particular support.

Eight months into their working relationship, Jas announces that he wants to apply for accreditation as a CBT therapist with the BABCP and asks Nina to provide a reference. His request is a surprise to Nina as she does not recall this having been raised previously. Moreover, she is not convinced that Jas has accumulated sufficient experience to be ready to take such a step.

Nina checks the contract, advises Jas that this was not an agreed aim and suggests that they work towards this over a period of time. Jas responds by saying that he distinctively recalls their discussing this as a possibility. If never explicit, it was certainly implicit, and he sought to commission supervision on this basis. He adds that he wishes to apply for promotion in his service based on his emerging skills in CBT and explains that achieving accreditation will support his case that he can bring added value to the service. Indeed, he explains that his manager is fully supportive of such a step.

- How would you encourage Nina to conceptualize this dilemma?
- What factors might be contributing to this dilemma?
- How would you advise Nina to proceed?

(We provide suggestions on how to approach this dilemma in Appendix 3.)

Tips for Supervisees No. 3

As a supervisee, it is important for you to have a 'voice' during the negotiation of the supervision contract and to input into shaping how supervision will proceed. This will enable you to maximize opportunities for learning and reflection. Listed below are some useful areas for you to think about and questions that you can ask your supervisor.

- *What kind of preparation would be useful for me to do before supervision?*

This question will help clarify your supervisor's expectations.

- *How can we separate clinical supervision from line management supervision?*

This will be an important question to ask if your supervisor and line manager is the same person. If your supervisor and line manager are different people, ask how information about your performance and competence will be shared.

- *What are the immediate, medium- and longer-term learning objectives that I am looking to achieve?*

This will help you think about how to make the best use of supervision.

- *From your experiences of supervision so far, what helps and hinders your learning?*

It will be useful to reflect on the supervisory styles and methods that support and inhibit your learning. Discussing the methods that facilitate or hinder you in the context of specific objectives can be a safe and containing way for you to share helpful and unhelpful experiences of supervision.

- *What opportunities are there in supervision to discuss or explore personal material?*

This question will clarify whether you can bring personal material to clinical supervision and how you will be supported.

- *What opportunities are there for support outside formal supervision arrangements?*

It is important to ask your supervisor about the availability and type of any additional support offered.

- *What opportunities will there be to review my supervision contract?*

As the contracting process occurs mainly during the initial stages of a supervisory arrangement, it might be helpful to periodically review its usefulness and establish whether certain aspects can be renegotiated as your CBT competences develop.

Conclusion

The supervision contract is the foundation of the supervisor–supervisee relationship. In this chapter, we have examined how a good contract specifies the responsibilities of each party and how, as a critical component of CBTS, it is necessary to devote sufficient time and energy to this task prior to commencing with the delivery of other supervisory interventions. We have also made the case that the supervisor's careful and attentive approach to this type of preparation represents an intervention in its own right and mirrors what is required of CBT therapists in establishing realistic and meaningful therapy contracts with their clients.

For the purposes of creating an effective foundation for supervision, it is important for the supervisor to excavate, acknowledge and manage expectations that the supervisee may be bringing, and work to establish an explicit and negotiated contract that is acceptable to all parties. This requires skills in negotiation as well as an understanding of the content areas of CBT contracts that are likely to optimize learning for an individual supervisee.

The approach advocated in this chapter is offered as providing a foundational architecture from which individual variations can, and should, be developed as a function of: (1) the supervisor and supervisee's values and beliefs (see Chapter 1); (2) the context in which supervision is provided (see

Chapter 2); and (3) the nature of the work being supervised, including the aims and objectives which have been agreed.

Chapter summary

✓ Preparing for CBTS is best achieved through underpinning the work with a clear contract that specifies the responsibilities and roles of each party and the learning activities that will be offered.

✓ Devising effective CBTS contracts requires a supervisor to attend to two aspects: the content of the contract and facilitating a process of negotiation.

✓ Common pitfalls include paying insufficient attention to the task of contracting as well as avoiding discussion about the more emotive aspects, such as evaluation of competence.

✓ Use of Proctor's (1988) normative, formative and summative framework can assist you in devising an effective contract.

PART II

Undertaking Supervision

In Part I we considered what needs to be in place in order to establish an appropriate, effective and ethical basis for CBT supervision. We considered the beliefs and values you have about CBT and supervision as a

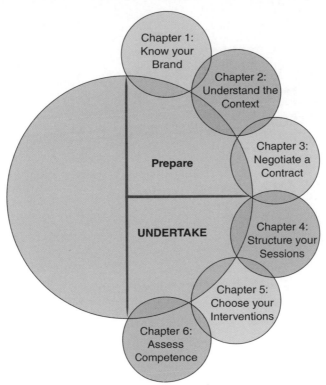

Figure 3   The PURE Supervision Flower: Undertake

basis for clarifying your particular 'brand'. We examined the context in which your CBTS is provided and how this will impact on what you offer. We then used this understanding to develop a contract that provides the basis for a learning journey while also establishing clear expectations and parameters for the work that is to follow.

Having completed the necessary preparations for undertaking supervision, in Part II we build on this by considering the content of supervision and the tasks, as supervisors, that you need to accomplish. This is the 'Undertake' element of the PURE Supervision Flower and comprises a focus on the second petals, as illustrated below:

Throughout Part II we encourage you to hold in mind the foundations you built through completing Part I of this book and how the ideas presented in each chapter might fit (or contrast) with your emerging understanding of your own personal 'brand' of CBTS.

FOUR   Structure your Sessions: Creating the Architecture of CBT Supervision

Learning objectives

After reading this chapter and completing the learning activities provided, you will be able to:

- Develop a structure that can support a consistent approach to selecting supervision interventions.
- Structure supervision sessions effectively as a function of supervisee need and stage of professional development.
- Develop a supervisory style which is congruent with your brand and context.

Introduction

In its broadest sense, the aim of CBTS is to enhance the clinical effectiveness of supervisees for the benefit of their clients. But how best can you achieve this in a way that remains consistent with the theoretical and procedural requirements of a CBT approach?

In the same way that CBT therapists emphasize the benefits of 'socializing clients to the model' prior to beginning therapy, so clarity concerning what to expect is likely to contribute to a smooth-running, effective and supportive learning experience. We would, therefore, concur with Bernard and Goodyear (2014) that, having established a supervision contract, a critical task is one of structuring the supervision experience in a way that affords clarity, sets boundaries and enables supervisors to identify specific interventions that will systematically support the development of their supervisees' knowledge and skills.

The aim of this chapter is to support you in developing an effective structure that paves the way for selecting supervision interventions that are optimal for your supervisees' needs. In the service of this aim, we begin by describing some of the challenges inherent in delivering effective CBTS of which supervisors need to be aware. We then identify what might be termed the 'hallmark features' of CBTS and examine some of the stylistic and procedural requirements that are specific to a CBT-oriented approach. Finally, we offer a range of frameworks that you can draw upon to structure the brand of CBT that you choose, or are required, to deliver.

By way of preparation, we invite you to first complete Learning Activity 4.1. The aim of this task is to orient you to the structure and style of CBTS by providing an opportunity to reflect upon your own experiences of being supervised in this model and how these experiences may have informed your own approach.

Learning Activity 4.1   Identifying the hallmark features of the CBTS you have received

Take some time to reflect on your own experience of receiving CBTS. What specific features were present that determined that the approach was CBT-oriented? Consider specifically:

1. Your supervisor's style of working.
2. The expectations your supervisor had of you as a supervisee.
3. The way in which the supervision contract was established.
4. The stated aims and objectives of your work together.
5. The types of issues you discussed (and did not discuss).
6. How the supervision sessions were organized, structured and delivered.
7. The range of methods used in supervision.
8. The ways in which the normative, formative and restorative functions of supervision were expressed (if you are unsure what these are, now is a good time to recap on the material in Chapter 3).

When you look back, how did these experiences shape your learning, development and practice as a CBT therapist? Which methods and aspects of the structure and style most effectively supported your learning and why? Which methods and aspects of the structure and style were least effective and why?

The challenges of providing high-quality CBTS

Providing consistently high-quality CBTS is a challenge. Training individuals to deliver competent CBT is an altogether more complex enterprise than it was in the late 1970s when the approach emerged as a treatment model for a limited number of specific disorders (Meichenbaum, 1977; Padesky, 1996). Supervisors today need to navigate a wide range of disorder-specific treatment protocols, be able to guide their supervisees in developing individually-tailored intervention plans for increasingly diverse clinical presentations and keep abreast of an expanding field of research and practice.

A further challenge for the conscientious supervisor is that competence itself is a fluctuating terrain. Even when supervisees are highly experienced therapists, their proficiency will vary from client to client (for example, as a function of client complexity), within an individual session (therapists are not necessarily consistently 'competent' across the duration of the therapy hour), and can be compromised by over-arousal or chronic stress (as might occur in the context of high levels of performance anxiety, overly large caseloads, or pressures resulting from organizational restructuring). Factors outside work may also exert a significant negative influence on a supervisee's resilience and capacity to learn. Learning and development cannot, therefore, be understood as a linear progression and supervisors will need to make session-by-session evaluations of what is required.

Given the challenges inherent in delivering high-quality CBTS, it is unfortunate that there are not, as yet, any empirically-substantiated models that could inform a more systematic approach to its delivery. As Reiser and Milne (2012: 162) comment, the under-developed state of the CBTS literature disadvantages both therapists and supervisors and remains 'an embarrassing situation given the empirical heritage of CBT'. Despite the absence of empirically supported guidelines, there are principles and frameworks that can usefully inform CBT supervisors' approach. The formal guidelines of credentialing bodies such as the BABCP, Roth and Pilling's (2007) competence framework (which we examine in Chapter 5) and the ethical codes of our professional bodies (see Chapter 10) all represent important sources of information for deciding how to organize the supervision experience.

What should CBTS look like?

In a helpful categorization of different types of supervision, Milne (2009) identifies the following principal formats:

1. Developmental models, derived from lifespan development theory.
2. Therapy models, whereby the concepts, principles and practices that underpin a particular therapeutic approach are replicated within supervision.

3. Supervision models that focus on the roles performed by the supervisor (see the normative, formative and restorative functions reviewed in Chapter 3).
4. Pragmatic models, whereby theoretically-informed explanations are de-emphasized in favour of more practical considerations, such as what might work best with a particular client at a particular point in time.
5. Evidence-based supervision, which aims to combine research with professional consensus on best practice in the pursuit of optimal supervisory interventions.

Although supervision may entail drawing on several of the above categories, and developmental constructs in particular have come to inform other formats of supervision (Bernard and Goodyear, 2014), it seems uncontentious to assert that CBTS would position itself broadly within the 'therapy models' category. Specifically, the delivery of CBTS can be expected to mirror the practice of CBT itself and will typically be:

1. Structured and directive.
2. Supported by a clear and transparent learning agenda (supervisees should know what to expect and what is expected of them).
3. Organized around specific aims, learning objectives and (where appropriate) operationalized goals that reflect meaningful outcomes for the supervisee, supervisor and other stakeholders who have an investment in the outcomes of supervision.
4. Organized around the principle of collaborative working.
5. Underpinned by a clear understanding of how progress will be evaluated and how the process of giving and receiving feedback will be managed.
6. Typically (although not dogmatically) organized around an agenda that is agreed at the start of each meeting.
7. Informed by a problem-solving focus.
8. Underpinned by a strong emphasis on experiential learning strategies and skills practice.

Consider the hallmark features of the supervision that you provide. What procedures, processes and style of delivery would enable an observer to identify your approach as CBT-oriented?

Consistent with these over-arching principles, a number of authors have attempted to provide descriptions of the activities that characterize a typical supervision session (Liese and J. Beck, 1997; Kennerley and Clohessy, 2010). For example, noting that the CBTS literature is currently in a transitional stage, Gordon (2012) has developed a ten-step structure, aimed at providing CBT supervisors with an accessible approach to organizing both the content of each session and the style of its delivery. The ten steps he proposes are outlined in Table 1 (NB: A third column has been added so that you can self-score on each of the criteria, and identify any personal areas of strength and development).

Table 1   Gordon's (2012) Ten-Step Model

Step	Brief description	Self-rating 1–10 (1 = very low level of skill; 10 = optimal level of skill)
Step 1	Clarify the supervision question. *Aim for a clear question which will promote learning*	
Step 2	Elicit relevant background information. *Keep it brief and structured, e.g. client problem statement, key points of history, formulation and progress to date*	
Step 3	Request an example of the problem. *This will usually include listening to a session tape extract*	
Step 4	Check supervisee's current understanding. *This establishes their current competence and gives an indication of the 'learning zone', where supervision should operate*	
Step 5	Decide the level or focus of the supervision work. *For example, a focus on micro-skills, or problem conceptualization, or on problematic thoughts and feelings within the therapist*	
Step 6	Use of active supervision methods. *Role-play, modelling, behavioural experiment, Socratic dialogue*	
Step 7	Check if the supervision question has been answered. *Encourage the supervisee to reflect and consolidate the learning*	
Step 8	Format a client-related action plan. *Formalize how the learning will be used within the therapy*	
Step 9	Homework setting. *Discuss any associated development needs, e.g. reading related literature or self-practice of a CBT method*	
Step 10	Elicit feedback on the supervision. *Check for any problems in the supervision alliance, or learning points for the supervisor*	

Adapting your structure and style to the idiosyncratic needs of your supervisees

Gordon's ten-step framework provides a useful structure for supervisors to reflect upon, critique and refine their approach. Nonetheless, how these features become translated into a specific style and format of delivery will depend on a broader range of factors, including the therapist's stage of career development and learning needs.

In our experience of providing consultation to CBT supervisors, it is not uncommon for them to alter their style and use of structure as a function of format and context. Consider, for example, how you might find yourself adjusting your style and use of structure to meet therapists' development needs in the following settings:

- A High-Intensity IAPT training, where a small group of trainee CBT therapists receive weekly supervision in order to achieve specific targets within a given time frame and the supervisor is working alongside a formal training programme to deliver a national curriculum.
- Monthly CBTS delivered to a highly experienced CBT therapist who is seeking a personalized milieu through which to extend an already well-developed set of CBT competences into a new clinical domain.
- 'Remedial' CBT-focused supervision where specific difficulties or learning needs have raised questions about competence to practise.
- Peer supervision between a group of experienced CBT therapists where the aim is to support the ongoing delivery of effective therapy alongside other functions that include discussions about managerial responsibilities and career development.

In planning a use of structure that is likely to create a 'best fit' with a particular therapist, we would advocate starting with a formulation of the therapist's general professional as well as CBT-specific needs. Of the many factors you might want to consider when compiling your formulation, the areas of personal and professional values, beliefs about CBT and contextual factors (which were examined in the Prepare phase of the PURE Supervision Flower) are useful starting points. In this chapter we consider two additional sources of influence: (1) the developmental stage of the supervisee, and (2) their preference for style of working.

The developmental stage of your supervisee

Developmental models of supervision (e.g. Stoltenberg, 1981; Stoltenberg and McNeill, 2010) propose that therapists progress through a series of stages. In order for optimal development to occur at each stage, different types of supervisory style and strategy are required. A range of models exist, with some proposing linear stages of development (e.g. Stoltenberg, 1981) and others informed by psychosocial developmental theory (e.g. Loganbill et al., 1982). However, perhaps the most widely applied is Stoltenberg et al.'s (1998) Integrated Developmental Model (IDM).

The IDM proposes that therapists progress through three stages of development, with shifts in self–other awareness, motivation and autonomy occurring at each stage. A brief description of each of these stages is summarized in Table 2.

Table 2 IDM Developmental Stages (Stoltenberg et al., 1998)

Level 1:	Supervisees have limited experience of the therapeutic modality in which they are being supervised. They are typically highly motivated to learn, wanting to progress rapidly through the anxiety that comes from being a novice. They are relatively dependent on the supervisor, with an under-developed capacity for autonomous practice and craving concrete answers to the challenges of therapeutic work. A concern with acquiring knowledge and skills to deliver the 'correct' response can result in a wish to imitate expert others, including the supervisor. This stage is characterized by limited self–other awareness (that is, a tendency towards self-preoccupation with relatively limited awareness of the client's internal and external worlds) and anxiety over evaluation.
Level 2:	Supervisees have moved beyond the initial phase of anxiety resulting in reduced self-absorption and an increased focus on the client (developing other awareness). This creates confusion, as supervisees have to grapple with therapeutic material in new ways. Simple instructions no longer seem adequate, which triggers feelings of ambivalence and resistance to the supervisor's recommendations. Thus, while there is a growing self–other awareness, motivation fluctuates, as does the ability for autonomous working. This stage is characterized by a dependency–autonomy conflict in which motivation varies as a function of therapeutic 'successes' and 'failures'.
Level 3:	Supervisees have achieved self- and other-awareness at a higher and more consistent level, moving towards what the authors have termed 'enlightened self-awareness'. As they begin to develop a personal therapist identity, motivation becomes more stable and the capacity for autonomous functioning increases. Self-doubt about professional competence occurs but is not paralysing in the way that is characteristic of earlier stages of development due to an emerging confidence in one's own professional judgement. Differences in knowledge and skill between supervisor and supervisee become less marked, with supervision adopting a more collegiate style.

Stoltenberg and Delworth (1987) have also proposed a higher level of development – the Level 3 Integrated therapist. This is where the therapist has integrated level 3 knowledge and skills across all domains of practice (assessment, formulation, intervention, etc.), and has a honed self-awareness of strengths and needs in the context of an individualized approach to working. This level is reserved for those 'master' therapists or experts in the field and is not necessarily attained by all.

Awareness of developmental stages can be a useful decision-making aid through enabling CBT supervisors to identify a structure that is consistent with the broad principles of CBTS while also accommodating individual differences. For example, at level 1, where supervisees have relatively limited experience of CBT (even if they come to this approach with experience in other models of therapy) and are typically both motivated and anxious, the IDM would suggest that supervisors use a highly structured approach which affords a greater sense of containment in the context of potentially high levels of anxiety. Optimal learning for level 1 therapists is supported by a supervisor who combines guided discovery with didactic input, direct instruction and clinical demonstrations to enable supervisees to address gaps in knowledge.

At level 2, motivation tends to fluctuate as a function of the supervisee's level of confusion and ambivalence. Identified by Stoltenberg et al. (1998) as a turbulent stage in therapist development, supervisors need to anticipate how supervisees might react against the structure of a CBT-focused approach. Here, it may be helpful to relax formerly highly structured ways of working in favour of a style of working that encourages greater autonomy. This may include inviting supervisees to take turns in setting the agenda and organizing the session (if supervision takes place in groups), and encouraging much more active sharing of ideas about each other's cases. This enables therapists to 'test out' their emerging proficiency within a framework that still enables supervisors to manage the process effectively.

At level 3, supervisees are focused on developing a more idiosyncratic approach to therapy, with a greater sense of relying on their own 'selves' as a resource of learning and development. Here, supervisees draw upon their own experience to reflect upon and critique their work; with core knowledge and skill consolidated, there is less didactic instruction in favour of collaborative working. However, there may also be greater levels of challenging which, as a function of the robustness of the therapist's knowledge, skills and confidence, are experienced as opportunities for enhancing learning. In group settings there will be an emphasis on sharing hypotheses, challenging ideas on what will be useful and offering recommendations based on past experience, with supervision resembling peer-facilitated learning.

The practical utility of developmental models for CBTS lies in their offering a heuristic for deciding on how to structure, organize and deliver supervision in ways that are consistent with the over-arching principles identified by authors such as Gordon (2012). Where developmental models are perhaps less informative is where supervisors need to adjust their style, approach and use of structure as a function of individual learning preferences. In certain cases, supervisor style has been found to trigger resistance (Quarto, 2002) with Tracey et al. (1989) finding that higher levels of reactance predicted therapists' preference for less structured supervision, at least among advanced trainees. As such, alongside developmental stage, preference for style of working must also be considered.

Preference for style of working

In reviewing approaches to group supervision, Proctor and Inskipp (2001) identify four common supervisor styles: authoritative, participative, cooperative and peer. This approach to categorization is mirrored in the literature on leadership, which has identified leadership styles as ranging along a continuum from autocratic (the leader makes the decision and then informs subordinates) to more collaborative or 'free-reign' approaches (where a team is permitted to function with a high degree of autonomy within specified parameters; see Tannenbaum and Schmidt, 1973).

Leadership models have relevance for CBT supervisors who, within the parameters of a CBT approach, need to consider how to adjust structure and style to the needs of a particular individual or group. In Figure 4, we present a variation of Tannenbaum and Schmidt's (1973) continuum of leadership behaviour, adapted to CBTS and, in particular, the style of the supervisor. Consider where you tend to position yourself on the supervisory styles continuum, which types of learner and learning need cause you to shift your position, and if it might be helpful to adjust your supervisory style in any way for those whom you are supervising currently.

Supervisor-led/'authoritative'
supervision style

Supervisee-led/'free reign'
supervision style

→

Supervisor functions as teacher and expert: 'Instructor-led discovery'	Supervisor uses Socratic dialogue to lead therapist/s towards a specific conclusion: 'Assisted discovery'	Supervisor presents options and invites responses: 'Supported discovery'	Supervisor draws on therapist's/s' existing knowledge, fills in gaps and enables therapist/s to synthesize understanding: 'Guided discovery'	Supervisor defines parameters of the dilemma and invites therapist/s to arrive at a solution: 'Peer-facilitated discovery'	Supervisor and therapist/s work together to generate useful questions that the therapist can then consider how to take forward: 'Mutual discovery'

Figure 4   The supervisory styles continuum

Drawing parallels between supervisor style and patterns of leadership can be helpful as therapists may vary in the extent to which they can thrive within learning environments that follow a predetermined structure. In their work on organizations and employee behaviour, Rajan et al. (2000) found that individuals differ widely in the extent to which they will follow someone else's 'script' and that individuals have specific preferences of which it is important for managers to be aware. Rajan et al. (2000) identified three specific categories which we would see as having implications for how CBTS is both structured and delivered. The categories are:

Actors: who prefer to follow a script that someone else has defined. In the context of CBTS, these therapists may particularly appreciate treatment protocols and/or value highly concrete guidance from supervisors.

Adaptors: who, while working within agreed frames, prefer to adapt their approach to meet specific client needs. In the context of CBTS, such individuals may particularly appreciate the clarity afforded by disorder-specific models but also want the flexibility to draw upon a range of ideas to create bespoke solutions.

Innovators: who prefer to experiment with a range of ideas to develop new possibilities for generating high levels of service. Such therapists prefer learning environments that allow for high levels of autonomy in decision-making and which encourage innovation and the adaptation of existing theory and practice.

These preferences for how we work also manifest in how supervisors approach the task of supervision. What type of CBT therapists, for example, are you seeking or being required to develop – actors, adaptors or innovators – and how does this translate into the style of supervision that you are providing? Equally, where would you locate yourself within the above preferences? Are you primarily an actor, adaptor or innovator and how do your preferences shape your approach?

Pulling it all together

Where supervisor style is aligned with both the developmental stage and learning preferences of a therapist the likelihood of optimizing the effectiveness of supervision is enhanced. In the service of formulating individual therapists' needs, you may find the type of planning tool provided in Learning Activity 4.2 a useful means of identifying and summarizing the key features of which you need to take account. (We have completed one as an example.)

Learning Activity 4.2   Planning your supervision style in the light of supervisee need and preference

Identify a current supervisee for whom you wish to plan an effective style and use of structure. Using the grid, insert both your formulation of their developmental stage (1, 2, 3, or even 3 Integrated) and their preference for style of learning. In the empty boxes in the grid, insert the implications of your assessment for your style of delivery of supervision.

Name of Supervisor: *Sarah C*

Name of Therapist: *Karine*

Context: *High Intensity IAPT Training - Term 1*

Agreed Learning Objectives: *To develop skills in case formulation and treatment planning; enhance cognitive restructuring with a specific focus on working with negative automatic thoughts*

Stage of Therapist Development in relation to these objectives: *Level 1 (case conceptualization and treatment planning); level 2 (cognitive restructuring with negative automatic thoughts)*

Learning Style Preference: *Requesting clear guidance and instruction, an opportunity to 'plug gaps in her knowledge' - Actor style preference?*

Therapist Developmental Stage	Supervisee Preference for Style of Learning		
	Actor	Adaptor	Innovator
Level 1	*Initial approach:* *1. Sarah to provide written examples of formulations and treatment plans from her own practice* *2. Instruction on how to approach case formulation (use of 'top tips' and relevant reading)* *3. Karine to bring written formulations and treatment plans to supervision for discussion*	-	-
Level 2	*Initial approach:* *1. Karine to role-play eliciting and revising NATs in supervision* *2. Sarah to provide clinical demonstrations* *3. Karine to bring regular recordings of sessions demonstrating her delivery of this skill for further guidance*	-	-
Level 3	-	-	-

Having read this chapter and completed the learning activities provided, we invite you to adopt once again the role of supervision consultant for Nina, our experienced CBT supervisor, who offers supervision to a wide range of colleagues as part of her professional role. This is followed by tips for supervisees on how to better understand and inform the supervisor's style of working.

Case Study 4

In a newly formed supervision group of mid-career professionals, Nina identifies that she is struggling to engage at least two of the three group members who bring to their post-graduate CBT training significant experience of working in other therapeutic modalities and some proficiency in CBT. One is looking for an open debate without appearing to recognize that her knowledge of CBT is quite limited. The other is more guarded in expressing her views but Nina notices that she nods in agreement whenever the other member criticizes Nina's style of supervision. The third person in the group appears more engaged in supervision and appreciates quite directive input which Nina is happy to provide, but whenever she does so, Nina notices how the other two members exchange fleeting glances. The group enjoys case discussion but seems to be reticent about engaging in skills practice.

Nina experiences her supervisory offer as being rejected by two members of this group and believes that she needs to find a way to engage these students. Drawing on the material covered in this chapter, consider your responses to the following:

- How would you encourage Nina to conceptualize this dilemma?
- What factors might be contributing to this dilemma?
- How would you advise Nina to proceed?

(We provide suggestions on how to approach this dilemma in Appendix 4.)

Tips for Supervisees No. 4

Once the supervision contract has been agreed, there should be a shared understanding of the expectations of supervision and clarity about practicalities and boundaries. The ideas below might help you gain optimally from the structure and style of your supervisor as your working relationship unfolds.

Think of two previous CBTS experiences, one negative and one positive. With particular reference to the supervisor's style in these different situations:

- What are the elements of supervisor style that help you learn best?
- What are the elements of supervisor style that help you least?
- Are there any supervisor styles that you might find yourself resisting?

After Stoltenberg et al. (1998), consider your stage of therapist development (level 1, 2 or 3) in different areas of practice (assessment, case conceptualization, intervention, etc.). Based on your self-assessment, consider:

- What types of supervisory intervention are most likely to facilitate your learning?
- What type or use of structure are you most likely to find helpful?
- What type or use of structure might you react against?

Use specific frameworks to identify your learning style and areas of development:

It might be useful to synthesize your reflections of your experiences of supervision from the questions above with your current learning objectives. You could refer to Roth and Pilling's (2007) CBT competences (see Chapter 5), or the Cognitive Therapy Scale-Revised (CTS-R) (Blackburn et al., 2001). After Rajan et al. (2000), consider also whether you would regard yourself as falling within the Actor, Adaptor or Innovator category. What implications might your learning style have for how you respond to your supervisor's attempts to structure the supervisory relationship? Do you and your supervisor have the same or different styles, and with what implications?

Conclusion

Regardless of the type of CBT you are supervising and your own particular brand, your supervisees need to become acquainted with the structure and style of supervision being offered to them. This provides the foundation and rationale for the selection of specific supervision interventions.

In this chapter we have introduced a range of models for thinking about the style and delivery of CBTS that are aimed at helping you retain fidelity to the model but which also afford sufficient flexibility to accommodate the idiosyncratic needs of those whom you are supervising. It is of course essential to familiarize yourself with any formal guidelines that relate to the CBTS you are expected to deliver (including training requirements if you are supervising as part of a CBT course) and to discuss with your supervisee how these will inform the structure of supervision and your particular style of delivery.

CBTS is a complex, multi-layered activity that requires supervisors to be able to navigate a shifting terrain. Learning poses threats to self-identity and prior beliefs about competence and skill, and supervisees expose themselves to multiple challenges when they open their work up to external scrutiny. Knowledge of therapists' developmental stage and learning preferences, couched within a formulation of their strengths and needs and the specific pressures and opportunities they face, will enhance the likelihood of organizing the supervision experience in ways that afford an optimal learning experience.

In the next chapter we consider how, based on the structure and style of your supervision, you can select interventions that are likely to ensure the aims of the supervision contract are realized.

Chapter summary

✓ It is important to underpin CBTS with a clear and specific structure.
✓ Despite the lack of a substantive evidence-base there are useful principles that supervisors can draw on to inform their approach.
✓ As a 'therapy model' of supervision, CBTS follows the principles and practices of CBT itself, which provides a foundation for the structure and style employed.
✓ In order to enhance the effectiveness of CBTS, it is useful to augment the existing CBT guidelines with developmentally-informed perspectives and knowledge of individual preferences for style of working. This enables supervisors to tailor the hallmark features of CBTS to the individual needs of the therapists they supervise.

FIVE Choose your Interventions: Selecting Methods to Enhance Proficiency

Learning objectives

After reading this chapter and completing the learning activities provided, you will be able to:

- Audit and evaluate the range of interventions that characterize your current supervisory practice.
- Be clear about what are essential and optional interventions in the context of your setting.
- Increase your ability to select supervision interventions that are optimal for the learning and development needs of an individual therapist.

Introduction

Having completed the learning activities from the previous chapters and identified an appropriate structure and style for your supervision, you are now well placed to identify specific interventions through which you can systematically facilitate the CBT proficiency of those whom you supervise.

One implication of the notion that good CBTS should mirror the practice of CBT itself is that a broad range of supervisory methods should be used. Choice of supervisory method also needs to take into account the strengths and needs, developmental level and learning preferences of the therapist, as well as the context in which supervision is mandated and delivered. In this chapter we focus on the competences that CBT therapists need to acquire, and consider some of the possible supervisory interventions that can be used to foster proficiency. Through drawing on current thinking about CBT competences and other approaches to guide the selection of specific supervision interventions, this chapter seeks to assist you in designing an effective learning process that will result in the improved performance of the therapists you supervise, and ultimately enhanced outcomes for clients.

Enhancing therapist proficiency through the supervision function

Competent therapists are able to draw upon and integrate knowledge, skills and attitudes in the service of client need (Roth and Pilling, 2007). Helping therapists to develop the ability to ground their clinical thinking in knowledge relevant to their discipline, apply this knowledge in ways that are appropriate to an individual client, and understand the rationale for the selection and application of this knowledge in specific contexts are some of the central tasks of supervision.

Hawkins and Shohet (2012), in a highly influential model, make the point that we are drawing on various experiences and bringing them into the room in supervision. They talk of 'seven eyes' through which we might view the encounter. They make the point very clearly that it is not just the therapist and supervisor who need to be seen, but also the client, the wider system and the parallel processes that are happening between each of these in the supervision session. Therapist proficiency is enhanced by enabling insights through these different viewpoints. In pursuit of this aim, supervisors need to offer a blended range of learning opportunities that can enable therapists to bridge the divide between what Williams (1995) terms 'campus and clinic'.

There are two principal tasks facing the CBT supervisor. The first task is deciding what specifically a supervisee needs to learn. The second is deciding which methods of learning are most likely to enable that learning to take place. Before we consider these tasks in more detail, we invite you to audit your own use of supervision interventions as a function of your context and style.

Learning Activity 5.1   Auditing your use of supervisory interventions

What methods of learning, or specific supervision interventions, do you use most and least often in your CBTS to support the growth and performance of those you supervise? Specifically consider how often you use:

	Always	**Often**	**Rarely**	**Never**
1. Case discussion				
2. Presentation of formulations				
3. Recommending and discussing reading materials				
4. Tips derived from your own clinical experience				
5. Didactic teaching on specific techniques				
6. Live observation or recordings of supervisees' sessions				
7. Clinical demonstrations				
8. Role-play rehearsal				
9. Guided discovery				
10. Working with the therapist's own cognitions, emotions and behaviours				
11. Homework for the supervisee				
12. Feedback (giving and inviting)				

What do you notice about the range of supervisory interventions that characterize your practice? Were any interventions always or never used, and if so, why? Overall, how would you rate the balance and blend of the different learning opportunities you provide? Does anything need to be changed to optimize your practice?

What are the competences that CBT therapists need to master? Taking a closer look

Muse and McManus define competence in CBT as 'the degree to which a therapist demonstrates the general therapeutic and treatment-specific knowledge and skills required to appropriately deliver CBT interventions which reflect the current evidence base for treatment of the patient's presenting problem' (2013: 485). CBTS is underpinned by an assumption that therapist competence is most likely to be achieved if supervision is structured (as we saw in Chapter 4), educational and focused on the acquisition and implementation of specific knowledge and skills (Liese and J. Beck, 1997).

Although CBTS encompasses a range of features, the selection of specific supervisory interventions will vary as a function of the career stage of the supervisee, the context in which supervision is taking place (e.g. initial training versus peer supervision between two experienced colleagues) and the chosen format (individual or group). While certain features may be non-negotiable (it would be unlikely that the supervisor would start to draw on concepts, principles and methods explicitly taken from another therapeutic approach), other features, such as modelling, experiential skills practice and case discussion, will need to be balanced in a bespoke fashion.

Proctor and Inskipp (1988) make a useful distinction between 'must interventions' and 'can interventions'. The 'must' category refers to those interventions that supervisors deem essential to ensuring that a supervisee follows through on a specific action (e.g. having direct access to samples of the therapist's work through live observation or audio- or video-recordings). The 'can' category refers to those interventions which confer greater autonomy for the supervisee to decide if, how and when to follow through on a specific action (such as a supervisor's recommendation for the supervisee to undertake self-practice/self-reflection in relation to specific CBT skills).

Drawing on CBT theory, we could consider the 'must' interventions as examples of conditional assumptions or rules for practice that, within the early stages of supervision, can be examined for their implications in much the same way that clients' assumptions are examined for their utility. Thus, supervisors can encourage those they supervise to embrace these assumptions not as impositions but as guidelines that can be tested out for their contribution to learning and development.

> Given the audit of your supervision practice in Learning Activity 5.1, can you identify the top three 'must' interventions that underpin your CBTS and how they inform your style of delivery? What also are your top three 'can' interventions and how do these inform your style of delivery?

In their work aimed at identifying the activities that typify proficient CBT for clients with depression and anxiety disorders, Roth and Pilling (2007; see also 2008b) have devised a map of competences which provides important clarification of the knowledge, skills and attitudes that underpin effective CBT. Through reviewing the efficacy of therapeutic approaches demonstrated in controlled trials, and studying the associated manuals detailing specific interventions and procedures, Roth and Pilling have identified over 50 competences that appear central to the delivery of effective CBT. Given the number and varying levels of competences outlined, the authors note that in its original format the framework cannot be used to assess competence, suggesting instead that competence measures identify and focus on assessing a subset of core competences. Nonetheless, the framework provides a comprehensive overview of competence in CBT, assisting therapists to identify the knowledge and skills they need to acquire, and supervisors to better understand what they need to teach. These competences have been organized into five domains, as shown in Figure 5.

Each of the five domains includes a range of activities which comprise a set of specific competences, as follows (NB: the full version of this framework and the details of the specific competences included within each domain can

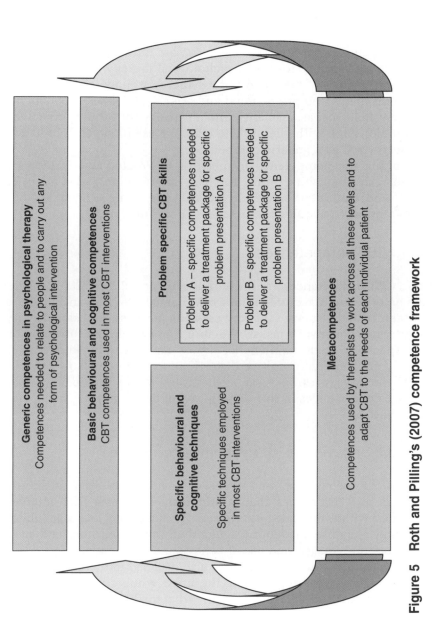

Figure 5   Roth and Pilling's (2007) competence framework

be downloaded from www.ucl.ac.uk/CORE. We would recommend that you familiarize yourself with this in addition to reading the summary below):

Generic competences

The competences identified as 'generic' are those that would typically be demonstrated in any form of psychological therapy. Often referred to as 'common factors', they incorporate therapist understanding of mental health problems and professional and ethical guidelines, the ability to conduct psychological assessments, and a capacity for forming effective working relationships with clients. The effective use of supervision would also be categorized as a generic competence.

Linking the competence framework to Proctor and Inskipp's (1988) notion of distinguishing 'must' and 'can' interventions, what might be your 'must' and 'can' interventions if you are supervising a therapist whom you believe needs to acquire competences in this domain?

Basic CBT competences

Basic CBT competences are those that Roth and Pilling (2007) suggest provide an orienting structure to the work that follows. They include the ability to organize and structure therapy sessions (through, for example, use of an agenda and homework tasks), the ability to explain the rationale for CBT, the capacity to elicit maintenance cycles, and a working knowledge of frequently encountered cognitive distortions and safety-seeking behaviours.

If you are working with a therapist whom you believe needs to acquire competences in this domain, what might be your 'must' and 'can' interventions?

Specific behavioural and cognitive techniques

The specific behavioural and cognitive competences refer to the principal methods and techniques that would feature in most CBT interventions. Identified within this category are activity monitoring and scheduling, exposure and response prevention, guided discovery, eliciting and modifying cognitions and images, and use of behavioural interventions. Use of formulation to inform treatment planning is also included in this category.

If you are working with a therapist whom you believe needs to acquire competences in this domain, what might be your 'must' and 'can' interventions?

Problem-specific competences

Problem-specific competences are those interventions and procedures described in disorder-specific treatment protocols for depression and the anxiety disorders for which there is empirical evidence of effectiveness. They are concerned with the knowledge and skills necessary to apply CBT concepts and methods to specific clinical conditions, based on the procedures for which effectiveness has been empirically substantiated. The framework details the assessment and treatment components of specific phobia, social phobia, panic disorder, obsessive-compulsive disorder, generalized anxiety disorder, post-traumatic stress disorder and depression.

If you are working with a therapist whom you believe needs to acquire competences in this domain, what might be your 'must' and 'can' interventions?

Metacompetences

The fifth domain of the competence framework refers specifically to what are termed 'metacompetences' – namely, those 'higher order' skills of thinking, reflection and procedural knowledge that enable a therapist to implement and adapt, pace and time specific interventions in response to client need. As Roth and Pilling (2007) note, these metacompetences are more abstract than those of other competence domains because they typically reflect the aims of the therapist and can only be inferred from the therapist's actions rather than observed directly. Both generic and specific metacompetences are identified. Whereas generic metacompetences include the application of clinical judgement, the pacing and timing of interventions, and the ability to balance fidelity to a treatment model with any relational issues arising, CBT-specific metacompetences include practising according to the philosophy of CBT, selecting optimal methods for individual clients, and the ability to manage obstacles and endings.

If you are working with a therapist whom you believe needs to acquire competences in this domain, what might be some of your 'must' and 'can' interventions?

Supervision strategies for promoting therapist development: How the competence framework can help

There are a number of ways in which use of the competence framework might assist the supervisor in selecting supervision interventions. Roth and Pilling (2007) comment that the framework has the potential to improve the quality of supervision by providing a clearer focus on the acquisition of those competences that have been empirically implicated in the delivery of effective CBT. In this context, the competence framework can provide a means of facilitating a dialogue with supervisees about specific areas of pre-existing skill and learning need. This may be particularly important early in a CBT therapist's career. As Drake (2009) observes, early on, it is often difficult for practitioners to know which domain of knowledge to focus on, let alone identify methods of learning that will optimally assist with the task in hand.

Roth and Pilling (2007) emphasize that the domains should not be interpreted as hierarchical, but rather as interrelated. For example, delivering disorder-specific CBT interventions is only likely to be effective if a therapist has an understanding of mental health problems (generic competence), is able to form an effective working alliance (generic competence) and has an ability to ensure that therapy is structured to ensure agenda setting and homework assignments (a basic CBT competence). Helping therapists understand how competences need to operate concurrently, and in complementary fashion, can assist therapists in developing a more sophisticated understanding of what competence is and pave the way for discussions as to how it may be acquired.

Using the competence framework to facilitate a dialogue around the nature of therapist competence can also challenge unrealistic and unhelpful beliefs about the nature of mastery. For example, helping therapists to identify areas of strength as well as need, the judicious application of supervisor self-disclosure concerning domains of competence that they are seeking to refine, and the fact that competence varies as a function of a wide variety of professional and personal factors, can highlight that excellence is an aspiration and ongoing commitment, rather than an outcome that can be definitively achieved. This awareness can demystify the supervision process and the process by which competence is acquired.[1]

> Take some time to look over the competence framework developed by Roth and Pilling (2007). What implications might it have for your practice as a CBT supervisor? Additionally, are there any domains of competence which you believe you need to develop as a CBT *therapist* in order to supervise them effectively in others?

Padesky's Supervision Options Grid

Padesky (1996) observes that competence requires both knowledge of cognitive and behavioural theory and an ability to apply this knowledge in a systematic fashion to the material encountered in the clinical setting. As a parallel to CBT itself, Padesky (1996) highlights how supervision needs to provide a balance of blended learning opportunities that afford data-based learning. These opportunities typically include case discussion, problem-solving and decision-making, didactic instruction on theory and technique, and treatment planning. They also include clinical demonstrations that provide learning on pacing, vocal tone and other forms of non-verbal communication, role-plays and homework.

---

[1] Therapists and supervisors can download a tool for assessing therapists' competences against the CBT framework (www.ucl.ac.uk/CORE). This provides a platform for identifying areas that might usefully form a focus of supervision at specific stages in a therapist's development.

In order to help supervisors make systematic choices about which supervisory interventions to use and when, Padesky (1996) has developed the Supervision Options Grid (see Figure 6).

		MODE				
		Case discussion	Video/ audio/live observation	Role-play demonstration	Supervisor- supervisee cotherapy	Peer cotherapy
F O C U S	Mastery of cognitive therapy methods					
	Case conceptualization					
	Client-therapist relationship					
	Therapist reactions					
	Supervisory processes					

Figure 6   Padesky's (1996) Supervision Options Grid

In the Supervision Options Grid, Padesky (1996) highlights how learning in supervision can be achieved by any of the identified 'modes' (the horizontal axis) and that the 'focus' of supervision (the vertical axis) will vary. Thus, at any given point in time, a supervisor may wish to prioritize the mastery of a specific skill, reviewing the case conceptualization, exploring the client–therapist relationship or the therapist's reactions or reflecting on the supervisory process itself, and may approach this through case discussion, live observation, role-play, etc. The task for the supervisor is ensuring that the selected intervention meets the need of the therapist. Padesky recommends that this can be achieved through supervisors:

- Building on the therapist's existing areas of strength (and then extending to areas that require development).
- Selecting modes of working and areas of focus that will enable the therapist to work towards the next level of competence or skill.

- Fostering conceptualization skills so supervisees become increasingly able to engage in self-directed learning.
- When problems arise, using a road map to pinpoint the problem and adopt a systematic approach to its resolution.
- Being attentive to what is not discussed in supervision.

There are a range of benefits for the supervisor and supervisee of adhering to such a structure, particularly in optimizing the formative function of supervision. Specifically, it enables the construction of a map of learning options that responds to different types of development need, protects against what Gambrill (2005) has described as the 'monomethod bias' (whereby one method of data-gathering is overused at the expense of a more balanced approach) and supports supervisors in thinking through their rationale for choice of supervision method. A further benefit of using the Supervision Options Grid is that it enables supervisors to audit their practice. For example, take a moment to reflect on your supervision practice in light of the options that Padesky (1996) identifies. Which of those do you use regularly, occasionally, rarely and never? Is your practice consistent or are there marked variations depending on whom you are supervising (and if so, what influences your choice)? Are there any methods that you would like to try (or think you should try) using more frequently? What impact do you think this might have?

Bennett-Levy's Declarative Procedural Reflective Model

The third model which we examine in this chapter is a more recent contribution that is grounded explicitly in information-processing theory. The Declarative Procedural Reflective (DPR) Model (see for example, Bennett-Levy, 2006; Bennett-Levy et al., 2009) is offered as a comprehensive framework for informing understanding of why different domains of skill develop at different speeds, and why diverse methods of instruction are required for the enhancement of specific skills. An extensive review of this model and its implications for practice is beyond the scope of this chapter (see Bennett-Levy, 2006, for a review). In brief, this model identifies three principal systems of therapist skill development: the declarative, procedural and reflective. Each of these systems develops optimally through use of different learning strategies, as illustrated in Figure 7.

The declarative system is concerned with factual information about particular aspects of therapy generally or CBT specifically (such as knowing about a specific model of depression or that CBT sessions are agenda-led). Procedural knowledge, in contrast, concerns rules of application that enable a therapist to discern what to do and when. This assists the pacing and timing of interventions as well as decisions about which intervention to introduce at any given point in time. As Bennett-Levy (2006) observes, this level of knowledge is often tacit, reflecting the operation of therapists'

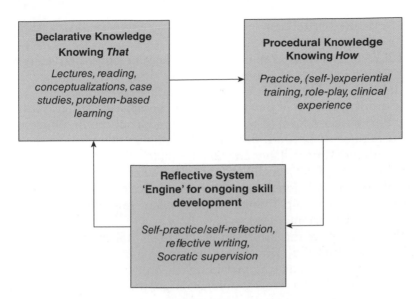

Figure 7   DPR Model of therapist skill acquisition and refinement
(adapted from Bennett-Levy, 2006)

cognitive strategies that have evolved over the course of their development as a result of refinements in decision-making and problem-solving, and the 'chunking' of knowledge to enable a much broader repertoire of procedural skill. Finally, the system through which expertise is acquired is the reflective system and that which Bennett-Levy argues is the central skill that supervisors should be aiming to develop.

The development of each of these systems is differentially responsive to different methods of instruction. Thus, while lectures, reading and observation are forms of didactic instruction that facilitate declarative learning, they will not assist the procedural knowledge that is required for the direct implementation of CBT skills. Although aided initially by grounding in teaching and clinical demonstrations, procedural knowledge is ultimately attained through experiential methods of learning and application in clinical settings, which provide the training ground for its refinement. For this reason, a balance of training methods is required. In a more recent development of this work, however, Thwaites et al. (2014) propose that central to the development of all three information processing systems is self-practice/self-reflection, which is integrative, not only impacting the reflective, procedural and declarative systems, but also helping to link them (see also Gale and Schröder, 2014). As such, use of self-practice/self-reflection can be understood as offering an integrative approach to both training and supervision and is 'ideally suited to enhancing the skills of therapists who have learned the basic techniques of CBT, and now wish to move towards developing therapeutic artistry by learning CBT "from the inside"' (Thwaites et al., 2014: 242).

Pulling it all together

A critical task for supervisors is deciding where to focus their energies at a specific point in time, as a function of the supervision contract that has been established and the therapist's baseline level of competence and skill. In our experience, it is not unusual for CBT therapists to struggle with identifying their baseline level of competence and one of the first interventions required of supervisors can, therefore, be training therapists in the task of self-assessment. Bennett-Levy and Beedie (2007) also describe how, during CBT training, there is typically an unfolding awareness of what CBT actually involves. The judicious use of a blended range of learning opportunities by supervisors can help therapists hone their emerging ability for self-assessment in important ways.

In their concept of the Informed Practitioner, Stober and Grant (2006: 6) have identified that the critical issue is not so much one of applying prescriptive interventions as it is providing 'theoretical frameworks, information, critical thinking, and methodological rigor that the practitioner can use to navigate the ever-changing waters of the ... intervention'. In seeking to equip therapists with this type of competence, supervisors do well to ensure that their choice of intervention is underpinned by a suitable framework, or frameworks, that can enhance the rigour of the decision-making process.

Of course, competence frameworks need to be used with considerable skill if they are to fulfil their potential as a method for improving client outcomes. As Gambrill (2007) cautions, if lists of competences are divorced from the decision-making process, there is a risk of 'bucket theory' thinking; that is, where the task of training becomes conceptualized as one of essentially pouring knowledge into students' heads.

It is also important to note that the use of competence frameworks is itself contentious. While the breadth of the debate is beyond the scope of this chapter, Wheelahan (2007) has observed that the increasingly widespread embracing of competence frameworks has a number of consequences. In particular, therapists are initiated into the world of professional practice through access to specific content, but not the systems of meaning which generated that knowledge. In the absence of those generative principles, the creation of new knowledge or the criteria to select the knowledge needed in new contexts is missing. Thus, being taught to supervise using specific content has the potential to leave supervisors struggling when supervisees present something outside that particular frame. Moreover, Drake (2011) has argued that while competence frameworks provide valuable scaffolding for practitioners at novice and intermediate stages, they may be less helpful for guiding the development of optimal performance among advanced practitioners. He concludes: 'While it is possible to deconstruct excellence into observable components ... it is less possible to reconstruct excellence from these components' (Drake, 2011: 140).

Having an awareness of the debates about competence frameworks acts as a reminder that the acquisition of competence is a complex activity that cannot be understood as a checklist of individual skills – a point made also by Roth and Pilling (2007). In working to facilitate proficiency across the spectrum of competences and domains, there are many methods of learning that can potentially be utilized. By drawing on the frameworks described in this chapter, and anchoring their use in a formulation of the supervisee's strengths and needs, the supervisor is better equipped to select methods from the wide range of interventions available.

Learning Activity 5.2   Recommendations for selecting your supervision interventions

Consider the recommendations outlined below and how you could implement them to support your supervision practice in your particular context. You may find it helpful to identify a specific supervisee and work through this list in relation to their needs.

1. Ask your supervisee to undertake a self-assessment of their competence and skill at the outset of working together. A variety of options exist but two possibilities are the Self-Assessment Tool developed for use with Roth and Pilling's (2007) competence framework, or a commonly used measure of therapist competence such as the CTS-R (Blackburn et al., 2001). This can help create a shared understanding of baseline levels of competence that can form the basis of an individual development plan.
2. Ensure that all the 'fundamentals' are in place for you to be able to make an informed decision about a therapist's development needs. Be certain that the therapist knows how to present a case and can extract the salient issues that need to be discussed from large amounts of clinical material. Also ensure that they can present a clear, concise and workable supervision question.
3. Have an understanding of the stage of development and learning preferences of your supervisee and how this might influence the use of specific interventions.
4. Identify specific skills and competence domains you will work on for the short term, medium term and longer term (depending on the duration of the supervision contract).
5. Identify which methods of learning will be most relevant to enhancing competence in specified areas.
6. Consider whether your intervention is aimed at the normative, formative or restorative level at any particular point in time. For example, didactic instruction may meet a need at the formative level but can also provide containment during a period of anxiety and may, therefore, also contain a restorative element.

Having read this chapter and completed the learning activities provided, we invite you to adopt, once again, the role of supervision consultant to Nina. This is followed by tips for supervisees on areas that may be helpful to discuss in supervision.

Case Study 5

Nina was becoming concerned about the lack of confidence that Sandra exhibited in her ability to deliver CBT. Sandra was a recently qualified clinical psychologist who, despite doctoral-level training, had avoided sharing recordings of her sessions and often asked for very concrete guidance on how to proceed, framing her supervision questions as 'What should I do?'. Nina would have anticipated Sandra to have greater confidence in her knowledge and expertise after an extensive training and previous CBT-oriented placements.

At the outset of supervision Nina asked Sandra to complete Roth and Pilling's self-assessment tool. A lengthy debate with Nina about the pros and cons of competence-based supervision had not resulted in Sandra completing the measure or any of the alternatives which Nina had suggested as a means of establishing baseline competence. Sandra's preference was for discursive supervision with a heavy emphasis on case discussion and individualized formulations, and a tendency to compare CBT unfavourably with other therapeutic approaches.

Sandra had just assessed a client who appeared to have relatively straightforward PTSD. Nina believed that the intervention of choice was clear, but Sandra was yet to bring a formulation and intervention plan to supervision. Nina was becoming suspicious that Sandra's apparent lack of confidence masked a lack of knowledge in key areas. She had no wish to shame Sandra but, as her supervisor and line manager, Nina was clear that she needed to understand what Sandra was, and was not, competent to provide.

- How would you encourage Nina to conceptualize this dilemma?
- What factors might be contributing to this dilemma?
- How would you advise Nina to proceed?

(We provide suggestions on how to approach this dilemma in Appendix 5.)

Tips for Supervisees No. 5

Take some time to review any supervision contract that has been established, and what has been agreed in terms of the structure, style and learning objectives of supervision. Having done so, see how you might use the ideas below to discuss the kinds of interventions your supervisor will be drawing upon.

Ask your supervisor about models that inform their approach to supporting your learning:

- Do they use a specific model (such as Padesky's)?
- Do they use the Roth and Pilling's (2007) competence framework to guide their thinking about your needs? If so, how? How would they recommend that you use it to monitor your own progress?

- What led to them to favour the model they use and how do they apply it? (Their choice may be based on very practical considerations rather than elaborated theoretical constructions. For example, supervisors often find it most helpful to hold in mind a simple and practical model that enables them to think constructively with you about client material.)

What type of supervision interventions can you expect (and how do these relate to your own expectations? Do you need to discuss these?)?

- What are your supervisor's 'must' and 'can' interventions? What is the rationale for these choices?
- What are your 'must' and 'can' interventions (i.e. features of CBTS that, if they were absent, would greatly concern you, and ones that it would help you to have included as part of your work together)? What is the rationale for these choices?

Seek formative and summative feedback regularly:

- Come to supervision with a clear sense of your own strengths and 'growing edges'. How does this compare with your supervisor's assessment of your competence and skill level?
- Ask your supervisor's advice about what method/s they would recommend you use to evaluate your competence and track your progress.
- Be open to feedback – even when it's uncomfortable to hear!

Conclusion

Friedberg et al. (2009) describe how good clinical skills depend on an ability to deal with the 'raw realities' encountered in the consulting room. They make the recommendation that those training in CBT should be assisted in developing an understanding of the sometimes bewildering scenarios with which they will be confronted. In addition, there is a considerable amount of material that CBT therapists need to master. In assisting the therapist in this endeavour, the supervisor's own decision-making can be optimized by ensuring that their selection of supervisory method is underpinned by a specific framework that can be explicitly articulated and shared. This is likely to provide greater clarity and transparency and offer a more systematic approach to learning and development throughout the supervisory engagement.

In this chapter we have introduced three frameworks that can guide the selection of supervisory interventions. The competence framework developed by Roth and Pilling offers a timely and detailed understanding of what potentially underpins the effective delivery of CBT and offers the supervisor a range of competences, embedded within specific activities and overarching domains, that can provide a rationale for targeting specific areas of development. Padesky's Supervision Options Grid represents a helpful, practical model for identifying a focus for action and mode of delivery that can be used in the service of a particular development need. Finally, the more elaborate model offered by Bennett-Levy (which we explore further in Chapter 7) provides an important guide for understanding why different domains of skill develop at different speeds, and why diverse methods of instruction are required for the enhancement of specific skills.

These are only three of the frameworks available that can support CBT supervisors in making choices about how to select supervision interventions in the context of an ongoing evaluation of their supervisees' development. In the next chapter we consider how, having applied your interventions, you evaluate your supervisees' competence and the implications of any evaluations that you make.

Chapter summary

✓ It is important to underpin your choice of supervisory intervention with a specific framework or model that can provide a rationale for your approach.
✓ It is useful to differentiate between essential ('must') and optional ('can') interventions when developing a learning plan for supervisees.
✓ Roth and Pilling's Competence Framework, Padesky's Supervision Options Grid and Bennett-Levy's DPR Model are three among a range of frameworks that can guide the development of a systematic approach.
✓ The use of such frameworks assists supervisees in developing an understanding of the sometimes bewildering dilemmas they will encounter in practice.

SIX Assess Competence: Developing an Effective Approach

Learning objectives

After reading this chapter and completing the learning activities provided, you will be able to:

- Decide how to organize the evaluative aspect of supervision in a way that makes sense for your context.
- Apply general recommendations from the literature to the needs of individual supervisees.
- Improve your evaluations of therapist competence.

Introduction

In the previous chapter we identified the knowledge and skills that CBT supervisors aim to foster in those whom they supervise. We drew specifically on Roth and Pilling's (2007) competence framework, Padesky's (1996) Supervision Options Grid, and Bennett-Levy's (2006) Declarative Procedural Reflective Model as three possibilities that can assist the selection of supervision interventions.

In this chapter, we focus on what is perhaps one of the thorniest aspects of supervision – namely, the task of assessing therapist competence and providing feedback on your evaluations. We begin by considering why this supervisory task is so critical and yet often so challenging. We then examine how you can develop a systematic approach to assessing the competence of your supervisees and, finally, offer guidance on how to deliver your evaluations, framing them in a way that increases the likelihood of your feedback being heard and used effectively. To orient you to the material that follows, we first invite you to complete Learning Activity 6.1.

Learning Activity 6.1   How do you evaluate the competence of those you supervise?

When you are supervising a CBT therapist (including in the context of peer supervision), how do you decide whether or not that individual is 'competent'? Specifically:

1. What performance evaluation criteria do you use?
2. What specific methods and instruments do you use?
3. How much knowledge of a therapist's practice, and over what time-scale, would you need in order to reach a judgement?
4. To which factors (e.g. theoretical knowledge, technical delivery, interpersonal qualities) do you attach most and least significance when you evaluate competence (and why)?
5. Who, or what, shapes your approach to evaluation? Whose expectations are accommodated in your approach to the assessment of competence?

The case for, and challenges of, effective therapist evaluation

The assessment of therapist competence is a defining feature of supervision. Indeed, in models of supervision where the approach closely resembles the style of the therapy being mastered, it is the evaluative component that differentiates the supervision from the therapy. Without assessment of performance being present, it is questionable whether the task being undertaken is actually supervision at all.

The evaluation of therapist competence in CBT serves a number of critical functions. Specifically, it supports the delivery of safe and effective practice (Falender and Shafranske, 2004) and is thus a vital part of a supervisor's duty of care to clients. Indeed, there is evidence to suggest that, certainly in the context of depression, therapist competence is implicated in the treatment outcomes obtained (Kuyken and Tsivrikos, 2009; Strunk et al., 2010). Additionally, the ability to accurately assess therapist competence is vital to the success of disseminating CBT into clinical services (Muse and McManus, 2013).

In terms of the formative aspects of supervision, evaluation also provides a direct means through which therapists can gain insight into the extent of their knowledge and skills. If carried out effectively, the evaluative component of supervision equips supervisors with an important means of interpersonal influence; through their supervisors' feedback, therapists are presented with an extrinsic motivation to hone their skills (Bernard and Goodyear, 2014).

Despite the critical importance of this task, supervisors have been found to provide insufficient feedback (Larson, 1998), and in particular to avoid constructive criticism (Hoffman et al., 2005). This may be because delivering evaluations is experienced as anxiety-provoking. Arguably, most individuals do not seek to become supervisors with the aim of reaching a verdict on a colleague's competence. As such, this aspect of the supervisory role may be perceived as incompatible with certain values that are core to the supervisor's sense of identity and purpose, including the desire to support another's growth (Cohen, 1987).

The evaluative component of supervision also brings into sharp focus the fact that in most cases (with the exception of peer supervision) the relationship is hierarchical. When conducting assessments of competence, the supervisor's focus shifts away from the formative and restorative functions of supervision towards the normative or managerial functions. This has significant implications for supervisees for whom supervisors then become not only teachers but also 'feared judges who have real power' (Doehrman, 1976: 10–11). This may in turn lead supervisees to withhold information on their clinical practice (Hess, 2008).

Additionally, as discussed in Chapter 5, clinical competence is neither dichotomous nor absolute but relative to stage of career development and professional context (Gray and Jackson, 2011). It is unlikely, for example, that a supervisor would use the same performance evaluation criteria for a CBT trainee on a High Intensity IAPT training programme as they would for an experienced accredited CBT therapist seeking to extend their skill set to a new client group following a change in role. However, it may be the case that the supervisor's context requires them to assess therapist performance against a set of predetermined institutionally- or nationally-defined criteria which will affect the ways in which judgements are formed and the extent to which a developmental formulation of the therapist's strengths and needs can be accommodated.

Supervisors' evaluations also need to be contextualized. It is important to be aware of whose needs any evaluation does and should serve. Who will be informed of any judgements made and with what implications? What are the ethical and legal implications of those evaluations? Moreover, the evaluation has both a present and a future focus. Is the evaluation one that relates to performance at a specific point in time (such as when evaluating a recording of a session)? Or is the evaluation concerned with developing a more global picture? Supervisors need to determine whether a therapist is competent in delivering CBT to current clients, but often must also seek evidence of competence to work with future clients. An example of a dilemma at this level might be where a therapist performs with sufficient competence in a particular sessions to achieve a 'pass' on a standard measure of proficiency but the supervisor harbours doubts about the therapist's ability to deliver CBT more generally. It can be seen, then, that evaluating therapist proficiency is fraught with challenges.

How to improve your evaluations of competence

As CBT supervisors, we have found it helpful to organize our approach to evaluation using a three-step method. These steps are outlined in Table 3 and then examined in greater detail.

Table 3   Three stages in conducting effective evaluations: a framework to guide you

1. Be explicit about the performance criteria you are using to inform your evaluations:

    a. Have a working definition of competence.
    b. Be able to explain any frameworks you are using as a basis for determining your choice of performance criteria.

2. Be explicit about the evidence you will use to inform your evaluations:

    a. Be clear about the types of data, data-gathering or instruments upon which you will base your assessments of competence and why.
    b. Know how you will implement these.

3. Manage the process effectively:

    a. Have a clear mechanism or procedure for delivering feedback.
    b. Anticipate how your feedback will be used by the recipient and any other stakeholders in the process.

1. Be explicit about the performance criteria you are using

To the best of our knowledge, there is no universally agreed definition of CBT competence. Moreover, there is no single method of assessment that can provide all the necessary information to arrive at a well-rounded conclusion about the quality of another's professional practice (Miller, 1990). In the absence of definitive criteria that can be readily imported into the supervision context, a number of scholars have offered frameworks through which judgements about another's level of skill might be formed. Miller (1990), for example, proposes the use of a hierarchical framework for the assessment of clinical skill. At the base of the hierarchy is 'knows' (knowledge), followed by 'knows how' (competence), then 'shows how' (performance) and at the top of the hierarchy, 'does' (action).

To elaborate, at the lowest level lies the knowledge needed to perform a variety of functions effectively. For example, does a CBT therapist 'know' Clark's model of social phobia to the extent that they could describe or reproduce it diagrammatically? There is, however, more to the competent delivery of professional practice than 'knowing'. The next level of the hierarchy denotes 'know how'. Knowledge remains inert if it is not utilized in ways that assist performance. It is the capacity for translating knowledge from a variety of sources into a formulation and action plan that signifies competence at the level of 'know how'.

'Knowing how' needs to take the form of 'showing how', where the therapist demonstrates the ability to act effectively and to implement their knowledge through, for example, simulations of therapy sessions such as role-play rehearsals and other forms of experiential learning. Finally, the top layer of the hierarchy is concerned with what a practitioner 'does' – that is, the act of functioning independently with clients and the myriad content and procedural adaptations that need to be made to optimize effectiveness for an individual client.

In reviewing the available methods for assessing competence in CBT, Muse and McManus (2013) draw on Miller's (1990) hierarchy to categorize and evaluate the contribution of different approaches. At the level of 'knowing', for example, they identify the benefit of essays and multiple choice questionnaires; at the level of 'knowing how', the use of case reports and clinical vignettes are identified. For 'showing how', standardized role-plays are valuable. Finally, formal ratings of CBT sessions using standardized instruments, as well as reviewing outcomes and other forms of client feedback, are necessary for evaluating competence at the level of 'doing'.

Miller's hierarchy provides a useful rubric for helping supervisors evaluate particular kinds of therapist strength and need. For example, it may be helpful to categorize emerging judgements about a therapist's proficiency through use of the following questions:

1. To what extent is this therapist competent in 'knowing' critical aspects of CBT (that is, do they have the necessary understanding of theoretical constructs, theories, principles and models to know what underpins effective CBT)?
2. To what extent is this therapist competent in 'knowing how' (that is, the practical aspects of effective CBT delivery. What, if any, aspects are absent? Can you identify these, comparing them against Roth and Pilling's (2007) competence framework)?
3. To what extent is this therapist competent in 'showing how' this knowledge is delivered (are there specific procedural aspects of delivery that are lacking)?
4. To what extent is this therapist competent in 'doing' CBT? (Do you see them as 'a safe pair of hands'? If not, why not? Can you map this back to a particular domain or competences in Roth and Pilling's competence framework?)

What is your definition of competence? If you were required to provide an operational definition, what would it be? After Miller (1990), what criteria would you seek as evidence of 'knowing, knowing how, showing how and doing'?

2. Be explicit about the evidence you will use to inform your evaluations

In order to form an opinion about a therapist's proficiency, performance criteria need to be translated into specific standards. As identified previously, evaluation of competence is likely to take multiple forms and ideally draws on a range of methods. However, in broad terms, assessments of proficiency are likely to fall into one of two categories: formative assessments and summative assessments. Formative evaluation is principally concerned with tracking and facilitating growth along a developmental trajectory to help steer the learning process (Robiner et al., 1993). In contrast, summative evaluation entails what Bernard and Goodyear (2014: 224) describe as '"the moment of truth", when the supervisor steps back, takes stock, and decides how the supervisee measures up'. This is when supervisors, in essence, reach a verdict.

When selecting methods of evaluation it is important to remember that any method used will shape what you do, and do not, attend to. Observation is not neutral and each tool provides merely one of many lenses through which to form an opinion. For example, the presentation of a case formulation couched within a case discussion will lead a supervisor to obtain a qualitatively different type of data from that obtained through listening to a therapy session and rating this on the Cognitive Therapy Scale – Revised (CTS-R) (Blackburn et al., 2001). In deciding upon your approach, you will need to consider whether you are in a position to make a relatively autonomous choice based on your own beliefs about what assists optimal evaluation, or whether this decision has been made for you (such as might be the case if you are supervising in the context of a CBT training course). A first step, therefore, is to identify the kind of data you need for the task in hand.

Learning Activity 6.2   What are your preferred methods of evaluation?

Consider the range of evaluation methods that you typically use as a basis for both formative and summative assessment. Examine the list below and, taking the last six months of your supervision practice as a sample, identify which methods have featured frequently, occasionally, rarely or never. Write those that are most typical for you in the box directly underneath.

- Case discussion
- Process notes
- Case reports
- Supervisee self-reports of strengths and needs

- Video or audio-recordings of therapy sessions
- Live supervision and/or joint working
- Role-plays/simulations
- Client self-reports of progress
- Outcome data derived from client's self-report inventories
- Instruments designed to evaluate CBT therapist competence, such as the CTS-R
- Any other methods not included above

Typical methods of formative assessment:	Typical methods of summative assessment:

Now examine your choices. What guides your preferences? By using these methods, which aspects of a therapist's work are you attending to and which might be overlooked? To what extent is your current repertoire of formative and summative methods optimal for the supervision you provide in your service context? Are there any alterations you might want to make at this time?

Wherever possible, methods of evaluation should be available to supervisees as a means of self-assessment and to enable them to calibrate their own judgements with those of their more experienced supervisors. However, there is currently a lack of performance measures that can reliably distinguish competent from incompetent practitioners (Robiner et al., 1993). In their review of the literature, Muse and McManus (2013) identify seven CBT-related scales which they categorize as either transdiagnostic (that is, assessing the general CBT competences demonstrated in a particular session) or disorder-specific (assessing the competences required to deliver a particular treatment protocol for a given disorder). Examples of the former would include the CTS-R (Blackburn et al., 2001) and the Cognitive Therapy Adherence and Competence Scale (CTACS) (Barber et al., 2003). Examples of the latter include the Manual-Assisted Cognitive Behaviour Therapy-Rating Scale (Davidson et al., 2004) for the purposes of assessing competence for the prevention of parasuicidal behaviour and the Cognitive Therapy Scale-Psychosis (Haddock et al., 2001) for use with psychosis.

Standardized measures provide an important vehicle for making pronouncements about overall levels of competence demonstrated in a particular session, as well as specific domains within CBT practice that represent areas of strength or development need (Muse and McManus, 2013). For example, for the frequently used CTS-R, a total score of 36 is typically regarded as evidence of competence demonstrated in a specific session. This score is attained through adding individual scores on each of the 12 identified domains: Agenda setting and adherence; Feedback; Collaboration; Pacing and efficient use of time; Interpersonal effectiveness; Eliciting of appropriate emotional expression; Eliciting key cognitions; Eliciting behaviours; Guided discovery; Conceptual integration; Application of change methods; and Homework setting. By distinguishing these domains of competence, and considering whether performance in one session is representative of the therapist's proficiency more broadly, it is possible to identify where the therapist is particularly strong (e.g. working in a clear, structured way where the Agenda is well set, the Pacing and use of timing are well demonstrated and Homework is carefully reviewed and planned) and limited (e.g. there are difficulties using Guided discovery and Applying change methods). This can then support your choice of supervisory intervention (e.g. by the supervisor modelling Guided discovery and then incorporating role-play of increasingly complex scenarios to enable the therapist to hone their skill and confidence in this domain).

Despite a growing number of instruments, their reliability and validity are, in many cases, yet to be substantiated. Moreover, implementing disorder-specific measures into routine clinical services is not always feasible. This may partly explain Bernard and Goodyear's (2014) speculation that supervisors tend to develop Likert measures that make sense in their particular work contexts and to the learning objectives agreed with the therapist. Where bespoke measures are used – particularly in the context of summative assessments that may have implications for a supervisee's future career – the authors recommend the need for clear descriptions of what each numerical score means and what constitute pass and fail criteria. The use of rubrics can assist with this process. For example, the CTS-R is underpinned by Dreyfus and Dreyfus' (1986) model of skill acquisition which posits five stages through which professionals pass in the process of acquiring expertise:

> **Novice**: Learns to recognize objective factors relevant to the skill and acquires rules for subsequent responses. Knowledge is 'context-free'. Self-performance is judged by how well learned rules are followed.

> **Advanced Beginner**: Develops more sophisticated rules based on experience, using both context-free and situational elements, but treats each aspect of the task separately and gives equal importance to all of them.

> **Competent**: Sees tasks within the context of a conceptual framework, makes plans within this framework and uses standardized and routinized procedures within a hierarchical approach to decision-making.

Proficient: Sees the client's problems holistically, prioritizes tasks and is able to make quick decisions. Combines analytical decision-making with intuition.

Expert: No longer uses rules consciously but has a mature and prac- tised understanding, and is able to use novel problem-solving techniques.

Ensuring that non-standardized measures are underpinned by a model of skill acquisition such as Dreyfus and Dreyfus' (1986) five stages can enable both supervisor and supervisee to have greater confidence in the process of evalu- ation. Whatever method or instrument is used, it is important that the supervi- sor is clear about the type of information that will (and will not) be yielded, that the method is built into the heart of the supervision process (rather than 'tagged on' to the formative aspects of supervision), and that it forms part of a multi-method approach to evaluation that is both systematic and under- pinned by clear performance criteria.

3. Manage the process effectively

It is critical that supervisors do all they can to create optimal conditions for the delivery of feedback. Both positive and corrective feedback have the potential to enhance performance, but in order to do so must be presented in ways that can be received, understood and acted upon by the therapist. This can be a challenge. Therapists draw heavily on their relational capabilities to create a safe and welcoming space for clients. Thus, the distinction between performance and self-worth can become blurred such that receiving correc- tive feedback may be experienced as an assault on the self (Bernard and Goodyear, 2014). For this reason, feedback can be experienced as threatening and supervisors need to attend to how they will create a safe environment in which potentially uncomfortable information can be conveyed clearly and respectfully. This entails thinking through how you will balance the evidence with the mechanisms through which you deliver feedback.

From within the supervision literature, a range of frameworks have emerged that can help supervisors structure their feedback. One useful approach has been offered by Hawkins and Shohet (2012) in the form of a mnemonic – CORBS – which can assist the process of delivery. CORBS identifies effective feedback as:

Clear: About the feedback that needs to be given.

Owned: Presented in a way that indicates recognition that the feedback is based on perception rather than truth (e.g. 'In my view...' versus 'You are...').

Regular: Occurring sufficiently frequently to be helpful as well as early enough in the process and close enough to the event for the recipient to act upon it.

Balanced: Including a balance of positive and corrective feedback.

Specific: Which is easier to understand and act on than general comments which can feel vague ('On the last three recordings you have asked me to listen to, I notice that you haven't discussed or agreed any homework tasks with the client' versus 'You don't seem to be able to set homework effectively').

Ensuring that your delivery is informed by a particular approach, and sharing this openly with supervisees, can go some way towards reassuring them that you understand and take seriously the impact of your assessments.

Based on your knowledge of the intended recipient, it is also helpful to consider your supervisee's 'readiness' to receive feedback. Drawing on your formulation of their values, perspectives and beliefs, are there any factors of which you need to take particular account in order to ensure that your evaluations are safe to hear? For example, a therapist producing neatly typed formulations and intervention plans may well be demonstrating a conscientious attitude to both data-gathering and preparation for supervision. However, this behaviour might also indicate perfectionistic tendencies that are underpinned by problematic cognitions about mistakes and deficits ('If I make a mistake it means I have failed and am a terrible therapist', or 'This measure of evaluation is too demanding to assess competence in "real world" services, so it's the fault of the measure that I failed this submission rather than my skills as a CBT therapist'). As Kimmerling et al. (2000) observe, like everyone else, CBT therapists have flaws in their information-processing skills that have both emotional and behavioural consequences.

Finally, it is important to think through the potential consequences of your evaluations – for you, as well as for others. Bernard and Goodyear (2014) advocate the importance of anchoring the task of evaluation within a strong administrative structure. Both supervisor and supervisee need to know that the wider organizational context in which any evaluations are couched is trustworthy and will be supportive of both parties. It is important to ensure that procedures are in place should one party have concerns about the fairness of any evaluation made. In the service of this, we recommend that you ensure you are able to answer the following questions:

- What is the role that your evaluations are expected to play – will they be 'career defining' for the person being evaluated?
- How will your evaluations be used and by whom?
- Where will you get support from, particularly if your summative assessments are not favourable?
- What pressures are you likely to encounter and how will you manage these?

How effective do you think you are at giving those you supervise both positive and negative feedback? What helps and what gets in the way? Can you identify any factors (including any emotional reactions, cognitions and safety-seeking behaviours) that prevent you from delivering your assessments of competence as effectively as you would like?

Pulling it all together

Ideally, evaluation should be a mutual and continuous process, embedded within a diverse range of activities and dialogues, rather than an isolated activity that is 'done to' the supervisee at a particular point during the contracted period of working together. Drawing on the work of a range of authors, Bernard and Goodyear (2014) offer a list of conditions which they propose enhance the likelihood that supervisor feedback will be heard and feel safe to receive. These include retaining an empathic stance towards the supervisee, addressing therapist defensiveness openly and non-judgementally, and warning against premature evaluations of competence, especially for those therapy skills that can only be accurately assessed over a longer period of time. It is important to avoid over-simplification, choosing to direct attention on a limited range of skills which are most easily measured at the expense of a richer, broader understanding of how a therapist works (Muse and McManus (2013)).

In Table 4 we provide a checklist of points to keep in mind as you consider how to frame your feedback and we recommend that you audit your usual practice in light of these. We then present a case study to help you consolidate the material covered in this chapter, which is followed by tips for supervisees.

Table 4   Recommendations for improving the effectiveness of your evaluations

Consider the recommendations outlined below and how you can implement them to support the evaluations you undertake in your supervision. You may find it helpful to use this as a means of auditing your approach with a specific supervisee, or your practice more generally.

1. Remember that supervisees welcome clear communication about expectations. Ambiguity (even when intended as a means of 'softening the blow') is unhelpful.
2. Make evaluation criteria explicit from the outset and encourage your supervisees to hold these in mind for the duration of the supervision contract.
3. Explain the difference between formative and summative evaluation and the role that each plays in harnessing development as a CBT therapist.
4. Ensure formative and summative evaluations are consistent with the performance criteria you are assessing.
5. Ensure that your supervisees are familiar with (and can self-assess on) any methods used for the purposes of formative and summative evaluation.

(Continued)

Table 4   (Continued)

6. Introduce evaluations early on. The sooner you include them, the easier it will be for supervisees to embrace them.
7. Do not shy away from giving corrective feedback where this needs to be provided.
8. Be clear about the purposes for which any evaluations will be used, by whom and with what implications. Will your evaluations stay between the two of you (unless a serious issue arises) or will they be shared with a line manager or the course director of a training scheme? Will they influence whether the therapist passes or fails a training programme?
9. Explain how you will give and prefer to receive feedback so that supervisees know what to expect, and take time to teach supervisees how to receive feedback if necessary.
10. Beware of forming impressions about a supervisee's competence too early in the process, as your own cognitive biases may be operating. If you have emerging concerns, consider what needs to be in place in order for you to form a robust judgement.
11. If you struggle with providing summative feedback, try role-playing this with a trusted colleague in order to experiment with different formats of delivery.
12. After Padesky (1996), ensure that you review your supervisee's entire caseload periodically. A range of factors (adaptive and maladaptive) may influence who supervisees decide to present. Keeping a sense of the entire caseload can enable you to develop a clearer picture of areas of strength and need.

Case Study 6

It was clear to Patrick that Leanne was happy with her feedback: a score of 40 on the CTS-R, which indicated a pass mark.

Leanne had been diligent about submitting recordings of therapy sessions for formal evaluation since the beginning of her placement and, as a result, her profile of scores had steadily improved. Initially her competence had been limited, but through the formal training she had received at the university and the site supervision Patrick had provided, Leanne was now consistently passing assessments on the CTS-R – both those submitted for formal evaluation and those she had asked Patrick to assess informally.

Despite her progress, a nagging doubt remained. For reasons that Patrick had difficulty pinpointing, he would not have been entirely confident about referring a member of his own family to Leanne – the benchmark criterion he always applied.

Now, nearing the end of her two-year Master's programme in CBT, Patrick's doubts intensified. Leanne could certainly deliver on the technical side; she knew how to explain vicious cycles to clients and understood common cognitive distortions and safety behaviours. And with a narrow range of clients he was confident that Leanne could be quite effective. But he wondered about her interpersonal skills, and in particular her ability to work with clients who were harder to engage.

Leanne was expressing her intentions to establish a part-time private practice on completion of her training in addition to wanting a full-time job in the NHS, and Patrick knew it was only a matter of time before she asked him for a reference. As the conclusion of her training drew nearer, Patrick wondered what he should do (if anything) with his concerns.

Drawing on the material covered in this chapter:

- How would you encourage Patrick to conceptualize this dilemma?
- What factors might be contributing to this dilemma?
- How would you advise Patrick to proceed?

(We provide suggestions on how to approach this dilemma in Appendix 6.)

Tips for Supervisees No. 6

When starting any new supervisory relationship, make sure that you have the opportunity to talk with your supervisor about the evaluative aspects of supervision and how these will be conducted. In particular:

Clarify the methods of both formative and summative assessment that will be used:

- Make sure you have access to the tools of evaluation that your supervisor will be using.
- Ask for clear information about which performance criteria will be used to inform your supervisor's thinking.
- Understand the rationale for any performance measures used.

Own the process of evaluation, rather than seeing it as externally imposed. Learn to see yourself as the primary assessor of your own performance:

- Ask your supervisor how you can become better equipped at self-assessment; seek their advice and recommendations.
- Explain how it is most helpful for you to receive corrective feedback. Help your supervisor understand what is most likely to enable you to hear both positive and negative comments.
- Know how you are likely to react to corrective feedback. Are there any assumptions or beliefs that might lead you to become defensive? If so, how can you work towards restructuring these so that they don't restrict your development?
- Ask your supervisor how they want to receive feedback from you.

Understand the implications of any evaluations:

- Depersonalize feedback from your worth as a human being. Corrective feedback will help you become a better therapist. However:

(Continued)

(Continued)

- Be clear about the consequences of any evaluations for your current and future practice and who will have access to these.
- Ask your supervisor about the process that would occur if there were serious concerns about your competence.
- Seek clarification as to the options available to you if you genuinely believed that your supervisor was negatively biased in their evaluations of your work.

Conclusion

The evaluation of competence is a vital task for the CBT supervisor, and makes an essential (if at times uncomfortable) contribution to the therapist's development as part of a broader quality control agenda. Effective supervision makes use of direct and frequent feedback in order to alert therapists to their strengths, gaps in understanding or experience, and difficulties arising from lack of self-awareness in key areas.

The recognition of clinical competence as a 'moving target with an elusive criterion' (Robiner et al., 1993: 5) means that supervisors are typically navigating a shifting terrain which requires a specific set of skills, coupled with considerable sensitivity, to define, articulate and share evaluations in ways that the recipient can hear. The ability to do so rests in part on the interpersonal sensitivity of the supervisor in the context of a clear understanding of the roles of each party and an effective supervisory alliance.

Chapter summary

✓ Evaluation is a central part of the supervisory role but can be difficult to conduct effectively.
✓ You can improve your effectiveness by being clear and explicit about the performance criteria you are using.
✓ You need to have a clear rationale for the assessment methods that will be used and how they will be used.
✓ It is important that you manage the process effectively through creating a safe environment.

PART III

Refining Supervision

In Parts I and II we considered what needs to be in place in order to establish an effective and ethical basis for CBT supervision through exploring the 'Prepare' and 'Undertake' quadrants of the PURE Supervision Flower.

In Part I we considered the values and beliefs you have about CBT and CBTS as a basis for clarifying your particular 'brand' of supervision. We examined the context in which you provide supervision and how this impacts on what you offer. We then considered how to develop a contract that provides a basis for achieving specific learning objectives and establishes clear expectations for the work that is to follow.

In Part II we considered the style and structure of CBTS, explored how to go about selecting supervision interventions and identified ways of developing a robust and effective approach for the assessment of therapist competence.

In Part III we help you develop your practice through attending to some of the many process aspects of CBTS. This is the 'Refine' element of the PURE Supervision Flower and attention to these areas will enable you to hone the delivery of your supervision offer once the fundamentals are in place. 'Refining' your CBTS entails a focus on the third quadrant, as illustrated below:

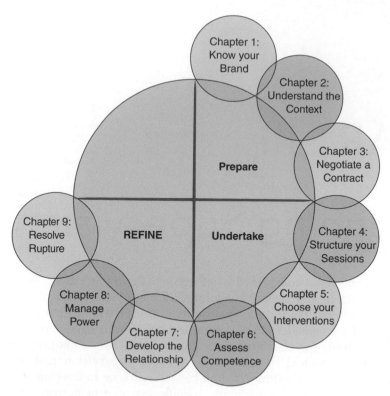

Figure 8 The PURE Supervision Flower: Refine

Throughout Part III we encourage you to hold in mind the foundations you built through completing Parts I and II of this book and consider how the ideas presented might fit (or contrast) with your emerging understanding of your own personal 'brand'.

SEVEN Develop the Relationship: Using the Supervisory Alliance as a Source of Learning

Learning objectives

After reading this chapter and completing the learning activities provided, you will be able to:

- Understand how the relationship in CBTS can be a valuable source of learning.
- Know how to make more effective use of the supervisory relationship in order to achieve key learning objectives.
- Formulate interpersonal issues that may arise in the context of the supervisory relationship.

Introduction

There is growing evidence that the quality of the relationship between supervisor and therapist plays an important role in both the therapist's experience of supervision and their performance in the work place (Olk and Friedlander, 1992). Despite this, in our experience, the guidance available to CBT supervisors on how to create an effective working relationship remains sparse.

In this chapter we examine the role of the supervisory relationship in supporting the effective delivery of CBTS. We consider the importance of the supervisory relationship as a vehicle for learning and development, and identify some of the frequently cited 'components' that comprise effective working alliances. Drawing on both the available research as well as the contribution of specific models and frameworks, we identify some approaches that can help you refine the quality of your working alliance in light of the style and structure you developed for your practice in Chapter 4.[1]

Towards an understanding of the supervisory relationship

We have seen how, as a therapy-based model of supervision (Milne, 2009), CBTS is expected to parallel CBT (Padesky, 1996). Thus, therapists might reasonably expect that their supervisors will seek to form a collaborative relationship, make use of guided discovery and facilitate psychological problem-solving to address the therapeutic dilemmas that are presented. CBT has, however, historically attracted criticism for failing to pay sufficient theoretical and empirical attention to the therapeutic relationship as a vehicle for change over and above its role in assisting the delivery of specific interventions (Safran, 1990a, 1990b; Safran and Muran, 2000). Thus, it is perhaps unsurprising that within the CBT literature, there has been a dearth of scholarly activity devoted to clarifying how the supervisory relationship might assist supervisee learning and development. Moreover, the privileging of competency-based supervision in the context of the competence movement (Falender and Shafranske, 2012), the outcome orientation of services in which CBT is delivered and caseload pressures have given rise to highly time-efficient models of supervision that are likely to prize task-focused over process-oriented elements. In such a climate, a diminished focus on the supervisory relationship is a distinct possibility.

Despite the lack of empirical evidence to support the assertion (see Milne, 2009), broad professional consensus affords the supervisory relationship a critical role in determining the effectiveness of supervision (Falender et al., 2004; Hatcher and Lassiter, 2007). Indeed, Ladany, Ellis and Friedlander (1999) claim that the relationship between supervisor and supervisee is a critical mediator of therapist development. Relational aspects identified as salient by both experienced supervisors (of different therapeutic orientations) and supervisees (at different stages of their careers) have included *attractiveness* (the collegial dimension of supervision that denotes warmth, support, openness and flexibility of approach), *interpersonally sensitive* (a relationship-oriented approach to supervision that

---

[1] The focus of this chapter is primarily how to establish a relational 'climate' that will support the learning and development of therapists rather than how to respond to any difficulties that ensue. We consider how to formulate and work to resolve ruptures in the supervisory relationship in Chapter 9.

signifies investment, commitment and perceptiveness) and *task-oriented* (an emphasis on being content-focused: goal-oriented, thorough, focused, practical and structured; Friedlander and Ward, 1984). Perhaps unsurprisingly, Friedlander and Ward (1984) also found that a task-oriented style was emphasized by CBT supervisors whereas psychodynamic and humanistic supervisors focused more explicitly on interpersonal sensitivity.

Traditionally, the supervisory relationship has been viewed through a psychoanalytic and subsequently a Rogerian lens (Lambert and Ogles, 1997). Nonetheless, Bordin's studies of the working alliance, emerging during the early 1980s (see Bordin, 1979, 1983), have become increasingly influential as a means of understanding and capitalizing on the relationships that characterize not just therapy but also supervision. Bordin's (1983) view of the working alliance centres on the notion of 'collaboration to change', which comprises three elements:

1. Goals (and the extent to which therapist and client, or supervisor and therapist can agree these).
2. Tasks (the extent to which there is agreement on the tasks necessary to achieve the goals).
3. Bond (the affective ties that develop out of working towards the goals, or a bond that is based on shared emotional experience).

These goals and tasks are compatible with the principles and procedures that typify CBTS. For example, if, as part of the 'Prepare' phase of the PURE Supervision Flower, a supervisor has established a supervision contract effectively, then all parties will have a clear understanding of both the goals that supervision has been designed to achieve and the means through which these goals will be accomplished. Additionally, the use of specific supervision interventions, linked back explicitly to the development of proficiency in key areas, will enable the therapist to appreciate how specific interventions can assist the development of competence in systematic ways.

Where CBT has been less explicit is perhaps in relation to its understanding of how the bond is formed and utilized within supervision. Although it is possible to contract for the goals and tasks identified, the affective bond is built moment-by-moment out of the interactions between therapist and supervisor and as material emerges.

Management of the relationship is principally the supervisor's responsibility (Nelson et al., 2001), requiring an ability to establish the working alliance, to ensure that supervision remains an effective environment in which to work and learn, and to manage seamlessly the continual transitions from 'gatekeeper', to coach, to mentor. Scaife (2001) also advocates that supervision needs to be a 'safe base'. Drawing on attachment theory, she proposes that the likelihood of developing a safe supervisory relationship is enhanced when supervisors:

- Demonstrate specific tasks and interventions to therapists before encouraging them to role-play such interventions (while supervisors can contract to include demonstration and role-play, it is through the continuous demonstration of ethical and respectful practice that supervisees feel encouraged to try new ideas).
- Share their experiences and work in an appropriately transparent way (e.g. by sharing recordings of their own practice or offering opportunities for observation).
- Are respectful in their reference to colleagues and clients (which demonstrates consistency, integrity and trustworthiness).
- Provide clear guidance and recommendations on how to address clinical dilemmas and demonstrate accountability (supervisors can agree in advance that they will provide guidance but it is the behavioural demonstration of accountability that underpins the bond and builds the working alliance).

These principles sit well within CBT and provide a framework for increasing the likelihood of creating a secure base in supervision. They not only support supervisors in identifying optimal methods of learning, but also enable therapists to feel sufficiently comfortable about engaging in 'safe to fail experiments' (such as role-playing a new technique) and revealing their practice for the purposes of feedback. As Ladany et al. (1996) found, not only is the perceived quality of the working alliance related to supervisee satisfaction with supervision, it is also related to supervisee willingness to disclose clinical material (see also Hess, Knox et al., 2008; Mehr et al., 2010).

The importance of investing time and energy in developing a positive working alliance in supervision is summarized by Bernard and Goodyear (2014), who report four critical outcomes. These are: (1) internalizing the supervisor, thus enabling the supervisee to recall what was discussed in supervision or anticipate what a supervisor might say in a particular situation (see Geller et al., 2010); (2) improving the therapeutic relationships that supervisees forge with their clients, thus enhancing an association between the therapeutic alliance and supervisory alliance (see Patton and Kivlighan (1997) and Bernard and Goodyear (2014), who, given the established link between the therapeutic relationship and outcome, infer that the supervisory relationship can affect clinical outcomes through the alliance between supervisee and client); (3) supervisee satisfaction with supervision (Ladany, Ellis and Friedlander, 1999); and (4) supervisees' adherence to treatment protocols, thus contributing to effective outcomes for clients (Holloway and Neufeldt, 1995; Patton and Kivlighan, 1997).

In summary, there are cogent reasons for believing that energy invested in establishing a bond with supervisees has a critical role to play in both the experience of supervision and the extent to which the learning agreement is successfully implemented.

Learning Activity 7.1   Identifying the relational climate of your CBTS

Take a moment to consider the type of relational climate that you seek to establish in the CBTS you provide. To what extent are you task-oriented? To what extent are you interpersonally-focused? How do you seek to balance the goals, tasks and bond-related aspects?

Reflect on occasions when you established and maintained a working alliance very effectively and less effectively. Can you identify the active interpersonal 'ingredients' that were involved in both positive and less positive relationships?

Having considered your responses to the above questions, consider whether the type of relationship you are aiming for is consistent from therapist to therapist, or whether there are differences as a function of format (individual or group), context or individual factors. If so, what informs the type of working alliance you seek to create in each case?

Making your supervisory relationships effective: Principles to guide your approach

Having identified some of the core components of an effective supervisory relationship, we turn our attention now to some of the features that increase the likelihood of establishing an empathic, collaborative and educational working alliance.

Drawing on the extant research, Bernard and Goodyear (2014) have catalogued the interpersonal behaviours and characteristics that typify 'lousy supervision', which occurs when supervisors:

- *Don't* reveal their own shortcomings to supervisees.
- *Don't* provide a safe environment in which the therapist can reveal doubts and fears about competence.

(Worthen and McNeill, 1996)

- *Don't* place the supervisee's learning needs above the service delivery mandate.
- *Do* ignore the supervisee's need for emotional support in a new context.

(Kozlowska et al., 1997)

- *Do* recruit their supervisee into the dynamics of the team.
- *Don't* support their supervisee's strengths (identify only their weaknesses).

(Wulf and Nelson, 2000)

- Feel threatened by a supervisee's competence and retaliate against them because of this.
- Avoid raising the issue if they sense that a conflict is emerging.
- Deny all responsibility for interpersonal conflicts arising.

(Nelson and Friedlander, 2001)

This list provides some useful insights into what supervisors should be aiming to avoid. Extending this to an identification of what supervisors actually *want* to aim for, Beinart (2004) offers the following 'pointers for good practice':

1. Establish a sense of safety (or a safe base).
2. Devote sufficient time to establishing the relationship in the early stages.
3. Use the contracting stage to clarify responsibilities, expectations, objectives and methods of evaluation.
4. Contract for the supervision relationship itself, in terms of preferred learning styles.
5. Manage power and diversity.
6. Set clear boundaries in relation to structure, availability and confidentiality.
7. Demonstrate your commitment, through your actions, to ensuring that supervision is effective.

These pointers can become the basis for a useful discussion in supervision. Using Beinart's list, for example, supervisors can reflect upon and talk with their supervisees about whether each of these aspects has been adequately embedded in supervision, or whether refinements are required to create an optimal learning environment.

Hawkins and Shohet (2012) draw attention to the critical importance of ensuring that the roles of supervisor and therapist are clearly identified at the outset. Where this does not occur, there is the potential for supervisees and supervisors to revert to sub-optimal patterns of relating that can undermine the alliance, and thus the learning agenda. In the supervision training they provide, Hawkins and Shohet (2012) describe how they encourage candidates to examine the variety of helping relationships that they have experienced in their lives, the needs they take to these relationships and the expectations they have in terms of anticipated response. This tends to yield the categories summarized in Table 5.

Inviting supervisees to reflect on helping roles can be particularly helpful when supervisors (including peer supervisors) are engaged in establishing the emotional climate and boundaries of the working alliance. It can also be a useful vehicle for 'unearthing' potentially problematic cognitions or behaviours, as well as providing a framework for facilitating effective discussions around any conflicts arising.

Table 5   Hawkins and Shohet's (2012) Helping Roles

Helping Role	What you take to them	What you expect
Doctor	Symptoms	Diagnosis, cure
Priest	Sins, confessions	Penitence, forgiveness
Teacher	Ignorance, questions	Knowledge, answers
Solicitor	Injustice	Advocacy
Coach	Poor performance	Improved performance
Judge	Crimes	Retribution
Friend	Yourself	Acceptance, listening ear
Mother	Hurts	Comfort
Car mechanic	Mechanical failure	Technical correction and servicing

© Hawkins and Shohet, 2012

Consider, for example, the following scenario in which one of us (SC) was approached by a trainee CBT therapist to complain about her experience of supervision with another member of the training team, and in particular her expressed dissatisfaction about the lack of apparent attention to her own emotional needs. On discussing her concerns further, it became apparent that her previous supervisor (operating within a humanistic framework) had elevated work on personal material to the heart of the supervision contract. As such, the boundary between the personal and the professional, and what was deemed appropriate to bring to supervision, differed markedly from this therapist's new experience on a CBT training course, where her supervisor had a more explicit focus on competence development.

In the context of discussing different models of supervision, drawing on Hawkins and Shohet's (2012) model also enabled the trainee to identify how she felt comfortable with the notion of her supervisor as 'friend' and 'mother' but found the notion of a supervisor operating in the roles of 'teacher' and 'coach' more challenging. Drawing on CBT concepts, it was then possible to engage the therapist in a conversation about assumptions that had the potential to negatively impact her experience of supervision ('If my supervisor is genuinely concerned about me, she will want to reassure me when I am anxious', 'If my supervisor challenges my practice, she must think I am a bad therapist').

> After Hawkins and Shohet (2012), think about which helping roles you tend to privilege as a supervisor, and the expectations you have of both your own supervisor and your supervisees. What cognitions underpin this? What behaviours follow from interpreting the various roles in this way?

Refining understanding of the supervisory relationship through CBT approaches

Although the assumption that psychotherapy theories can be easily 'imported' into the supervision context is widely held, it is important to note that this perspective is not without its critics. Beinart (2004), for example, comments that while therapy models have much to contribute, there are fundamental differences that render therapy models insufficient for the tasks of supervision. Specifically, supervision is an educative process in which therapists' performance is evaluated and (depending on context) the development of a professional identity assisted. Indeed, it has been argued that the use of therapy models to inform supervision practice may have hindered the identification of suitable directions for research and practice (Bernard and Goodyear, 2014). It is perhaps for this reason that a number of scholars have sought guidance from models developed in non-therapeutic contexts in order to seek a more sophisticated understanding. Beinart (2004), for example, has highlighted the role that models of adult learning (e.g. Kolb, 1984) and reflective practice (Schön, 1983) can play in facilitating professional learning.

Given the growing complexity of professional practice (Lane and Corrie, 2006) and the increasingly diverse client groups to whom CBT is delivered, there cannot be one simple view but rather, a diversity of thinking in the context of a growing understanding of how interpersonal relationships influence both physiological and psychological processes (Gilbert and Leahy, 2007). As noted previously, CBT has attended to this aspect of professional practice relatively late in the day compared with other approaches to therapy and supervision, and as Bennett-Levy and Thwaites (2007) observe, relational skills have tended to receive considerably less attention in the CBT literature than conceptual and technical skills. However, features of the supervisory relationship are starting to appear more centrally in the CBT literature, including the role of the relationship in enhancing the process of reflection.

Greenwald and Young (1998), from a schema-focused perspective, describe how the supervisory relationship can be a form of learning for both participants, requiring the supervisor to maintain a stance of confident humility. Bennett-Levy and Thwaites (2007) have also argued that the working alliance between supervisor and therapist is essential for effective interpersonal skills training, and that supervisors need to be able to model this effectively. Thus, the growing awareness of the impact of interpersonal relationships is starting to have implications for both how therapists are trained to form and maintain effective therapeutic relationships, and how supervisors can capitalize on the supervisory relationship to facilitate therapist development in this domain.

The work of Bennett-Levy and Thwaites (2007) has perhaps a particular contribution to make to understanding the interpersonal aspects of effective therapy and also supervision. It also offers a means of conceptualizing the difficult-to-define sense that supervisors sometimes experience whereby a therapist appears to be technically proficient, but lacking in interpersonal sensitivity.

As described in Chapter 5, Bennett-Levy (2006) has provided a framework for therapist skill development – the DPR Model – that differentiates declarative, procedural and reflective systems of information-processing. To recap briefly, the declarative system contains the verbal propositional knowledge-base of therapy (namely, that which we can write, read or talk about) and includes three types of knowledge: interpersonal, conceptual and technical. An example of declarative interpersonal knowledge might relate to knowledge of how collaboration is understood within CBT.

The procedural system refers to the rules that govern action and how declarative knowledge is operationalized in practice. This system has a variety of sub-components that contain both interpersonally-oriented (interpersonal perceptual skills, therapist beliefs and assumptions, interpersonal relational skill and self-schema) and therapy-specific skills (conceptual and technical skills). An example of the procedural system being implemented effectively in an interpersonal context is when a supervisor adapts their style of delivery (e.g. more or less directive) as a function of understanding a therapist's stage of career development and how that individual learns best.

The reflective system is a short-term representational system which is formed, as required, to assist with reflection on specific matters that require attention. Understood as the principal process through which professionals move from competence to excellence (e.g. Schön, 1983), the reflective system comprises three elements: focused attention (on a particular problem); mental representation (of that problem) and cognitive operations (to try to resolve the problem). Bennett-Levys et al. (2009) highlight that reflective practice has always been central to CBT ways of working (guided discovery is essentially a reflective process). Their work, however, provides a means of considering in greater depth the function of the reflective system in the unfolding process of supervision. In preparing for and undertaking supervision a contract for the work is established and a sessional process agreed, but the supervisor might also need to adapt to the issues that emerge. It is not always possible to know, in advance, what these issues might be. An example might be where, in the context of a case discussion, a supervisor suspects that a therapist's personal material (cognitions or emotions) is negatively impacting the work and needs to decide whether and how to raise the therapist's awareness of this.

Bennett-Levy and Thwaites (2007) also make the distinction between personal 'self-schema' and professional 'self-as-therapist schema'. Self-schema contains our beliefs about self, others, the world, our knowledge and skills and our values. Predating therapist training, the self-schema essentially comprises our sense of who we are: how we think and behave, our 'maps' of the world, and our sense of identity. In contrast, self-as-therapist schema is formed in response to developing a new therapist identity as professional training takes place and new conceptual and technical skills are acquired. Some aspects of the self-as-therapist schema may also predate training in the sense of providing the initial motivation for seeking therapist training (e.g. a desire to help others, and an interest in people's stories). We might also hypothesize that, for some, there is the development of a 'self-as-supervisor' schema which may give rise to attitudes and beliefs concerning a desire to nurture the talent and capability of others, and a belief in adult learning as a means to enhancing therapeutic outcomes for clients. All of these schema are brought into supervision for good or ill.

The DPR model proposes that self-schema are critically linked to interpersonal perceptual skills, therapist attitude and interpersonal relational skills. Given that our interpersonal style transcends our work as therapists and reflects who we are and how we conduct ourselves more generally, challenges in the interpersonal domain are more keenly felt (and potentially more threatening to self-esteem) than challenges in the conceptual and technical domains. For this reason, the model emphasizes the supervisor modelling a process in which such issues can be addressed. Specifically, Bennett-Levy and Thwaites (2007) recommend that the supervisor normalizes difficulties in the interpersonal realm, empathizes with the difficulty of acting effectively when strong emotions are activated, validates the therapist's attempts to deal with interpersonal issues and makes appropriate use of self-disclosure. They also highlight the need for clear boundaries – how and when to address interpersonal or personal issues and when not to, confidentiality agreements and a rationale for experiential learning – and helpfully refer to the work of Worthen and McNeill (1996) and Gilbert (2007), who emphasize the need for supervisors to create a sense of safeness, non-judgemental acceptance, affirmation, empathy, care, warmth and encouragement to explore. This means seeking permission to raise sensitive issues, but also being open to feedback from supervisees on issues that seem to them not to be going well.

Learning Activity 7.2   Using the DPR Model to conceptualize a supervisory dilemma

Identify a recent supervision dilemma in which you were puzzled by, or concerned about, the way in which a supervisee presented their work. It may be that you heard or saw something in a recording of a session that led you to wonder about the therapist's interpersonal skills, or it may be that a specific intervention was delivered by the therapist in a clumsy manner.

Can you formulate your puzzle or concern using the DPR Model? Specifically, can you locate the source of the difficulty in the declarative, procedural or reflective systems? How did you respond to this dilemma at the time and how might you now, using the DPR Model as a basis for your understanding? (You may find it helpful to return to Chapter 5 to consider specific supervisory interventions.) What does DPR add or detract from your current approach to understanding interpersonal processes in supervision?

Pulling it all together

Having read this chapter and completed the learning activities provided we invite you to adopt, once again, the role of supervision consultant and consider the following scenario in which Nina needs some assistance. This is followed by hints for supervisees on points to hold in mind in relation to establishing an effective supervision relationship.

Case Study 7

Nina is a participant in a monthly group supervision session in a small service of six staff and three trainees. The group essentially functions as peer supervision, although Nina is one of the more experienced therapists. At each meeting, time is given for staff to present their formulation of cases they are working with and one member presents, in detail, their formulation of a client's needs and how they developed their understanding of the critical issues. The formulation is open for discussion to all members of the group. Nina operates as a member of that group, which is chaired on a rotational basis from within the team. However, she is also the manager of the service.

One member of staff, while happy to present the short versions of her formulations, does not like to present more detailed versions. She takes the view that as there are evidence-based interventions available, it is not necessary to develop a full formulation. When questioned about the evidence-base for her formulations she becomes defensive. Another member of staff, who is a long-standing friend of this person, frequently adds comments in support of her stance even though her own formulations are very detailed and she is well respected for her work. The trainees, whom Nina is encouraging to write fully evidenced formulations, are confused by the stance taken in the supervision group. They tell Nina outside the group that they find it difficult to raise questions in the sessions because of the confusion.

As the manager of the service, Nina is concerned that weakly evidenced formulations are being used to justify the intervention. As a participant in the group, she feels increasingly frustrated that one member refuses to engage fully in the supervision process, and is apparently supported by her friend. As the manager responsible for the trainees, Nina is also concerned that they are finding it difficult to raise the questions and seek the guidance that would assist the development of their proficiency.

Drawing on the material covered in this chapter, consider your responses to the following:

- How would you encourage Nina to conceptualize this dilemma?
- What factors might be contributing to this dilemma?
- How would you advise Nina to proceed?

(We provide suggestions on how to approach this dilemma in Appendix 7.)

Tips for Supervisees No. 7

Give some thought to the type of working relationship you seek to develop with your supervisor, clarify how your supervisor is approaching your working relationship, and reflect on any factors that might help or hinder the development of this. You may find it helpful to consider the following themes to guide you:

Prepare for supervision by reflecting on your own relationship history:

- What has been your past experience of supervisory relationships, both good and bad? What was it about the relationship that contributed to the experience being helpful or unhelpful?
- How have different supervisors attempted to combine the goal, task and bond elements of the supervision relationship? What was the experience like for you in each case?
- After Hawkins and Shohet's (2012) work on helping roles, what types of helping roles have you tended to seek in supervision, and what have you been offered? What has been the impact?
- How have your reactions to supervision been shaped by your own relationship history and schema, with what effect?

Talk with your supervisor about how they understand the role of the supervisory relationship as a vehicle for change and development:

- Ask your supervisor about any models that inform their approach to developing working alliances.
- Be clear about what helping role/s you would like your supervisor to perform. To what extent are these compatible with your supervisor's understanding? What, if any, options exist to negotiate around roles?
- Develop some personal criteria that will enable you to reflect upon the supervisory relationship as it unfolds so that you are confident you can monitor its effectiveness for you. If it is not working as you had hoped, see if you can identify what is unhelpful and consider what steps you might need to take (Chapters 8 and 9 may prove helpful here).
- Be clear about the boundaries of supervision, what is expected and what can and cannot be supported. Seek clarification as to when and how personal issues (deriving from self-schema and self-as-therapist schema) can be identified and addressed, and the limits of confidentiality relating to any self-disclosure on your part.

Conclusion

Relative to other areas of CBT, the literature on the supervisory relationship is in its early stages, necessitating a consideration of the wider literature on supervision in order to develop a more sophisticated understanding of the complexities of the supervision process. Nonetheless, a number of features of the supervisory relationship are appearing more centrally in the CBT literature, including the role of the relationship, how to establish a working alliance, and how this can support the learning process.

As Milne (2009) remarks, the different facets of the supervisory relationship are not fixed. Rather they are ever-changing and manifest in the context of an unfolding interpersonal exchange. The supervision relationship is a process requiring ongoing refinement.

Chapter summary

✓ The role of the relationship is increasingly recognized as having an important role to play in CBTS.
✓ Therapists come to supervision at different stages of their career development and the approach to supervision will need to take account of diverse needs.
✓ There are a number of ideas and models emerging that can provide useful guidance on how to structure and refine the supervision process with specific reference to the supervisory relationship.
✓ By understanding the schema relating to self, therapist and supervisor and how these operate in supervision, we can refine the effectiveness of our supervisory relationships.

EIGHT Manage Power: Creating a Balanced Relationship within Supervision

Learning objectives

After reading this chapter and completing the learning activities provided, you will be able to:

- Better understand the operation of power in CBTS and how this can enhance or detract from optimal supervision experiences.
- Identify when issues relating to power are manifesting in supervision.
- Identify ways in which you can work constructively with power in the CBTS you provide.

Introduction

Power is a highly emotive facet of the cultures in which we live and work, and permeates our interpersonal interactions in complex and subtle ways. It is reasonable, therefore, to assume that power issues will also impact supervision.

The aim of this chapter is to help you reflect upon power as it relates to the CBT supervision that you provide. By doing so, we hope to enhance your awareness of how dilemmas relating to issues of power might manifest in your supervision practice (so that you can recognize them more swiftly and easily) and to offer some ideas as to how you can respond effectively when they arise.

Debates about power in the context of the psychological professions are, of course, extensive and a comprehensive review of this literature falls beyond the scope of this chapter (the interested reader is referred to Lane and Corrie, 2006; Milioni, 2007; Corrie and Lane, 2010). Here, we draw selectively upon different perspectives that have relevance to the types of dilemma encountered as CBT supervisors seek to enhance the development of the therapists with whom they are working. As you read through this chapter, you may find it helpful to hold in mind a specific example where manifestations of power and its management appeared to be a critical factor in how the supervision unfolded.

Power in therapy and supervision: A brief introduction

Power is a social psychological construct that refers to the ability to influence the beliefs and actions of others (Bernard and Goodyear, 2014). In the literature on both therapy and supervision, the issue of power has been noted to be a critical factor worthy of scholastic investigation. Proctor (2008), for example, comments that therapy is typically organized and delivered in ways that make it easy for therapists to have power over their clients. Specifically, clients enter therapy in the hope that their therapists can assist them in making changes which they have been unable to achieve unaided. This gives the therapist implicit licence to seek detailed, personal information and form opinions on what may or may not be optimal in the pursuit of any identified objectives. In CBT we are also given licence to encourage clients to engage in uncomfortable activities, such as behavioural experiments and exposure.

The management of power is relevant to all forms of therapy not solely (or even principally) CBT. Nonetheless, Proctor (2008) argues that CBT has tended to obscure issues of power through an appeal to the neutrality of science, and calls for the field to give 'serious consideration' to this matter. Given that CBTS seeks to replicate the CBT style of delivery, Proctor's challenge is arguably equally relevant to supervision. Supervisors of CBT therapists have a responsibility to consider how they can avoid the misuse of power and to take seriously the possibility that such misuses can occur despite laudable intentions.

Beyond the context of peer supervision, all supervisory relationships entail what Bernard and Goodyear (2014: 99) term an 'asymmetry in power'. This reflects the normative, formative and restorative functions that we examined in Chapter 3. As such, power is not necessarily negative (Moskowitz, 2009), but its safe and competent use does depend on the supervisor's ability to inhabit their authority. As Bernard and Goodyear (2014: 99–100) observe: 'The supervisor's greater power can be problematic if the supervisor is oblivious to it, abuses it, or (more typically) has difficulty assuming it comfortably. Indeed, learning to handle that power confidently and effectively is an essential task for new supervisors to master.'

Learning Activity 8.1 Eliciting your views on the power imbalance in CBTS

Consider the role that power plays in the CBTS you provide. (If this proves difficult, you might find it helpful to focus specifically on those aspects of the supervisor's role concerned with the management and evaluation of performance.)

Using a 0–10 point rating scale, where 0 = entirely uncomfortable, 10 = entirely comfortable and 5 = tolerably comfortable (with room for improvement), rate yourself on the following:

1. How comfortable are you about your use of power in the CBTS you provide?
2. How confident are you in your ability to manage the power asymmetry effectively?

Based on your ratings, can you elicit specific cognitions (particularly assumptions, standards and beliefs) about power and its role in CBTS? Do these cognitions suggest that you understand power in supervision as:

1. A positive aspect of the working alliance – something you can harness for the benefit of your supervisees, their clients and other stakeholders?
2. Problematic – an aspect of supervision that has the potential to cause significant difficulties?
3. An aspect of supervision that can be either good or bad and, if so, what are the mediating factors that you believe make it good or bad?

Conceptualizing power in CBT supervision

Within the CBT supervision literature, there is a paucity of guidelines on how to develop what might be termed 'anti-oppressive practices'. There is also a dearth of recommendations for CBT supervisors who seek ways of helping those they supervise to develop competence in this aspect of their work with clients. Nonetheless, the field does offer some useful principles that can provide pointers for how to understand and work with dilemmas relating to power.

From a behavioural perspective, the role of power can be explored in terms of how, as a sanctioned authority figure, the supervisor is authorized to grant and withhold rewards and punishments in the relationship, and under conditions of choice how contingencies influence behaviour (Rachlin, 1976). Combining behavioural and cognitive perspectives, a CBT approach would recognize that the structure of knowledge and how this leads to action has to be taken into account. In looking at knowledge, action and control, we can consider both the external control of behaviour (the social constraints in the supervisory relationship) and the mediating internal representations of events observed in 'verbalisable knowledge' (Martin and Levey, 1987). Thus, while behaviour is a function of the environment, it is also a function of choices made by the individual in relation to others (Krasner and Ullmann, 1973). It is also necessary to consider how social phenomena shape the construction of our behaviour (Kagan and Duggan, 2011). For example, those working with LGBT clients have reported how negative views from society can become internalized repressive dialogues (see Ross et al., 2008). It is important, therefore, for supervisors to pay attention to how they might externally (and unhelpfully) control a supervisee's behaviour as well as how potentially oppressive dialogues may come to be internalized by individual supervisees.

In her analysis of the supervisory relationship, Holloway (1995) sees the task as one of creating a balance between power and affiliation. Power can refer to either 'power over' or 'power with'. As Holloway (1995: 41–42) explains: '[The] relationship is the container of a dynamic process in which the supervisor and supervisee negotiate a personal way of using a structure of power and involvement that accommodates the supervisee's progression of learning.'

Each party brings to the working alliance personal and relationship histories which will influence the course of supervision through the level of involvement and extent of the bond that develops. Both parties influence the distribution of power and the ways in which power manifests in the working alliance. A useful starting point to the effective management of power (that is, capitalizing on and seeking to maximize 'power with' as opposed to 'power over') may therefore be to understand what each party brings to CBTS in terms of beliefs and values that emanate from personal history as well as membership of specific social, cultural and professional communities (Chapters 1 and 2 of this book provide some useful ideas on how to approach this).

Holloway's (1995) classification system of the different types of power that can manifest in supervision draws on the earlier work of French and Raven (1959), who described the following variations as typically operating in interpersonal relationships:

Reward power: The perception that the other person has the power to reward us.

Coercive power: The perception that the other person has the power to punish us for non-compliance.

Expert power: The perception that the other person has knowledge, competence and skill in a particular area of expertise.

Referent power: Power stems from perceived interpersonal attractiveness, whereby the person in authority is respected, admired or popular.

Legitimate power: The other person's power is a legitimate aspect of a socially sanctioned professional role.

> Conceptualizing the above categories from a cognitive-behavioural perspective, what assumptions and beliefs about self and other, the self as supervisor, self as supervisee and the supervision process might be related to each of these power stances? What types of behaviour could each of these categories give rise to? You might also find it helpful to consider which forms of power tend to be present in the CBT that you supervise.

It is possible to map the diverse tasks of CBTS on to different types and uses of power. For example, when CBT supervisors operate within the formative function, and deliver supervisory interventions such as clinical demonstration or specific recommendations based on their experience, this is an example of supervisors exercising both expert and legitimate power in ways that are role appropriate. When engaging in tasks that seek to evaluate performance, the supervisor moves into a normative role, exercising the categories of reward power (and perhaps being perceived by supervisees as exercising coercive power). When undertaking this task, the power resides largely with the supervisor rather than taking the form of sharing power. In reflecting upon the implications of this, Gilbert and Evans (2000) propose that the interpersonal distance between supervisor and supervisee varies as a function of the type of power being exercised and the way in which that particular type of power is managed.

The supervisor needs to be comfortable with navigating shifts in and out of different modes of power and remain attune to any forms of power that there may be a desire to avoid. For example, in Chapter 6 we noted how the evaluative component of supervision (considered here as the exercising of reward power) can be uncomfortable for supervisors, while nonetheless being vital to therapist development and the supervisor's broader quality control agenda. In contrast, a tendency to favour the more interpersonally comfortable aspects of supervision that are associated with the restorative aspects of supervision may in fact reflect an unhelpful use of referent power. In such a situation, the supervisor may be privileging a desire for popularity based on their own emotional needs over other forms of power that are more appropriate to the learning agenda.

Identifying different categories of power can assist CBT supervisors in a variety of ways. First, it provides a means for supervisors to identify the different forms of power that may be operating, and how these might be shaping the interpersonal climate of supervision with specific supervisees – with either intended or unintended consequences. Second, awareness of the different categories of power can assist supervisors in managing the working alliance (see Chapter 7) as well as resolving ruptures (see Chapter 9). By better understanding why certain reactions occur with individual supervisees (as we shall see shortly, supervisees also exercise power) as well as providing therapists with a framework of understanding, it becomes possible to increase the likelihood of a more transparent approach to this aspect of the supervisory process.

Negative and positive manifestations of power

A review of the supervision literature highlights that the misuse or abuse of power by supervisors is not as rare in its occurrence as the professional community might like to believe. Examples of the negative use of power include pathologizing supervisees and attempting to give them therapy instead of supervision; demanding supervisee self-disclosure; selectively attending to and commenting on the supervisee's limitations (at the expense of their strengths); verbally attacking supervisees and insisting on adherence to a supervisor's preferred approach; and sexual contact or unwanted sexual advances (Porter and Vasquez, 1997).

In their qualitative study investigating supervisees' perceptions of the use of power in supervision, Murphy and Wright (2005) found that reported abuses of power were rare but misuses were more common, suggesting that even when significant abuses do not occur, more subtle forms may be in operation. Certainly in relation to supervision with trainees, there is a growing literature which points to the detrimental effect that supervision can have on therapists' sense of competence and anxiety (Friedlander et al., 1986). In response to negative experiences, supervisees report feeling traumatized, exploited and doubtful of their abilities (Nelson and Friedlander, 2001). In Nelson and Friedlander's (2001) study, a poor supervisory experience also occurred with supervisors who were seen as remote or too busy to bother with the needs of trainees. This left trainees feeling dismissed, disappointed and lacking the guidance they wanted.

A lack of clarity in the expectations between supervisor and therapist can also create challenges. Olk and Friedlander (1992) found that this was particularly problematic where responsibilities were ambiguous, as in dual role relationships (e.g. where the supervisor was both training director and supervisor, or both clinical supervisor and line manager). Here, there are two aspects that can create challenges. The first is where power can be seen as an inequality of relations in terms of the organizational structure (such as where one party is a line manager of the other). The second is where a person 'proclaims' their power in order to emphasize the differential between themselves and their supervisees (that is, there is a 'power play' at work in the relationship; Jaworski and Coupland, 1999).

Although much of the literature has been directed towards the actions of supervisors, it has also been noted that supervisees, too, can misuse their power. In a study investigating 'supervisor-directed deviance', Liu et al. (2010) found that 'abusive' supervision was positively related to revenge cognitions directed towards supervisors (that is, the thoughts and beliefs of a self-identified 'victim' about inflicting damage or injury on the supervisor who is perceived as responsible for causing harm). Perceptions of supervisors having been abusive are typically associated with negative feelings that can trigger rumination as to how 'justice' might be achieved. This in turn can lead to actions that create a rupture in the working alliance. Bradfield and Aquino (1999) also found that perceived injustices produce cognitive and behavioural responses that can result in acts of resistance to the power held within the service or larger organizational context.

Although Liu et al.'s (2010) study examined these processes in a corporate rather than a clinical context, their findings have relevance for understanding the manifestations, and misuse of, power that can occur in CBTS. This includes a variety of attempts to undermine or even sabotage supervision, such as:

- A supervisee 'bad-mouthing' a supervisor to other colleagues.
- A supervisee making an official complaint against a supervisor in the absence of real grounds for doing so.
- A supervisee continuously challenging or rejecting a supervisor's advice.
- Withholding information about a client or critical aspects of the therapist's own practice that undermines the supervisor's effectiveness in assisting competence development.

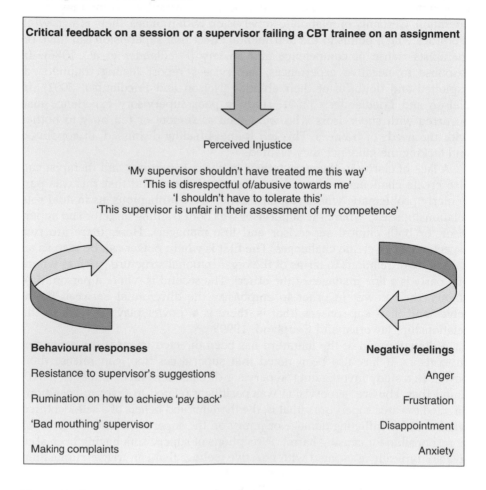

Figure 9 The vicious cycle of revenge: supervisees' inappropriate use of power

In Figure 9, we provide an illustration of how a supervisee's inappropriate use of power might operate in the context of CBT supervision.

Liu et al. (2010) highlight how encouraging awareness of this type of vicious cycle can enable supervisees to reflect upon what has occurred and to make a conscious choice about how to respond to the experience of injury – including whether or not to seek more adaptive attempts at 'justice-seeking'. More appropriate responses might include use of CBT methods to identify any cognitive distortions and modify unhelpful cognitions that perhaps exaggerate the extent or meaning of the injury; sharing what is experienced in a respectful way with the supervisor; and requesting an opportunity to work with the supervisor to engage in shared problem-solving in order to work towards a desired future outcome.

> It is possible to see how such a vicious cycle might operate for a supervisor as well as supervisee. In reflecting on your supervision practice (however uncomfortable this question may be to engage with), can you identify any occasions where you may have engaged in a misuse of power? If so, what form did this take? Did you realize it at the time or only subsequently? Retrospectively, can you identify any emotions or cognitions that were driving your response? What steps might you need to take to protect yourself and your supervisees from this happening in the future?

One way of developing greater understanding of supervisors' misuse of power is through the concept of 'supervisor countertransference'. Although this would be rejected by some as inappropriate terminology for CBTS, the concept affords some clarity on unhelpful interpersonal processes emanating from the supervisor and has indeed also been considered from a CBT perspective (see Rudd and Joiner, 1997). In their investigation of supervisor countertransference, Ladany et al. (2000) describe the following cues that led supervisors to become aware that this interpersonal process was occuring:

- Experiencing a strong emotional reaction when interacting with a supervisee (either positive or negative).
- Experiencing emotional reactions that were markedly different from those experienced in the context of working with other supervisees.
- Experiencing a gradual shift in feelings towards the supervisee or the work of supervision.
- Discussions with colleagues (especially those providing supervision of supervision).

In identifying the sources of supervisors' reactions, Ladany et al. (2000) note how participants' reported triggers included the interpersonal style of the supervisee or some aspect of the supervisor's own psychological issues. Bernard and Goodyear (2014) augment this with Lower's (1972) earlier findings that cite the supervisor's own personality characteristics, conflicts reactivated by the supervisory situation (in CBT terms, a reactivation of core beliefs and assumptions) and reactions to the individual supervisee.

Table 6 Recommendations for practice

CBT emphasizes transparency of approach, collaboration, and shared problem-solving. In thinking about how to harness the effective use of power in your supervision, and making power visible in your relationships, we recommend that you capitalize on these underlying principles by using the following steps:

1. Discuss power openly when you are establishing the supervision contract (the ideas contained in Chapters 1–3 can help you identify different ways of approaching this).
2. Discuss the different forms of power, how they might manifest in supervision and what represents the ethical use of these. This includes being transparent about how information will be used (and with whom such information will be shared), how supervisors will provide instruction in order to shape behaviour, and accepting responsibility for any mistakes made.
3. Anticipate ways in which the unhelpful use of power could manifest in supervision and any unhelpful reactions that could emerge from this. (You may find it helpful to use the vicious cycle in Figure 9 to guide your discussions.) Then develop a shared plan as to how you will both/all take responsibility for finding a solution.
4. Ensure that you have adequate time for self-reflection when maladaptive power issues begin to emerge. This is a good time to draw on self-practice/self-reflection strategies (see Thwaites et al. (2014) as well as the ideas discussed in Chapters 7 and 9 of this book).
5. Ensure you have consultation in place to provide you with 'supervision on your supervision' when you suspect that power issues are manifesting in unhelpful ways. Power plays are emotive and evoke thoughts, feelings and action tendencies for which it is important to seek support. Receiving consultation on your supervision can also enable you to identify and modify any unhelpful cognitions you may have about exercising an appropriate use of power in supervision.

As noted previously, power is not necessarily negative in its consequences and may actually be beneficial to the supervision process (Murphy and Wright, 2005). Consider, for example, a situation where a relatively inexperienced therapist is being pushed by service demands to work with more complex clients before their supervisor considers this to be appropriate or safe. The supervisor can play an important role in initiating dialogue with service managers about the needs of the service, therapist and clients in order to consider what other options may be available and thus provide the therapist with a buffer against expectations that may be difficult to navigate from a position of relative inexperience.

Robertson (2012) distinguishes between personal (aggrandizement) and social (for a wider good) motivations for power. Bernard and Goodyear (2014) also make the helpful distinction between power as dominance and power as social influence. In doing so, they highlight how all interpersonal behaviour is communication, and that all communication is an act of influence (Watzalwick and Beavin, 1976). Reconceptualizing power as influence can broaden and enable supervisors and supervisees to reframe their interpersonal interactions as a process of mutual influence, even while, in many cases, the supervisor retains role-based power (Bernard and Goodyear, 2014). What is critical, therefore, is that CBT supervisors feel confident about, and are effective in, exercising their power in ways that are transparent, containing and reassuring such that they come to support, rather than hinder, effective learning. By demonstrating a personal ease with the use of power, CBT supervisors also model for therapists how they might manage this aspect of their interpersonal relationship with clients. Some recommendations for practice are outlined in Table 6.

Power as social control in the supervisory relationship

Before we conclude this chapter, it is important to acknowledge – albeit briefly – some of the wider debates about power and the psychotherapeutic professions as these inevitably impact supervision as national and global level influences (see Chapter 2).

The place of psychotherapy as an agent of social control (Corrie and Lane, 2010) has been a matter of contention in the literature certainly since the 1970s. More recently, McClelland (2014) refers to its role as an ideological dimension in how we think about illness or 'deviant' behaviour. This is extended to the oppressive effects of inadequate services to minority groups and the marginalization of professionals from these communities (Jackson, 1977; Hobson, 2012). That these debates are about discrimination in services more generally and not specific to CBT does not mean that we can ignore them. Indeed, there is an increasing focus around alternative liberation theories and CBT has not been without its exponents. For example, Radical Black Behaviourism (Hayes, 1991) was an early call in the 1970s to behaviourists to engage in approaches that challenged power relationships in society, thereby changing life opportunities. Kelly (2006) has noted the collaborative and non-judgemental nature of CBT as offering value to marginalized groups. Its contribution as an anti-oppressive framework (to challenge oppressive internal dialogues) has been explored by Ross et al. (2008), with Watts (2004) examining CBT and social justice.

Certainly, as access to psychological therapies has become a UK Government priority, lack of use of services by minority communities has been an issue (Glover et al., 2010). Approaches to address this include that offered by Anderson and Goolishian (1992), who advocate a way of working where the client is seen as an expert in their own experience in ways that honour their cultural background. The CBT practitioner retains expertise in their way of working, which is then offered to the client to assist their process of change. Mpofu (2014) has gone further, claiming that many orthodox therapy services fail to recognize the different ways in which communities conceptualize health and illness, and ignore the sources of support and advice that such communities trust. He advocates the creation of CBT services which are accessed via community leaders as the first line of referral, rather than the medicalized settings in which many therapeutic interventions are still delivered. His position is not dissimilar to Milioni (2007), who argues that certain ways of defining health (medical, psychological and pathological) and practices that signify otherness (clinical settings, appointments and note-taking) perpetuate positions that compromise clients' egalitarian status, leaving them disempowered.

Seen in this light, without an awareness of such issues, we cannot work towards a politically and ethically aware supervision practice. Ross et al. (2008) show how they have adapted a standard CBT model (Greenberger and Padesky, 1995) to include the idea that marginalized groups might incorporate society's negative views about them into an internalized dialogue (the notion of 'internalized oppression' described earlier in this chapter). The aim, they suggest, is to help marginalized groups recognize those dialogues and challenge them. Equally, as supervisors, we need to be alert to how strict adherence to a model may need to be tempered by understanding of the client's (and supervisee's) story. If we fail to do so, we might miss the impact of such internalized oppressive dialogues. Understanding the background and culture of our supervisees helps to raise awareness of these issues.

Learning Activity 8.2   Learning about your supervisees

How much do you seek to discover about those to whom you are offering CBTS? When working with a supervisee, consider which of the following you would typically and rarely enquire about.

	Always	Often	Rarely	Never
1 Life stage				
2 Gender				
3 Race				
4 Ethnicity				
5 Culture				
6 Religion				
7 Social class				
8 Sexual orientation				
9 Disability				

Identifying those areas that you enquire about most and least, why do you think this is the case? Are there any features that you believe it would be beneficial to attend to more fully in the light of seeking to identify any internalized oppressive dialogues relevant to your supervisees and their clinical practice?

Pulling it all together

Having read this chapter and completed the learning activities provided, we invite you to adopt the role of supervision consultant for Patrick. This is followed by tips for supervisees on points to hold in mind in relation to negotiating power in the supervisory relationship.

Case Study 8

Patrick has been asked to take over the supervision of a new trainee, Seiko. He agrees reluctantly, as in a previous role he had line managed her. The person who was supervising Seiko has had to withdraw through illness and no one else is available.

The reports Patrick has received about Seiko confirm that she is focused and works hard to ensure that she creates technically correct formulations. The reports of her work are positive. This does not surprise him as he previously experienced her as diligent, although tending to want to stick rigidly to the organizational protocol (she referred to this as 'fidelity to the model').

After three sessions, Patrick can see that the formulation offered for a depressed client looks technically accurate but he wonders about the depth of exploration undertaken. In response to suggestions from Patrick, Seiko states that she is following the protocol for the service and is confused as to why he is asking for information that sits outside the standard process. Patrick attempts to assist Seiko in understanding that sometimes there is value in looking beyond standardized approaches, but he is met with a series of repetitions. He is hearing features of the story that point to the importance for the client of exploring his experience of discrimination which seem to be ignored by Seiko. Seiko states that Patrick is asking her to discard the protocol and questions why he is trying to make her work this way. She asks if she is allowed to change supervisor.

Drawing on the material covered in this chapter:

- How would you encourage Patrick to make sense of this situation?
- What might Patrick be doing that could be seen as the use of power to negate the supervisee's experience or her preferred stance on CBT?
- How would you advise Patrick to proceed?

(We provide suggestions on how to approach this dilemma in Appendix 8.)

Tips for Supervisees No. 8

Although CBTS is a collaborative process, the evaluative component inherent in supervision will raise issues around power. With this in mind, it might be helpful to:

Think about aspects of yourself (e.g. life stage, gender, ethnicity, culture, religion, disability, etc.) and the possible assumptions accompanying these factors that could influence:

- Your understanding of the client's presenting concerns and their context, the therapeutic relationship and intervention.
- Your expectations of supervision.
- Your professional identity.
- Your relationships at work.

From this, consider how you might raise these issues in supervision. For example, can some of these factors be explored in your conceptualization of the client's presenting concern? Could this be an agenda item for discussion? Would it be helpful to include any discussion about power in the supervision contract and review this on a regular basis?

Reflect on occasions in supervision where you discussed a clinical dilemma but felt dissatisfied or unhappy with the outcome. With these scenarios in mind:

- What beliefs and assumptions were triggered about the supervisory process, your supervisor or the specific CBT skills and strategies suggested, particularly in relation to issues of power?
- How did you feel when these cognitions were triggered? How did you respond? For example, did you seek support from experienced colleagues in the service or from your peers? Did you complain about your supervisor? Were there opportunities to explore the situation in supervision and to problem-solve jointly? It might also be useful to consider whether the process of self-reflection by itself could be helpful in managing how these issues are raised in supervision.

Conclusion

Issues of power are ever present in the supervision encounter. We can try to ignore them but we do a disservice to ourselves, our supervisees and their clients if we do. Power can be harnessed in ways that are positive and which enhance the quality of the working alliance, or misused in ways that marginalize and undermine. It is the responsibility of the supervisor to ensure that they are able and willing to work effectively with the power that is inherent in the role. As Kadushin (1992: 20) observes: 'The supervisor must accept, without defensiveness or apology, the authority and related power inherent in his [*sic*] position. Use of authority may sometimes be unavoidable. The supervisor can increase its effectiveness if he feels, and can communicate, a conviction in his behavior.'

In this chapter we have explored a number of ways in which issues of power may be present in supervision. Refining our work through feedback as events happen is a key part of creating effective supervision. What is left unsaid is left unaddressed to the detriment of both supervisor and supervisee.

Chapter summary

✓ Supervision involves an inevitable power differential that must be recognized and managed.
✓ Supervisors need to be comfortable in inhabiting their power.
✓ As issues of power emerge in supervision we need to refine our approach to embrace them rather than respond defensively.
✓ Finding ways to address emergent, power-related dilemmas can be used as a basis for strengthening the supervisory relationship.

NINE   Resolve Resistance and Ruptures: Working with Relational Challenges

Learning objectives

After reading this chapter and completing the learning activities provided, you will be able to:

- Draw on the literature on resistance and rupture in order to refine your supervision approach.
- Recognize when resistance or rupture is occurring, or likely to occur, and identify factors that may be contributing to this.
- Take steps to avoid or repair ruptures in your supervision in order to facilitate effective learning.

Introduction

Theoretical accounts drawing on social cognition (Miranda and Andersen, 2007) and on collaboration (Bordin, 1979) and negotiation (Safran and Muran, 2000) have led to a view that the alliance is an intrinsic part of the change process. In Chapter 7 we considered how to capitalize on the supervisory relationship as a vehicle for therapist development and in Chapter 8 explored how CBT supervisors need to engage effectively with power in the context of an unfolding interpersonal process. However, what happens when the therapist rejects our response to their supervision question, or declines our supervisory guidance? Does their continued refusal to countenance the ideas we offer represent 'resistance' and signal an emerging rupture, or does it indicate a need to change our approach? Additionally, how can we best respond when we detect a negative change in a supervisee's interpersonal behaviour towards us – whether this takes the form of overtly hostile acts or more passive responses, such as disengagement?

In this chapter we provide guidance on how to work with both resistance and ruptures. For the purposes of aiding understanding and offering potential solutions, we conceptualize resistance as feedback on a schematic mismatch between supervisor and supervisee and rupture as a potential or actual breakdown in the working alliance. We make the case that supervisors need to be able to recognize both in order to ensure that supervision is not derailed at times of relational challenge.

The inevitability of relationship challenges in supervision

The supervisory relationship is not a static entity. Rather, it is a dynamic and unfolding process that is impacted by a diverse range of influences emanating from the supervisor, supervisee and the interaction between them. Moreover, once the client is added to this relational equation (Bernard and Goodyear (2014) view the supervision alliance as essentially a three-person system), and the influence of local, national and global level influences is considered, the potential complexity of the supervisory relationship becomes apparent. It does not follow, therefore, that a relationship established effectively at the outset of supervision will remain that way for the duration of any supervision contract.

Moments of resistance or rupture occur in all authentic and meaningful relationships. Indeed, Lesser (1983) comments that there may be good reason to be wary of a supervisory relationship that appears to be too comfortable; such apparently positive relationships may indicate a superficial engagement and a desire to avoid the struggles of undertaking therapeutic work. Scholars seeking to understand the working alliance refer to the continual process of weakening and strengthening, disruption and restoration that characterize such relationships (see Bordin, 1983). As an unfolding interpersonal process, periods of resistance and rupture are, therefore, to be anticipated, and addressing them becomes central to therapy (Katzow and Safran, 2007) and to supervision (Prasko and Vyskocilova, 2010).

Towards an understanding of resistance in supervision

In the context of therapy, resistance has been defined as 'anything in the patient's behaviour, thinking, affective response, and interpersonal style that interferes with the ability of that patient to utilize the treatment and to acquire the ability to handle problems outside of therapy and after therapy has been terminated' (Leahy, 2001: 11). In supervision, resistance can take multiple forms, including refusing to play recordings, failing to undertake agreed tasks or frequently seeking reassurance.

Shohet (2012) conceptualizes resistance as feedback on something that is not yet fully understood. The source of the resistance can be the supervisor as well as the supervisee. Thus, difficulties in the working alliance can be reframed as a process about which both parties need to be curious, rather than an occurrence that becomes a battle of wills. Contemporary CBT approaches similarly view moments of impasse as potential 'clues' to the difficulties that clients experience and thus worthy of exploration. Katzow and Safran (2007) advocate that rather than responding to apparent resistance by challenging the client's cognitive distortions, therapists should 'join' with the resistance by validating the client's experience and collaboratively exploring its origins. Extending this approach to the supervisory alliance, identifying and examining resistance in a non-defensive manner can pave the way for a process of shared discovery and, ultimately, a strengthening of the working relationship.

Given Nelson et al.'s (2008) conclusion that difficulties often occur when supervisors fail to recognize or manage conflict effectively, a useful (if uncomfortable) starting point for supervisors is to reflect on their own possible contribution to what is occurring. This is particularly likely where interactions between supervisor and supervisee challenge core beliefs, assumptions or standards about self, other or change, and prevent supervisors from attending fully to the moment-by-moment events emerging in the room. Beliefs about professional status, roles, and the tasks and process of supervision can also form a point of resistance. For example, to the extent that we as supervisors believe we must have answers, we can find no place for expression of personal doubt which may create internal tension. Thus, we label the supervisee's reaction as resistant whereas their reaction might be feedback to us that we are inappropriately exercising control.

Before we identify some ways of understanding resistance, first consider your responses to the following exercise.

Learning Activity 9.1   Examining your experience of resistance in supervision

As a CBT supervisor, what types of resistance have you encountered? Have they been relatively 'major' and obvious to you, or more subtle and difficult to detect? Have any occurred which you were only able to identify with hindsight? What specific form did they take? For example, they may have taken the form of supervisees asking personal questions or subtly questioning your expertise. Alternatively, they may have involved a persistent rejection of your supervisory guidance, or defensiveness at being evaluated in a specific way. Once you have an overall sense of the types of resistance you have encountered, ask yourself the following questions:

1. What caused me to notice it?
2. What was my initial reaction?
3. How did the resistance 'play out' in the session/s?
4. What, if anything, changed over time?
5. Was a resolution achieved? (If so, what was it? How did we reach that resolution?)
6. What did I learn from this experience?
7. What would I now do differently?

CBT perspectives on resistance

Rudd and Joiner (1997) have attempted to find a way to conceptualize interpersonal influences that draws explicitly on CBT principles. They advocate the use of a therapeutic belief system which enables a consideration of the relationship at both the overt (automatic thoughts and feelings) and tacit (enduring cognitions such as assumptions, standards and beliefs) levels. Adapted here to the supervisory relationship, beliefs about the supervisor can be understood as moving along a continuum from victimizer, to collaborator, to saviour. For the supervisor, active beliefs about the therapist may fall along a continuum of aggressor, to collaborator, to dependent (helpless). Each 'shift' along the continuum is associated with specific core beliefs, assumptions and automatic thoughts, along with emotions and behaviours.

The therapeutic belief system can be applied to each party's beliefs about themselves and supervision. For the purposes of understanding resistance in supervision, a focus on each party's conceptualization of the other may be particularly illuminating. Consider, for example, the dilemmas that might arise when:

- The supervisor holds beliefs about the therapist as a collaborator (potential cognitions may include: 'This therapist is committed to learning from me and is open to benefitting from what I can offer') and the therapist holds beliefs about the supervisor as a 'saviour' (possible cognitions may include: 'My supervisor will teach me everything I need to know'; 'I can rely on my supervisor to solve my clinical dilemmas').
- The supervisor views the therapist as a potential aggressor ('This therapist has a reputation for making complaints') and the therapist views the supervisor as a victimizer ('This supervisor is going to undermine me so I need to protect myself').
- The therapist views the supervisor as a collaborator ('My supervisor is going to help me learn and is committed to my development') and the supervisor views the therapist as dependent or helpless ('The therapist has limited capability and needs a high level of didactic input to learn how to do CBT properly').

Rudd and Joiner (1997) propose that one of the strengths of the therapeutic belief system is that it enables practitioners to unearth those tacit beliefs and associated emotional and behavioural responses that are central to the conceptualization and resolution of resistance or rupture in a particular situation. This helps the supervisor shift from a reactive position towards one of reflection, neutrality and curiosity.

In Leahy's (2007) social cognitive model, it is recognized that the current therapeutic relationship may reflect previous relationships with significant others. Using the analogy of a game, Leahy (2007) understands the personal schema of client and therapist as creating mismatches. Each plays to their own set of interactional rules thereby playing the game in different ways. The result is manifest forms of resistance as each party seeks to affirm current schemas and protect themselves from loss.

Leahy (2007) proposes the following categories of resistance which we have adapted to the context of supervision (while these categories have been proposed as emanating from the supervisee, it is also important to consider the extent to which the supervisor is contributing to these resistances):

- **Validation**: That is, the supervisee gets stuck by seeking from the supervisor validation for how difficult the client, therapy or supervision is for them. They complain, catastrophize or withdraw if you try to refocus them on the agenda or the learning objectives of the supervision contract.
- **Victim**: The supervisee insists that they are not the cause of any difficulty and that the fault lies with another. They claim that they are being inadequately supported in their service and poorly guided by the supervisor.
- **Moral**: The supervisee believes that asking them to change would violate their personal moral or ethical code. They insist from an absolute, perfectionist stance and any proposed alternative that recognizes individual differences is rejected.
- **Schematic**: The supervisee's personal schema limit the potential for change. They operate a confirmatory bias in interpreting experiences to fit their current schema. They reject suggestions that challenge their current schema.
- **Self-consistency**: This is the desire for events to be predictable, which can result in a tendency to justify previous poor decisions. Supervisees resist suggestions to change course because too much effort has already been put into their plan.
- **Risk aversion**: The supervisee struggles with change as this involves an increase in uncertainty. Any suggestion meets with a demand for more information, more reassurance and a focus on the negative consequences of taking the proposed action.
- **Self-handicapping**: There is an avowed intent to move forward but the supervisee engages in self-sabotage, openly resisting suggestions or making half-hearted efforts to change that confirm that the suggestion was doomed to fail.

> How might Rudd and Joiner's therapeutic belief system and Leahy's frameworks of schema mismatches help you conceptualize and work with resistance? Can you identify any areas of application where this approach might help?

Resistance, if addressed, does not generate a rupture in the supervisory relationship but can be considered feedback that some aspect of the working relationship needs to change. Its occurrence provides feedback that a rupture could potentially occur. In the next section, we consider how supervisors can understand and respond to rupture.

Towards an understanding of ruptures in CBTS

In contrast to resistance, ruptures refer to a breakdown in the collaborative relationship between patient and therapist (Katzow and Safran, 2007). Again, although offered in the context of conflicts that occur in therapy, these definitions readily transfer to the types of relational dilemma that can occur in CBTS.

Ruptures may take the form of minor disruptions as a function of fluctuations in the alliance or significant breakdowns in the ability of a supervisor and therapist to work together in order to fulfil the objectives of the supervision contract. They can manifest as confrontational behaviour in which the supervisee openly rejects a supervisor's advice, or disengagement from the supervision process (Katzow and Safran, 2007). Alternatively, a supervisor may only become aware that a rupture has occurred when a therapist complains about the experience of supervision to a third party, such as a line manager or (in the context of a placement) a clinical tutor.

In their summary of the literature investigating negative events in supervision, Nelson et al. (2008) conclude that ruptures often occur when supervisors fail to recognize or manage conflict effectively. Reasons for this are noted to include a lack of awareness that tensions are arising, a reluctance to raise such issues for fear of compounding the situation, or difficulties knowing how to respond. More recently, Bernard and Goodyear (2014) have identified the following principal sources of rupture:

1. Conflicts that arise in response to an error made by the supervisor or a miscommunication between supervisor and therapist. These types of error or miscommunication are particularly likely to occur when the supervisor adopts an evaluative role (Burke et al., 1998). This underscores the importance of having clear and explicit evaluation criteria that are agreed at the contracting stage.
2. Periods of tension arising in the context of the supervisee's stage of development. For example, in Chapter 4 we considered how, at level 2 of Stoltenberg et al.'s (1998) stages of therapist development, therapists

experience a 'dependency–autonomy' conflict that can manifest as ambivalence towards the supervisor, supervision or CBT itself.

3. Conflicts arising in response to interpersonal process and supervisee expectation. We explore this in greater detail later in the chapter.

These findings point to the need for supervisors to develop specific skills in relationship management that extend beyond the ability to train therapists in the technical mastery of CBT. The identification, containment and ultimate resolution of ruptures may even represent a domain of supervisor competence in its own right. At the very least, it is important for supervisors to be equipped with methods for understanding and managing any ruptures that may arise.

Leahy (2007) has identified a range of personal and interpersonal schema which can hamper therapeutic engagement with clients. At least some of these are likely to be a feature of ruptures that occur in supervision so you may wish to consider (as non-judgementally as you can!) which, if any, apply to you, and may have been implicated in any difficulties experienced:

- **Demanding standards**: Supervisors with obsessional or perfectionistic traits may see their supervisees as lacking the discipline necessary to conduct CBT effectively.
- **Judgemental**: Supervisors hold a view that some therapists are simply not up to the task of delivering high-quality therapy. Feedback is direct and blunt, with a tendency towards 'micro-management' of supervisees.
- **Needing approval**: Supervisors experience a strong need to be liked by their supervisees. Any difficulties are construed as a sign of being disliked or having done something wrong. In consequence, giving and inviting feedback is avoided.
- **Need for superiority**: The supervisor views supervision as an opportunity to show off their special talents. Supervision of a difficult case may begin with grandiose claims (expressed directly or indirectly by the supervisor) that the therapist has finally found 'the right supervisor' who will help solve all dilemmas.

(You may also find it helpful to consider whether any of these schema seem relevant for the supervisee where a rupture has occurred.)

Seeking a solution: Responding to resistance and ruptures

Assuming that you have been able to identify and conceptualize resistance and rupture, what options exist for their management and resolution? Shohet (2012) emphasizes the importance of supervisors maintaining moment-to-moment self-awareness of their subjective experience. A first step, therefore, might be to attend to your own emotions, cognitions and any reactive tendencies as they arise, and to seek to formulate what is occurring. In the service of this aim, Shohet highlights the following possibilities:

- **Personal sense of irritation with supervisee**: Where this emerges, ask yourself if the irritation is a signal that a core belief about what should or should not happen in supervision has been activated.
- **Resistance as a form of mirroring**: When experiencing resistance from supervisees, ask what, in your own behaviour, may be reflected in their reaction.
- **Resistance as a reflection of cultural issues**: Different cultures view illness and well-being differently. What appears to be resistance might be an attempt to relate a new concept to an existing cultural understanding. Ask yourself what positive commitment to exploration or change might underpin the resistance.
- **Resistance can be used to protect an underlying vulnerability**: Recognize that supervision can be an uncomfortable place. Ask yourself how the resistance might help the supervisee move through the discomfort and find the courage to go forward.
- **Recognize when to challenge and when not to**: If the resistance can be redirected, change can happen. Explore with the supervisee how they might be able to redirect the energy.
- **Blindness where core professional beliefs are challenged**: It is difficult, as a supervisor, to go beyond the norms of the context in which you work. If your core beliefs are challenged, seek supervision outside your service context to help identify different perspectives.

As a CBT supervisor you are in a leadership role and so hold ultimate responsibility for the management of any ruptures occurring. This means that supervisors have to pay attention to de-escalating ruptures as they emerge and, where possible, work towards restoring a productive working relationship. In the context of their work on leadership, Hersted and Gergen (2012) suggest that when the focus is on de-escalating animosity and restoring productive relations, useful courses of action include the following:

- **De-construct the realities**: They propose that most conflict results from differing interpretations of reality. The challenge is to help participants recognize that their way of seeing is but one of multiple perspectives rather than 'the truth'. Here, you might ask them to tell the story from the other's point of view, enquire into possible doubts they have about their own account, or bring others into the story.
- **De-polarize the differences**: In addition to the hardening of perspectives that conflict generates, differences also become polarized. Here, you might ask participants to consider some potential benefits in the opponent's view and seek acknowledgement that there are different interpretations of the same event.

- **Search for commonalities**: One of the most useful ways to address conflict is to search for commonalities; that is, aspects on which the different parties agree. For example, you might ask each party to consider shared goals, values or outcomes.
- **Avoid using power**: If you adopt the position of ruling on disagreements you are likely to cause alienation. You might ask each party to reflect on the process and seek commonalities in order to avoid resentments going 'underground'.
- **Focus on the 'We'**: The authors propose that conflict often arises as a result of people's participation in differing social traditions. Trainee CBT therapists, for example, are not yet part of the tradition of the supervisor or professional service provider. If the supervisor adopts the power position, the trainee is likely to comply with, but not necessarily embrace, the core values. Here, the supervisor might focus on the 'we' (that is, what are we trying to achieve together?) and the process of relating (how we can give meaning to our conversations). Through this process, supervisor and supervisee can come to share a professional tradition.

Using a process such as Hersted and Gergen's enables supervisors to unhook from judgementalism and apply curiosity. In doing so, it becomes possible to create a collaborative basis for deciding how best to proceed. In pursuing such a process of dialogue, it is also important to remember that CBT emphasizes the value of live observation. Where there are doubts about a supervisee's willingness or ability to engage in dialogue, or where the nature of the rupture renders the approach unworkable, having a colleague observe your supervision or listen to a recording of a session can aid impartial problem-solving. The effective management of ruptures is often optimally supported through 'supervision of your supervision', which complements all of the methods described.

Learning Activity 9.2   Understanding ruptures in your supervision

- Think of an example where a supervisee was continuously resistant to your suggestions to the point of a potential rupture. What feelings did this provoke in you? Reflect on any beliefs or values that were challenged by this supervisee's stance. What issues did you identify? How might these have contributed to the potential rupture?
- Think of an example where a significant rupture occurred. What feelings did it provoke in you? Reflect on any beliefs or values that were challenged by this supervisee's stance. What issues did you identify? How might these have contributed to the rupture?

- As Lesser (1983) commented, there may be good cause to be wary of a relationship that appears to be too comfortable. If you believe that you have never experienced a rupture in supervision, consider if you might be organizing the work in such a way that avoids the emergence of any authentic challenge. If so, what might you do to address this?

Beyond the supervisory dyad: Trauma-organized systems and their contribution to rupture

Throughout this book, we have consistently highlighted context as a critical influence. The workloads of staff in professional services, the distress they may experience through engaging with clients' stories and the pressure to meet service standards with limited resources are the realities of working in what Bentovim (1992) terms 'trauma organized systems'. Bloom (2011) has looked at how a wide variety of human service delivery organizations might be 'trauma organized' (i.e. where trauma arises because of continual adaptions to stress and adversity which gradually impede service delivery to clients and damage the workforce). She draws our attention to parallel processes operating at the organizational level. Thus, clients present their experiences of trauma while trying to deal with their pain and loss. They are met by providers who bring to their work their own personal histories of pain and loss and who, in addition, are deeply embedded in systems under significant stress.

The result of these complex interactions (with leaders struggling with competing demands from those they manage as well as those to whom they are answerable, staff with different professional backgrounds and beliefs, and clients who fail to respond to treatment) is a potentially pernicious recapitulation of the experiences of those the providers are trying to help. The argument that Bloom (2011) makes is that ruptures are more likely to occur in these working contexts. The outcome can be a lack of safety, miscommunication, an inability to contain emotion and organizational amnesia. In response to these ruptures, management may become more autocratic, silence dissent, narrow the focus for decision-making (such as ruling out alternatives) and generate disempowerment, all of which promote latent acts of resistance from staff (Tehrani, 2011a).

The solution for Bloom is to apply our collective knowledge of trauma and loss to our attempts to manage the environments in which we work. She sees it as particularly problematic when individuals see that the organization fails to live up to the ideals they see as central to its functioning. Lane (1983; see also Vinten and Lane, 2003) points to a similar process. In consequence, in broadening our understanding of the manifestation and management of ruptures, it could be argued that we need to become more skilled in identifying our own (and our supervisees') experiences of trauma or loss in order to understand the meaning we have attached to any impasse occurring, and to recognize the triggers that will re-activate the thoughts, feelings and behaviours associated with it. For example, if the supervisee has experienced an abuse of power in their own life or in a previous experience of supervision, encountering this in their client's story may result in a resistance to responding to it in therapy that may be paralleled in supervision. To respond effectively to this, McNab (2011) reminds us we must be open to examining our own processes and genuinely open to receiving feedback.

Pulling it all together

Having read this chapter and completed the learning activities we invite you to adopt the role of supervision consultant for Patrick. This is followed by tips for supervisees on points to hold in mind in relation to maintaining an effective supervision relationship.

Case Study 9

Patrick has been asked to supervise Jason, who joined the service as a newly qualified CBT therapist six months previously. Jason has brought to supervision a case that has been worrying him for a while.

The client, an 18-year-old male, was involved in a major car accident which left him with life-changing injuries. He was in a car that he thought belonged to the driver's parents but which turned out to be stolen. Following the accident, his friends abandoned him at the scene. A passer-by called for an ambulance. The client was charged and given a suspended sentence. Twelve months later, he is having flashbacks from the accident and meets diagnostic criteria for PTSD.

Jason finds that all efforts to get the client to focus on the goals of therapy have been met with resistance. The client wants to go back over his early childhood experience of being placed in foster care. Jason is becoming increasingly frustrated by his inability to move the client on from those experiences to talk about current issues.

In listening to Jason's dilemma it seems to Patrick that Jason is pushing the client to account for his experience in terms of a somewhat rigid approach, rather than listening to the story the teenager wants to tell. His gentle enquiries into this are met with an angry response from Jason that this is not helping as he needs to get the client to move forward (he has already used half the allocated sessions).

More generally, and for some time, Patrick has sensed Jason's growing irritation in supervision, but in their most recent session Jason quizzed Patrick explicitly about his knowledge of CBT for PTSD. Patrick felt put on the spot and although he answered the questions posed to him, believed that he did not acquit himself as the knowledgeable supervisor he wanted to convince Jason that he is capable of being. Patrick, in turn, is feeling increasingly irritated by Jason, sensing in him both a strong sense of entitlement and air of superiority that Patrick regards as a tell-tale sign of a narcissistic personality. He starts to dread supervision with Jason.

Drawing on the material covered in this chapter:

- How would you encourage Patrick to conceptualize this dilemma?
- What factors might be contributing to this situation?
- How would you advise Patrick to proceed?

(We provide suggestions on how to approach this dilemma in Appendix 9.)

Tips for Supervisees No. 9

The supervisory relationship is always evolving. As such, putting effort into developing and maintaining the relationship is a necessary and complex process, involving a variety of relational skills. Three approaches you can take to support you in maintaining an effective relationship with your supervisor are as follows:

1. Learning through reflection on previous supervisory relationships

Recall an experience of supervision when you discussed a clinical issue and were dissatisfied with the discussion that took place. What factors led to that dissatisfaction? Now recall an experience of supervision when you discussed a clinical issue and found the response helpful. What factors were present? What stance by you and/or the supervisor differentiated these experiences in terms of their impact on you?

2. Reflecting on the current supervisory relationship

Which aspects of your current supervisory relationship feel most and least useful to your work as a therapist? How have you approached (or could you approach) raising any concerns? What might you do to help your supervisor become more aware of any concerns?

3. Clarify the boundaries of supervision

Was the issue of managing challenges addressed in the original supervision contract? If not, what might you do now to raise the possibility of reviewing the contract in order to include this? To what extent is there clarity about the boundaries of supervision? What can and cannot be discussed and what level of self-disclosure by you and your supervisor is welcomed. Self-disclosure might be particularly important to think through if you are receiving group supervision.

Conclusion

Concepts such as resistance and rupture have increasingly found a place in CBT and CBTS and the emerging models and frameworks provide a helpful means of conceptualizing and responding to such phenomena. This supervision literature draws attention to the need for supervisors to be aware that their own thoughts and feelings influence responses within supervision and calls for supervisors to be alert to early signs of resistance that may signal an impending rupture.

Some therapists (and indeed supervisors) may not be willing participants in the process, but are delivering CBT because they are required to, or because they believe that without doing so, they will be professionally disadvantaged. Thus, just as Friedberg et al. (2009: 108) describe CBT as 'more often than not a messy business. ... Rarely is it the tidy matters portrayed in most texts, manuals and articles', so the same might be said of supervision. There are many agendas that accompany each supervisor and supervisee into the consulting room, any of which has the potential to enhance or disrupt the learning agenda.

In addition to the supervisor's and supervisee's internal process, broader organizational and societal influences have also been identified. The literature on trauma organized systems provides an example of this. Dryden and Feltham (1992) previously noted that therapy as a response to individual issues can desensitize us to the need for wider social change. Resistance and rupture can be regarded as a normal part of the developing supervisory relationship. Treated as such, they represent opportunities for feedback to us and our supervisees. Working with them creates the space to refine our approach as issues emerge. The contract can be renegotiated based on those refinements to the benefit of all.

Chapter summary

✓ Resistance happens for the supervisor as well as the supervisee; there is a need to explore the beliefs that sit behind this.
✓ Ruptures are not necessarily pathological but can be understood as expressions of a moment for change.
✓ Supervisors need to consider how they make it possible for supervisees to offer resistance to their approach without this precipitating a rupture.
✓ By understanding the schema underpinning resistance we can refine the supervisory relationship.

PART IV

Enhancing
Supervision

In Parts I, II and III we explored the 'Prepare', 'Undertake' and 'Refine' quadrants of the PURE Supervision Flower.

In Part I we considered the values and beliefs you have about CBT and about supervision as a basis for clarifying your particular 'brand' of CBT supervision. We examined the context in which your supervision is provided and how this will impact on what you offer. We then used this understanding as a basis for considering how to develop a contract that offers a clear basis for the work that is to follow.

In Part II we considered the style and structure of CBTS, explored how to go about selecting supervision interventions and identified ways of developing a fair and systematic approach to the assessment of therapist competence.

Then, in Part III we explored how you can refine your practice through attending to some of the many process aspects of supervision, including establishing a working alliance, managing issues of power and working effectively with any ruptures that might occur.

In this final section, we consider how to 'Enhance' your practice as a CBT supervisor through examining how to approach ethical dilemmas, how to self-assess your level of knowledge and skill, and how to create a plan for your professional development. The latter includes an emphasis on self-care. 'Enhancing' your CBTS entails a focus on the fourth quadrant of petals, as illustrated below:

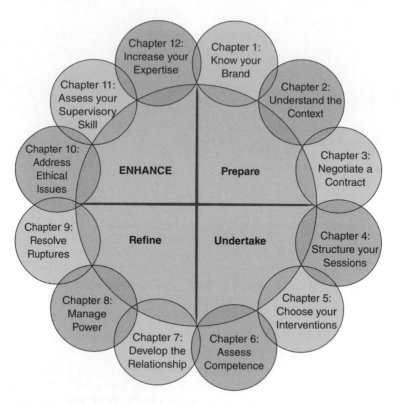

Figure 10   The Pure Supervision Flower: Enhance

Throughout Part IV we encourage you to hold in mind the foundations you built through completing Parts I, II and III of this book, and consider how the ideas presented might fit (or contrast) with your emerging understanding of your own personal brand.

TEN   Address Ethical Dilemmas: Developing a Coherent Approach

Learning objectives

After reading this chapter and completing the learning activities provided, you will be able to:

- Identify ways of conceptualizing ethical dilemmas encountered in CBTS.
- Consider ethical practice from the perspectives of compliance with an external code, as a matter of professional maturity and in relationship to others.
- Explore when it might be appropriate to use different approaches to resolve specific issues.

Introduction

Undertaking psychotherapy gives rise to unavoidable ethical dilemmas. As Goldfried and Davison (1994) observed, any attempt to change another person in the name of improving their mental health is fraught with issues of an essentially moral nature. This is equally true of supervision. CBT supervisors attempt to shape the performance of those whom they supervise in order to assist the acquisition of proficiency and improve outcomes for clients, while also fulfilling their obligation of safeguarding the public against poor practice.

By their very nature, ethical concerns tend to defy simplistic solutions. This chapter does not, therefore, seek to offer prescriptive approaches. However, a consideration of ethics in CBTS draws together many of the themes already examined in this book. If you have completed the work that the PURE Supervision Flower recommends – that is, you have 'Prepared' adequately (Chapters 1–3), thought through how you 'Undertake' supervision (Chapters 4–6) and worked to 'Refine' your approach (Chapters 7–9), you will be well equipped to manage the ethical dilemmas you encounter. The purpose of this chapter is to add to that foundation by describing three frameworks that offer diverse perspectives on how to approach ethical issues.

We begin by considering traditional approaches to understanding ethics through the application of an external code. We then invite you to consider your own level of ethical maturity and the extent to which you are sensitive and responsive to ethical dilemmas. Finally, consistent with our previous discussion about the importance of context (Chapter 2), we examine ethics as a model for understanding contextual relationships. By approaching ethical issues in this way, we attempt to provide a more nuanced approach to examining complex dilemmas as they relate to the delivery of supervision.

Ethical dilemmas and CBT supervision

Ethics is a branch of philosophy that examines what is right and wrong, moral and good (MacIntyre, 1998). When we make a choice to work as therapists, and indeed as supervisors, we commit ourselves to forming psychologically intimate relationships with those whom we seek to serve. As Pope and Vasquez (2011: 323) observe, the work of therapy carries with it both 'great influence and great vulnerability'. They claim that the extent to which such relationships prove helpful depends upon the degree with which therapists prove able to meet their ethical obligations in relation to issues of power, trust and caring.

Supervisees also place themselves in a vulnerable position when they reveal their work, and their beliefs and feelings about that work. Without genuine concern for the well-being of supervisees and respect for their values, strengths and vulnerabilities, supervision runs the risk of being experienced as exposing, unsafe and undermining. Supervisors are also obliged to make judgements about proficiency that have potentially career-defining implications, especially where supervised practice is a prerequisite for qualification and subsequent accreditation. Supervisors cannot evade their professional, moral and legal responsibility to protect the public from poor practice, even where this conflicts with the remit of advancing the learning and development of an individual therapist. Ethical concerns, therefore, lie at the heart of CBTS and an understanding of ethical responsibilities is essential.

In our experience of providing consultation to CBT supervisors, there are a number of recurring ethical dilemmas for which supervisors request guidance, including those described in Table 7.

Table 7   Common ethical dilemmas that can occur in CBTS

1. In the context of pre-qualification training, how to respond to significant doubts about a supervisee's competence, despite their consistently passing formal assessments.
2. How to manage a supervisee's inability or unwillingness to respond to constructive criticism.
3. How to raise doubts about a therapist's competence in the delivery of CBT when the therapist regards themselves as competent and receives positive feedback from clients.
4. What to do when a therapist is reluctant to use a particular intervention for reasons that the supervisor does not regard as valid (e.g. a refusal to use interoceptive exposure for panic disorder on the grounds that the client could not tolerate the distress that this would cause and hence seeing it as an unethical action; see Olatunji et al. (2009) for a discussion of therapists' avoidance of exposure-based treatments for this reason).
5. How to manage tensions arising from being both the therapist's CBT supervisor and line manager (in their survey of CBT therapists accredited by the BABCP, Townend et al. (2002) found that dual relationships were reported as common).
6. The therapist is intent on using an intervention they have just learned about because they find it interesting and want to 'try it out'. There is no apparent consideration of whether this is in the client's best interests, or any attempt to link decision-making back to a formulation that can guide intervention planning.
7. The demands of the supervisor's clinical service dictate that there is little time available for professional development and any CPD activities need to be self-funded. It is difficult, therefore, to develop a suitable knowledge management strategy that can enable the supervisor to remain abreast of developments in the field of CBT that are necessary to providing effective supervision.

As a CBT supervisor, what ethical issues have you encountered? How have you conceptualized them and attempted to address them, and with what degree of success? Additionally, what have you used as guidance to manage the dilemma (e.g. guidelines from professional bodies, local service protocols, reading about ethics)?

Frameworks for working with ethical dilemmas: The external, internal and relational

Having identified some common ethical dilemmas that can occur in CBTS, what are the options for formulating a response? In this section we consider three frameworks that can assist supervisors in considering how to respond. These are:

1. Ethics as a universal set of principles which are externally mandated and with which we are required to comply. We draw upon the BABCP's code of conduct as an example of the application of such general principles.
2. Ethical maturity: that is, practitioners' internal sense of moral behaviour which includes a sensitivity to ethical dilemmas and willingness to engage with them.

3. Ethical issues as dilemmas arising in the context of a relationship with others where we are required to negotiate what is moral in order to arrive at a shared understanding of an appropriate course of action.

1. Understanding ethics as drawing on universal principles which are externally mandated

An important manifestation of ethics as a branch of philosophy is its translation into guidelines that can inform practitioners' decision-making and provide a basis for the regulation of their behaviour (Bernard and Goodyear, 2014). It is also argued that ethics can provide a universal underpinning to the laws that govern our relationships with society. As practitioners we are subject to both statute (e.g. laws on discrimination and equality) and common law. In particular, two areas concern us: the law of contract governing the agreements that we make with others and the law of tort governing our responsibilities towards others and acts of negligence. It is also the case that our professional and, in some cases, statutory bodies tell us what we must and must not do. These precepts exist as either rules (to which we must conform) or guidance (to help us decide if our acts are appropriate). If we genuinely hold a view that we have acted within guidelines and are seen as competent by our professional body and act within its professional code, we are not likely to be judged as negligent in a court of law. (For example, in Bolitho v City and Hackney Health Authority (1997) 4 All ER 771 it was held that it will very seldom be right for a judge to reach the conclusion that views genuinely held by a competent expert are unreasonable.)

For most professionals, a consideration of ethics often begins with reference to a code of conduct and many professional bodies define a code of conduct which they expect members to uphold. The BABCP code is offered as an example of this (British Association for Behavioural and Cognitive Psychotherapies, 2010; see Table 8). In its full format (available at: www. babcp.com/files/About/BABCP-Standards-of-Conduct-Performance-and-Ethics.pdf), these standards inform CBT practitioners on what is required in relation to each of these 15 items listed in Table 8.

Professional body codes of conduct have to be consistent with common principles of law since the latter would take precedence in any court proceedings. Such codes represent examples of a more general duty of care. We are expected to act competently not negligently and to reasonably fulfil our contractual obligations to our clients. These precepts build on general principles of law, such as equity, proportionality, good faith, human dignity, and it is these principles that enable judges to make decisions about a case where a specific rule does not apply (Voigt, 2008).

Table 8   Standards of conduct, performance and ethics

YOUR DUTIES AS A MEMBER OF BABCP

The standards of conduct, performance and ethics you must keep to.

1. You must act in the best interests of service users
2. You must maintain high standards of assessment and practice
3. You must respect the confidentiality of service users
4. You must keep high standards of personal conduct
5. You must provide (to us and any other relevant regulators and/or professional bodies) any important information about your conduct and competence
6. You must keep your professional knowledge and skills up to date
7. You must act within the limits of your knowledge, skills and experience and, if necessary, refer the matter to another practitioner
8. You must communicate properly and effectively with service users and other practitioners
9. You must effectively supervise tasks that you have asked other people to carry out
10. You must get informed consent to give treatment (except in an emergency)
11. You must keep accurate records
12. You must deal fairly and safely with the risks of infection
13. You must limit your work or stop practising if your performance or judgement is affected by your health
14. You must behave with honesty and integrity and make sure that your behaviour does not damage the public's confidence in you or your profession
15. You must make sure that any advertising you do is accurate

© British Association for Behavioural and Cognitive Psychotherapies (2010)

Increasingly, the common features said to underpin law have been noted to be present in the ethical frameworks used by the professions (Lane et al., 2010). This universality has been marked in a number of projects considering the possibility of universal codes for professions. For example, the Universal Declaration of Ethical Principles for Psychologists (International Union of Psychological Science, 2008) was the culmination of a global collaboration and research into codes governing professional practice across cultures and the ages. It seems that for as long as groups have combined to form associations to deliver services to others, codes of conduct have emerged. The Universal Declaration asserts that ethics lie at the core of every professional discipline and argues that there are four principles covering all professional work:

1. Respect for the dignity of persons and peoples
2. Competent caring for the well-being of persons and peoples
3. Integrity
4. Professional and scientific responsibilities to society

Learning Activity 10.1   Applying the four principles to dilemmas encountered in CBTS

Consider the ethical dilemmas that we presented in Table 7 and work through these drawing upon the four principles in the Universal Declaration.

For example, in the first scenario – *In the context of pre-qualification training, how to respond to significant doubts about a supervisee's competence, despite their consistently passing formal assessments* – we could explore this as follows:

The significant doubt for this supervisor (which may not be shared by others given that the supervisee is passing their coursework assignments) raises an integrity issue: namely, the supervisor has to decide whether or not to voice their concern. If they decide to raise the concern, there is the issue of how competence is being assessed and what is being missed in the assessment process that fails to capture the supervisor's doubts about competence. However, raising this question brings into question the issue of respect for the student who has (diligently) passed all the assessments asked of them. How can the supervisor's concern be handled in a way that respects the supervisee's dignity?

If the concern is not raised, the dilemma becomes one of the supervisor's failure to address their professional and scientific responsibilities to society. In meeting this responsibility, the supervisor needs to think through the potential consequences of their evaluations (for themselves as well as the supervisee) and to be confident that the wider organizational context will be supportive of the process which the supervisor is initiating.

Having worked through the examples provided in Table 7, you might also find it helpful to apply these four principles to any additional ethical dilemmas that you have encountered in your own practice.

2. Understanding ethics as a matter of ethical maturity

Chapter 1 of this book introduced the idea that supervisors have an individual professional brand and considered how to identify the value-base that underpins this. This idea is extended here to include ethical maturity as part of who you are and what you bring to supervision. In contrast to the view of ethics as a set of universal principles which are externally mandated, the concept of ethical maturity (see Carroll and Shaw, 2012) privileges an understanding of ethical issues as derived from our own personal (internal) moral decision-making and our ethical maturation as professionals. This perspective conceptualizes ethical behaviour as much more than compliance with an external code. Rather, it is about having an internal moral compass to guide our actions which enables us to remain accountable to ourselves as well as others. As Carroll and Shaw (2012: 139) explain, ethical maturity is concerned with having:

...the reflective, rational, emotional and intuitive capacity to decide actions are right and wrong or good and better, having the resilience and courage to implement those decisions, being accountable for ethical decisions made (publicly or privately), being able to live with the decisions made and integrating the learning into our moral character and future decisions.

There are six components to the Carroll and Shaw (2012) framework:

1. Ethical Sensitivity

   - awareness of self, of harm, of consequences, of impact of behaviour, of intention

2. Ethical Discernment

   - reflection, emotional awareness, problem-solving process, ethical decisions

3. Ethical Implementation

   - what blocks me/what supports me, how to implement decisions

4. Ethical Conversation

   - defending the decision, going public, connecting to principles

5. Ethical Peace

   - living with the decision, support networks, crisis of limits, learning from the process, letting go

6. Ethical Growth and Development of Character

   - utilize learning to enrich moral self-knowledge, to extend ethical understanding, become more ethically attuned and competent.

It is possible to explore an ethical issue from the perspective of any one, or several, of these components. Returning to the examples provided in Table 7, it could be considered that the therapist who is intent on using an intervention because they have just learned about it and want to 'try it out' (example 6) is displaying a lack of Ethical Sensitivity (that is, insufficient awareness of self, of potential harm to the client and of the intention behind the decision). In contrast, a therapist's reluctance to use a particular intervention (such as exposure) on the basis that a client will experience emotional discomfort (example 4 in Table 7) may be categorized as a lack of Ethical Discernment, such as difficulties with problem-solving or decision-making. Once the relevant component has been identified, supervisors can then consider options for developing the 'moral compass' in each of the areas where issues arise. This helps supervisors move beyond the external frame (that is, what therapists must or must not do) in order to understand the degree of competence with which a supervisee approaches ethical issues, thus providing a developmental basis for discussion.

> How might you apply the notion of ethical maturity in the CBTS that you provide? What areas might this lead you to explore?

3. A relational view of ethics

Ethical dilemmas happen in relationship with others. Hence, ethics can also be conceptualized as a relational matter where supervisors become aware of ethical issues through their relationship with supervisees, and in the context of a contractual relationship with them and a wider social group (clients, employers, etc.). A third possibility for examining ethical issues is therefore to view ethics not as precepts but as matters of dialogue and collaboration within a relationship (Gergen, 2001).

Collaboration is elevated to the heart of all aspects of CBT. For example, in the context of case conceptualization, Dudley and Kuyken (2014) describe the collaborative process as central to combining the perspectives of therapist and client in order to develop a shared understanding. Indeed, the importance of that collaborative process goes back to the birth of CBT with Meichenbaum's (1977) contention that what is critical is the common conceptualization that evolves between client and therapist. Applying the idea of a common conceptualization to an ethical dilemma in supervision, a relational perspective would seek to identify how supervisor and supervisee can come to a shared understanding, through the dialogue that takes place between them, rather than resolving the issue by looking externally to a code.

The relational approach to understanding and addressing the ethical dilemmas encountered in CBTS can be helpful in a number of ways. For example, in Table 7, example 5, the challenge of dual relationships was identified. Resolving this cannot be through reference to an external code but requires full engagement in a collaborative dialogue between supervisor and therapist to identify and address the inevitable tensions. The supervisor and supervisee will have to come to an agreed position (rather than one imposed by either party, or an external stakeholder) in order for the relationship to work.

Gergen (2001) emphasizes the necessity of attending to the process of relating itself, which leads us to reflect on what is unfolding as supervisors engage their supervisees in discussing their clients' needs. So how might we pay attention in a collaborative dialogue to this process?

Epstein (2006) suggests a consideration of the following, which we have adapted to supervision:

- Respecting the supervisee's constructions of the world (e.g. understanding your supervisee's values and respecting their perspectives in the way you form your contract; see Chapters 1 and 3 of this book for some ideas as to how to approach this).
- Avoiding unilateral authority-based decisions (e.g. not imposing your 'expert' view on the supervisee; see Chapters 4 and 8 of this book).
- Broadening the circle of participation (e.g. recognizing that supervision happens in a context; see Chapter 2).
- Focusing on the relationship (e.g. commitment to ongoing work to sustain the alliance; see Chapters 7 and 9).
- Avoiding person blame (e.g. pathologizing a therapist's resistance to your view; see Chapters 8 and 9).
- Emphasizing affirmation as opposed to censure (e.g. actions to build rather than undermine the confidence of the supervisee; Chapters 6 and 8).
- Reflecting on the participatory process (recognizing that supervision is always a process in which both parties should feel enabled to fully engage; see all chapters in this book).

> How might you apply this form of dialogue in your own approach to CBTS? What areas of exploration might it lead to? Are there any that it might hamper?

Combining the external, internal and relational approaches

Supervisory relationships exist within boundaries which define what is and is not part of our practice. We are able to draw the lines which identify issues as lying within or outside our boundary of competent and responsible activity. The ethical dilemmas that confront us tend to occur at the margin of those boundaries. Issues which clearly sit outside belong to another domain (such as when an act is illegal or in obvious breach of a code of conduct) and will tend to be referred elsewhere (such as to statutory authorities). It is at the margin that they trouble us; we recognize that we have to respond but cannot readily identify how to do so.

One way to address ethical dilemmas in supervision is to consider them through each or all of the perspectives described in this chapter: the external, the internal and the relational. These provide potential boundaries to guide discussion. For example, starting with the universal principles might enable a discussion around issues such as respect and responsibility without needing to move directly to code violations, and can therefore be a productive way to help the supervisee think about what any action might mean for those involved. (In the first scenario in

Table 7, for example, application of the universal principles might enable the supervisor to reflect on issues of integrity and respect, as well as the potential impact of different courses of action.)

If an initial exploration generates the need to explore further, it may help to consider Carroll and Shaw's (2012) concept of ethical maturity. (For example, in scenarios 4 and 6 in Table 7, a consideration of the different components of ethical maturity may enable the supervisor to identify specific areas of ethical development that need to occur.) Finally, you may decide that an ethical dilemma is best addressed through collaborative dialogue, as no external code can provide a solution and what is needed is a process of negotiation in relation to different worldviews. (For example, in scenario 5 in Table 7, the tensions in the dual relationship need to be explored through dialogue rather than resolved through appealing to an external code.)

Learning Activity 10.2   Applying the external, internal and relational perspectives to your supervision practice

Having explored three approaches (external, internal and relational) to understanding ethics, consider a supervision case where you felt uncomfortable about the practice of a therapist whom you were supervising and believed that you were confronted with an ethical dilemma. (If you have not had such a case, define a situation that would lead you to feel uncomfortable.)

Taking the external, internal and relational approaches in turn, how you might address your dilemma? What considerations does each approach enable? What considerations might be disabled by using that approach? Finally, reflect on what you have learned and how you might apply this to enhancing your future practice or that of your service.

Pulling it all together

Having read this chapter and completed the learning activities provided, we invite you to adopt, once again, the role of supervision consultant for Patrick. This is followed by tips for supervisees on how to approach ethical concerns with their supervisors.

Case Study 10

Patrick is supervising Moses, a male trainee CBT therapist, who has a placement at a girls' high school. The client that Moses brings to supervision is a 15-year-old girl. Moses has been working with her to address a marked decline in her school grades which was found to be a consequence of her low mood and symptoms of depression. The client has made good progress using CBT to address her negative thoughts about herself, her world and her future.

During the penultimate session, the client asks Moses for help. She believes that her parents are planning to send her abroad for the holidays but suspects that they have a husband in mind for her and that this has already been agreed between the families. She is desperate to avoid this situation. She is brought to school by her brothers and has little freedom outside school. She asks Moses if he will buy her a train ticket (she offers the money) so she can run away. She is very upset in the session. He tells her he cannot buy the ticket and will have to think about the implications of this and talk to his supervisor. She makes him promise not to tell the school or her parents.

Moses is both distressed by his client's predicament and confused about what steps to take and is anxious for Patrick to provide clear guidance on what he should do. Patrick, too, feels anxious about how to address this in the way that meets Moses' stage-appropriate dependence for guidance and his ethical and legal responsibilities to the client, his service and his professional body.

Drawing on the material covered in this chapter, consider your responses to the following:

- What factors might be creating this dilemma for Patrick?
- How would you encourage Patrick to conceptualize this dilemma? What would you encourage him to explore with Moses in this case?
- How would you advise Patrick to proceed?

(We provide suggestions on how to approach this dilemma in Appendix 10.)

Tips for Supervisees No. 10

Supervisors not only evaluate supervisees' competence, but also have a safeguarding role. However, supervisors can also engage in ethical violations (Ladany, Lehrman-Waterman et al., 1999). This is important to bear in mind when considering any ethical issues that arise in your clinical work and how these are supported. You may find it helpful to ask your supervisor explicitly how ethical dilemmas can be addressed in supervision in a way which feels supportive.

You might find it helpful to adopt an external approach:

- Develop awareness of the code of conduct or standards of practice of the relevant professional body as well as those of the organization where you work. These could include those of the BABCP, the Health & Care Professions Council, the British Psychological Society and guidelines from NHS Trusts.

(Continued)

(Continued)

- Consider the sources of support that might be available to you from your training establishment or place of work should you feel your supervisor might be transgressing ethical boundaries. Become aware of what you can and cannot expect.

You might find it helpful to adopt an internal approach:

Consider a past experience of an ethical dilemma:

- What schemas, assumptions and values were brought to awareness? How did these make you feel?
- What helped you to manage the dilemma?
- What principles or guidelines influenced your response?
- In terms of the concept of ethical maturity, which of the six components were the most challenging to apply?
- What did you learn about yourself, the way you work, or your values?

You might find it helpful to adopt a relational approach:

- Regularly monitor the supervisory relationship and the supervision contract. As discussed in Chapter 7, this might help you think about whether your development and learning needs are supported.
- Consider what you might do to assist your supervisor in helping you explore ethical issues.
- Depending on the nature of the supervisory relationship, it might be useful to ask your supervisor about any ethical dilemmas they have faced and how they have managed them.

Conclusion

Pope and Vasquez (2011: xi) describe ethical awareness as a 'continuous, active process that involves constant questioning and personal responsibility'. Ethical dilemmas present an opportunity to challenge your own thinking and the field in which you are operating, and thereby enhance your practice.

In this chapter we have argued that it is important to approach ethics and ethical dilemmas as something more than a matter of ensuring conformity to the code of practice of a professional body. Clearly these are important, but codes of conduct, professional standards and the laws to protect society are best seen as the starting point of, rather than the conclusion to, the ethical considerations that occur in practice.

If a simple solution is available and agreeable to all parties, there is unlikely to be a dilemma. It is at the margins of our practice that concerns arise. Dilemmas occur because a problem is messy (Lane, 1990) and does not fit a neat cause–effect category. In aspiring to an enhanced approach to ethical considerations in CBTS, we have explored three approaches: the external, the internal and the relational. If ethical issues are considered in terms of the universal principles of respect, competence, integrity and responsibility, our work can be seen as underpinned by a single set of assumptions. Guiding our work may also be an awareness of ethical maturity and our ability to judge, act and live with the consequences of our actions. This approach takes ethics from being a matter sitting outside us (external) to a matter for us and our values (internal). As supervisors, we also act in relation to others, individuals and communities. The nature of those relationships and the way they come to generate meaning for us also provides a perspective from which to consider ethics as arising in our relational responsibilities to, and with, others.

Having a coherent way to approach ethical dilemmas has a number of benefits including, but not restricted to, understanding and resolving the issue in front of us. That understanding, if we take our ethical responsibility seriously, enables us to refine our practice to the benefit of all within our community.

Chapter summary

- ✓ The role of supervisor brings with it responsibilities that give rise to ethical dilemmas.
- ✓ Ethics are often seen as a matter of compliance with a code of conduct, but can also be seen as embodying universal principles of respect, competence, integrity and responsibility.
- ✓ We can consider our practice as based not solely on a code but as a reflection of our ethical maturity, in which we draw on our own values and level of awareness, or based on relational responsibilities emerging in the way we relate to each other within our communities of practice.
- ✓ These three approaches, external (codes), internal (maturity) and relational (collaboratively constructed), result in different ways of addressing dilemmas, all of which can offer benefits to those whom we seek to serve.

ELEVEN Assess your Supervisory Skill: Building Methods to Evaluate Practice

Learning objectives

After reading this chapter and completing the learning activities provided, you will be able to:

- Be aware of the competences needed to supervise effectively.
- Identify your strengths and development needs as a supervisor.
- Devise a process to obtain feedback on your supervisory competence.

Introduction

Becoming an effective CBT supervisor relies not only on subject matter expertise, but also on an ability to self-assess proficiency so that practice can be enhanced over time. The aim of this chapter is to enable you to assess your supervisory skill, with a view to deciding how to progress your professional development (which we consider further in Chapter 12).

The position taken in this chapter is that in order to be fit for purpose, self-assessment of supervisory skill needs to adopt an holistic and contextualized approach that takes account of the literature documenting specific competences, but which goes beyond a 'checklist' approach. If you have worked through the different petals of the PURE Supervision Flower and engaged with the learning activities provided in Chapters 1–10, you will already have an emerging understanding of your areas of strength and development need. In this chapter, we provide some further 'lenses' through which you can reflect upon and refine your proficiency.

In the service of this aim, we begin by considering the 'what' of effective supervision, identifying specific skills and competences highlighted in the supervision literature. We then consider 'how' you might personalize this to your particular service and needs while retaining a systematic approach.

What do we know about the effective supervisor?

As we have seen throughout this book, facilitating the therapeutic competence of others is a complex task requiring of supervisors the ability to perform a variety of roles and undertake a wide range of activities. Although the literature has identified diverse characteristics and skills that typify the effective supervisor, Bernard and Goodyear (2014) propose that supervisor competence can be distilled into two over-arching categories: (1) knowledge of the area of practice that the supervisee is learning to master; and (2) the ability to deliver supervision effectively.

Bernard and Goodyear's (2014) categorization can provide a starting point for conducting a meaningful and robust analysis of supervisory practice. Focusing on the former, for example, CBT supervisors might seek to ascertain their subject matter expertise through relevant reading and further training on specific disorders, self-assessment on Roth and Pilling's (2007) CBT competence framework and gaining feedback on their CBT practice using a standard measure of competence such as the CTS-R. In seeking to learn more about how to deliver supervision effectively, supervisors might devise a strategy that combines updating knowledge of theory and research, seeking training in supervision, organizing 'supervision of supervision' and evaluating their practice through use of specific measures.

For supervisors seeking measures to inform the development of their expertise, there is now a range from which to choose. In their 'Supervisor's Toolbox', Bernard and Goodyear (2014) reproduce a variety of useful measures spanning supervisee needs (Muse-Burke and Tyson, 2010); supervisory styles (Friedlander and Ward, 1984); supervisor self-efficacy scale (Barnes, 2002); the supervisory working alliance (with versions for both supervisor and supervisee) (Efstation et al., 1990); and a group supervision scale (Arcinue, 2002). These are generic measures although they still add value for those CBT supervisors seeking to enhance their approach (see Bernard and Goodyear (2014) for access to these).

Within this broad categorization of subject matter and supervision expertise, different authors have conceptualized supervisory skill from diverse perspectives. Hawkins and Smith (2006), for example, differentiate competences (the ability to apply or demonstrate a specific intervention or skill), capabilities (the ability to apply an intervention in the right way at the right time and in the appropriate context) and capacity (a human quality relating to the person of the supervisor and how they are 'present' in relationship to others). Meanwhile, Falender et al. (2004) have identified four distinct domains of supervisor skill:

1. Knowledge (theories and models of therapy; knowledge of professional/ supervisee development).
2. Skills (the ability to assess the learning needs and developmental level of the supervisee; relevant teaching skills; competence in providing formative and summative feedback effectively).
3. Values (being respectful; empowering the supervisee; valuing ethical principles; being committed to lifelong learning).
4. Context (knowledge of the immediate system and its expectations; socio-political context and creating an appropriate climate within supervision).

Learning Activity 11.1   Self-assessing your effectiveness as a CBT supervisor

Drawing on the methods that you would typically use to self-assess your practice, and using a scale of 0–10 (where 0 = absence of proficiency and 10 = optimally effective), how would you rate your effectiveness as a CBT supervisor on the following:

1. Knowledge of CBT in the areas of practice which you are supervising (i.e. CBT-specific theory, research and practice).
2. Knowledge of professional/supervisee development (theory, research and models specific to current thinking about supervision).
3. Supervisory skills (the ability to assess the learning needs and developmental level of the supervisee; relevant teaching skills; competence in providing formative and summative feedback effectively and delivering supervision in ways consistent with a CBT approach).
4. Values (being respectful; empowering the supervisee; valuing and demonstrating ethical principles; being committed to lifelong learning).
5. Context (knowledge of the immediate system and its expectations; socio-political context and creating an appropriate climate within supervision).

Reflecting on your ratings, do any specific areas stand out as priority development areas for you?

What are the competences that underpin effective CBTS?

It is important to note that when considering supervisor competence, different professional bodies may privilege different domains of knowledge and skill. CBT practitioners and supervisors are often members of more than one profession and may, therefore, be subject to different requirements in terms of how proficient supervisory practice is defined and understood. For example, the BABCP requires that supervisors are also accredited CBT practitioners. In contrast, the British Association for Counselling and Psychotherapy does not require supervisors to be accredited counsellors; those from other professions can offer supervision. Traditionally, the British Psychological Society did not require supervisors to be qualified in supervision but rather focused on experience in their core profession. However, the Society now has a generic supervision register that requires training and ongoing CPD, although membership requires different training depending on the area of practice (counselling, clinical, forensic, etc.).

As the confines of this chapter prevent us from considering the competence requirements of all the professions providing CBT, we have selected just one as an example that has particular relevance to CBT supervisors at this time: namely, the competence framework for the supervision of psychological therapies devised by Roth and Pilling (2008a). Although the authors note that much of the content is pan-theoretical, its initial application has been concerned with the competences necessary to support the delivery of CBT interventions in the context of IAPT services.

The supervision competence framework identifies four domains of supervisor competence: generic, specific, model-specific and metacompetences. Generic competences include the ability to form a supervisory alliance, structure sessions, and apply principles of adult learning to foster therapist development, whereas specific supervision competences refer to the ability to conduct supervision in different formats, assist therapists in practising clinical skills and making use of live observation. Model-specific supervision competences concern the application of supervision to the cognitive and behavioural therapies. The CBT (model-specific) competences are emphasized as needing integration with the other domains identified and are organized under the following headings:

1. Supervisors' expertise in CBT (such as the ability to draw on knowledge of the principles that underpin CBT).
2. Adapting supervision to the supervisee's CBT training needs (e.g. the ability to identify the supervisee's level of knowledge of and experience of using the CBT approach).
3. Structuring supervision sessions (e.g. working collaboratively to establish an agenda for the supervision session and to appropriately prioritize items for discussion).
4. Specific content areas for CBTS (e.g. fostering knowledge of diagnosis and the ability to devise formulations of clients' needs; draw upon basic, specific, problem-specific behavioural and cognitive-behavioural competences while maintaining an effective working relationship with clients.
5. Specific supervisory techniques (drawing upon a blended range of observational and experiential methods of learning such as role-play rehearsal and listening to audio-recordings of segments of therapy sessions to enhance supervisee learning and proficiency).
6. Monitoring the supervisee's work (the ability to assess the supervisee's CBT competences using appropriate measures and methods).

Finally, the domain of metacompetences refers to adapting the process and content of supervision to supervisees' needs, giving feedback, managing concerns about supervisees' ability to use supervision effectively and addressing major issues about supervisees' competence or fitness to practice.

> Review the broad domains of the supervision competence framework described above. (You might also find it helpful to download the full competence framework from www.ucl.ac.uk/CORE.) As you reflect on your supervisory practice, do any priority areas emerge as worthy of development at this point in your career? If so, how might you translate these into specific learning objectives?

Translating general principles into a personalized approach

Frameworks that attempt to identify the specific competences underpinning effective supervision provide important information about the knowledge and skills required. If they are to fulfil their potential as aids to learning and development, the identified competences need to be translated into a form that makes sense for the needs of the individual supervisor.

How a supervisor approaches the task of enhancing their proficiency at the start of their supervisory career may be quite different from how an experienced supervisor approaches this task. Moreover, there is an important distinction between acquiring and retaining competence. What is needed to build competence initially is not necessarily what is required to ensure that knowledge and skills remain fit for purpose over the longer term. Thus in order to accurately self-assess supervisory skill and formulate an appropriate response, self-assessment needs to be 'pitched' at the right developmental level. Two approaches can assist this endeavour. These are: (1) a consideration of the literature that seeks to understand how supervisors (like therapists) progress through specific stages of development; and (2) thinking about competence development in the format of supervision being provided. These are considered next.

Competence in the context of supervisor development: A stage theory perspective

As supervisors gain experience, they will (ideally) accrue knowledge and skill, develop an enhanced self–other awareness and undergo changes in sense of self-efficacy that are communicated to supervisees through enhanced interpersonal effectiveness. In Chapter 7, we examined Bennett-Levy and Thwaites' (2007) distinction between self-schema and self-as-therapist schema, which the authors see as having important implications for interpersonal therapeutic skills. We would also see this concept as highly relevant for the development of supervisor 'presence'. Specifically, changes in knowledge and skill that are acquired through experience foster changes in perception that can help crystallize a unique supervisor identity. It is through this identity that the 'human quality' to which Hawkins and Smith (2006) refer in their notion of capacity is communicated to, and experienced by, supervisees.

The development of what we might consider to be a 'self-as-supervisor schema' is likely to progress through a series of stages, in the same way that therapist development has been conceptualized as stage-dependent. Several models of supervisor development have been proposed, each of which privileges specific themes and time-scales but which have in common the attempt to clarify the shifts in self-efficacy, perceptions of role, and relationship with others that occur with experience. As their stages parallel the stages of therapist development outlined in their Integrated Developmental Model (see Chapter 4), we consider here Stoltenberg and McNeill's (2010) model, which identifies four levels (Table 9).

Table 9 Stoltenberg and McNeill's (2010) stages of supervisor development

Level 1:	Supervisors (like level 1 therapists) are anxious and eager to 'get it right'. This can create a tendency to be overly structured and lacking in flexibility in pursuit of the desire to deliver supervision 'correctly'. Stoltenberg and McNeill (2010) note that because level 1 therapists are similarly driven by a desire to know 'how to do therapy properly', a level 1 therapist and level 1 supervisor can be an effective pairing. An example might be a relatively recently accredited CBT therapist delivering site supervision to a student who has recently begun an IAPT training. Here, the supervisor may well come across as knowledgeable and skilled through clarity of approach. However, at level 1, a supervisor may be less equipped to manage the process aspects of supervision and less able to adjust their approach as a function of a therapist's learning needs and interpersonal style.
Level 2:	As for therapists, level 2 is associated with conflict and ambivalence. For supervisors at this stage of development (identified as short-lived), there is a growing appreciation that supervision is a complex undertaking that poses many challenges. Motivation can fluctuate, and there is an inclination to be overly focused on the supervisee, which can create a tendency to experience frustration and blame the supervisee at the expense of retaining objectivity. At this stage it is important for supervisors to have access to consultation on their supervision to remain a consistent and helpful presence.
Level 3:	Level 3 supervisors now have consistent motivation in the supervisor role and are able to function autonomously, although 'supervision of supervision' is accessed as needed. At this stage of development supervisors are increasingly able to accurately and effectively appraise their own practice.

(Continued)

Table 9   (Continued)

Level 3 Integrated:	Finally, at level 3 Integrated, these 'master supervisors' are able to work effectively with supervisees at all levels of development and have a personalized approach to their practice. At this level, supervisors are often sought out to provide consultation to less experienced supervisors at earlier stages of development.

Using Stoltenberg and McNeill's model, what would you see as being your stage of supervisor development? On what evidence are you basing this evaluation? How might this stage 'show' in your practice in terms of areas of strength and limitation, and specific competences identified in the supervision competence framework?

Although a lack of evidence has been noted (Russell and Petrie, 1994), stage theories may, nonetheless, provide insight into themes that can enable supervisors (and those who train them) to formulate 'the next steps' of their development and the specific types of instruction that may be required (Heid, 1997).

Tharp and Gallimore (2002) describe how a learner progresses through the zone of proximal development (ZPD). A term coined by Vygotsky, the ZPD refers to 'the distance between the actual developmental level as determined by independent problem solving and the level of potential development as determined through problem solving under adult guidance or in collaboration with more capable peers' (Vygotsky, 1978: 86). Applied to CBTS, James et al. (2006) propose that the ZPD can help supervisors conceptualize those skills that a therapist can deliver independently and those which they may be able to deliver with optimal supervisory assistance. This applies equally to CBT supervisors. For example, at level 1, a supervisor may be relatively dependent on others for their learning. Observing experienced supervisors, obtaining feedback on recordings of sessions and role-playing challenging scenarios (such as giving corrective feedback or managing ruptures) are likely to be particularly beneficial. At level 2, there is a transition away from instructor-led learning towards a consciously employed self-regulation. Here, ensuring that live observations are augmented by reflective practices through which supervisors can articulate their formulations and choice of intervention may be useful.

By level 3, the learner has emerged from the ZPD, practice is no longer actively developing and performance becomes more automatic. Here, there is a risk of habitual responding that may undermine effective practice. At level 3, the need for direct observation of practice may take on a new importance, as might use of measures to gain feedback. Here, supervisors need to remain open to critiquing their practice to prevent what Vygotsky (1978) refers to as 'fossilization'. In the final stage that Tharp and Gallimore (2002) describe, what has been automatic comes back under conscious control and can therefore be subjected to reflection and modification. At level 3 Integrated, supervisors are able to draw effectively on multiple sources of feedback to hone their approach. At this level also, supervisors may find that demand for their services goes beyond the traditional expert–apprentice role into other forms of delivery. These are considered next.

Competence as a function of supervision format

Traditionally, supervision has been understood as a role played by experienced practitioners who pass on the codified assumptions of the past to the present generation. However, today supervision is increasingly seen as a 'whole career' activity and hence the role it plays extends beyond this traditional model.

Increasingly, supervisors need to be able to work with CBT therapists at all stages of their careers. The need for many supervisors to support experienced professionals as well as trainees can blur the distinction between a process that is developmentally-focused and one which is concerned with adherence to external mandates. Moreover, as supervisors mature in their knowledge and experience, it is possible that they are required to deliver supervision in different or more flexible ways. All of these factors have implications for how supervisor competence is defined and developed. Exploring this issue in relation to the field of coaching, Lane (2011) identified four possible formats of supervision which have implications for how proficiency is understood and developed: the Expert–Apprentice Model; the CPD Model; the Peer Mentoring Model; and the Process Model. Each of these is considered in turn.

Expert–Apprentice Model

In this role the supervisor holds both content and process expertise and mentors a junior partner to develop their practice in an apprenticeship model. We would see this as being the principal format of supervision on which the existing CBT literature has focused. An example of this would be where an experienced CBT supervisor works with a small group of therapists in the context of a CBT training course.

When working from the expert–apprentice model, supervisors will be attentive to competence frameworks that relate to both the skills of the therapist and their own supervisory competence in facilitating these. A high level of subject matter expertise will be required and CBT-specific measures of supervisory competence may also be beneficial. Milne (2009) has argued that if supervision is a professional competence, then it should be possible for this to be observed reliably. Assuming this is the case, evaluations of competence can be obtained and instruments devised to assist evaluation and supervisor development. Thus, a number of measures have emerged. The Supervision: Adherence and Guidance Evaluation Scale (SAGE) (Milne et al., 2011) is based closely on the Dreyfus (e.g. Dreyfus and Dreyfus, 1986) taxonomy of competence that underpins the CTS-R, using the seven-point rating scale of 'absence of feature' through to 'expert'. James et al. (2004) have also developed a supervision scale – STARS-CT (Supervision Training Assessment Rating Scale for Cognitive Therapy) – for assessing competence in the delivery of CBTS.

An additional instrument, the Supervisor Evaluation Scale (SES) (Corrie and Worrell, 2012; Appendix 11B), similarly draws on Dreyfus's taxonomy, tracking evidence of a supervisor's abilities as delivered in the context of a specific supervision session. The SES avoids a narrow, prescriptive approach to competence in favour of four broad domains in which the supervisor is afforded considerable flexibility in how the competence is demonstrated. The four domains are:

A. Session Structure and Planning.
B. Facilitation of Supervisee Learning.
C. Development of CBT-Specific Competences.
D. Management of the Session.

CPD Model

In this model both parties (or members of a supervision group) possess content and process expertise and may work together across areas of practice, service or disciplinary boundaries. Supervision is concerned with refining practice in the context of a negotiated process for continuing professional development. An example might be where two accredited CBT therapists from different professional backgrounds (such as nursing and psychology) and working within different clinical specialisms (mental health and cancer services) come together to enhance their CBT skills in specific areas. Because supervision takes the form of learning between colleagues at a similar level of development, the power differentials of the expert–apprentice model do not apply. However, as supervision may review working practices with different client groups, it is important to define the specific areas on which feedback is sought.

In addition to the measures considered previously, a further approach for gaining feedback is the 'ORCE' method (Psychological Testing Centre, 2012). ORCE is a trans-theoretical process that can be adapted to any area of professional practice as there is no predetermined competence model in play. Commonly applied in occupational psychology for the assessment and development of competence, it can, therefore, be adapted to the assessment of supervisory competence.

Use of the method begins with agreement about what would constitute an example of a competence, behaviour or process that the individual seeks to explore. A specific event is then Observed. This might be a sample from a video-recording of a supervision session. The observer watches that sample and Records (writes down) what they observe, recording all that happened rather than looking for specific examples of the competence in question. Following this, the recording is reviewed to see whether there is any evidence that can be Classified as an example of the competence under consideration. Finally, that evidence is Evaluated to see if it is a positive or negative example of the behaviour (i.e. whether the competence was effectively or ineffectively delivered).

To give an example of the ORCE method as applied to supervision, consider a supervisor who seeks to refine their approach to delivering capsule summaries (a supervisory technique identified in the supervision competence framework). From a <u>R</u>ecording of a supervision session, it proves possible for an <u>O</u>bserver to <u>C</u>lassify a piece of behaviour as an example of the use of a capsule summary. A positive example of the use of capsule summaries might be the evidence that the supervisor did indeed provide regular summaries throughout a session. A negative example would be where this was implemented in a rushed manner at the end of the session, without seeking feedback from the supervisee as to whether this was consistent with their experience.

As a tool for developing evaluation skills, ORCE is very powerful and in occupational practice peers are often taught how to evaluate each other through multiple assessments on this basis (Seegers, 1989). This could be a useful development for supervision training in the field of CBT.

Peer Mentoring Model

In some fields, such as coaching and mentoring, and certainly in industry, the idea that (even inexperienced) peers can mentor each other is widespread. An example of this might be where, in the context of a CBT training course, trainee therapists meet in self-directed learning groups to support the development of one another's knowledge and skill. In this type of supervision, peers play the role of thinking partners (Lane, 1994) or create with others a time and space to think (Kline, 1999). Where a structured model for running sessions is provided, it enables peers to ask appropriate questions to help their colleagues explore issues of concern (McNicoll, 2008). In McNicoll's approach, peers choose from a set of cards the format for questioning that best fits the issue they want to explore.

One approach to enhancing self-evaluation of practice in the context of peer mentoring is to draw on the concept of triangulation commonly used in qualitative research (Hammersley, 1996). Triangulation is based on the assumption that examining a situation from diverse viewpoints assists the development of a coherent three-dimensional picture. In applying this to self-assessment of supervisory skill, you might seek to examine aspects of your practice and find the coherence (or lack of) in your approach. Gosling (2010) has used this approach to explore practice in services working with children. By comparing self-reports on practice with case material on file and live observations, three perspectives on the same practice were possible. Peers working in mentoring groups can similarly seek varied sources of information on the question they are exploring. Applying this approach to the analysis of CBTS might include a practitioner providing a description of their own practice (the aims, objectives, theoretical perspectives brought and process used), to which could be added a process report and a video-recording of a supervision session. This would provide triangulated data as the basis for exploration, which may be experienced as easier with one another than with other supervisors since the evaluative component of supervision is less of a focus than in the expert–apprentice model.

Process Model

Effective supervision is also possible where the supervisee holds the content expertise and the supervisor sits outside that knowledge-base, but is an expert in the process of supervision itself. Although less common in CBT than other disciplines, it is argued by groups such as the Association of National Organizations for Supervision in Europe and the European Association for Supervision that supervision is a professional practice in its own right. Expertise in the process of supervision, and in the process of learning, enables practitioners to work across multiple areas. For a wide range of interventions (e.g. working with refugees, in mental health, psychosocial care, process consultancy and peer counselling), individuals are providing supervisory support outside their content expertise (Stern et al., 1994).

Given an expertise in process consultation, there may be occasions when a supervisor may not need content expertise in CBT. However, the boundaries would need to be carefully managed and the code of ethics governing the work would also need to be negotiated to ensure that supervision remains capable of meeting the development needs of the supervisee and, by extension, the needs of the client. An example, outside CBTS but relevant to it, is the use of process consultation in development work. The consultant does not possess the local knowledge so has to rely on participants as experts in their context (Schein, 1997).

A further step in this analysis, again borrowed from occupational psychology, is to create a narrative (supported by the evidence). You might each consider a particular supervision event and create a narrative around the Situation observed (its context and purpose), the Task attempted (the objective of the session), the Actions undertaken in pursuit of that task (what was done) and the Results achieved (what happened). A participant in process supervision might be asked to provide examples of when the experience was positive (or not). They then structure their understanding of this experience in terms of the STAR. Students are often taught to use this as a way of structuring responses to questions (Careers Advisory Service, University of Bath, 2013). A process perspective is concerned not just with what happened but also with how any understandings emerged. For example, with Situation, the narrative is concerned with describing the context and purpose and how participants came to define it in the way that they did (that is, what process was occurring between them to reach any agreed description). This approach enables both parties to examine the extent to which the actions taken match the agreed objective of the session, and make use of interventions that address the supervisee's needs.

Reviewing Lane's four types of supervision, consider those forms of supervision you have delivered. What different forms of knowledge and skill might be particularly important for each of the types in which you are involved and can you identify any development needs relating to these? For example, if you are delivering CBTS in the context of an expert–apprentice model, are there any specific competences in which you need to enhance your proficiency? If you are delivering a process model, what specific knowledge of learning, professional development and consultation in supervision might you need to do so effectively?

Learning Activity 11.2   Honing your approach to self-assessment for future practice

Consider how, up until now, you have approached the task of self-assessing your strengths and limitations as a CBT supervisor. In particular:

1. What specific methods have you used to determine your level of proficiency?
2. What (if any) measures have you used?
3. Upon what sources of feedback have you relied?

Based on the material covered in this chapter, are there any new methods for informing the self-assessment of your proficiency that it might prove helpful to introduce? If so, how might you go about doing so?

Pulling it all together

Having read this chapter and completed the learning activities provided, we invite you to adopt, once again, the role of supervision consultant for Nina who has been approached by Patrick for consultation on his CBTS. This is followed by some suggestions on when and how supervisees might be in a position to support the development of their supervisors' knowledge and skills.

Case Study 11

Patrick explained to Nina that he wanted to organize some 'supervision of his supervision' away from his place of work, in order to reflect on his practice and consider how best to develop his supervisory skill. He contacted Nina after he found her details on the BABCP website and, impressed by her credentials, believed that she might be the person to assist him.

(Continued)

(Continued)

After an initial discussion, they decided to meet in person in order to establish whether they could agree a basis for working together. When Nina asks Patrick what he sees as his primary areas of learning and development, he seems to struggle to identify clearly what he needs, but describes some of the challenges that he has faced recently, as he has begun providing CBTS for the first time. (These are the challenges that you will have read about in the preceding chapters.) Nina is unfamiliar with Patrick's work. However, she senses from how he describes his supervisory practice that he might need some assistance in establishing clear learning objectives derived from a robust understanding of his current skill level as a supervisor and his stage of supervisor development.

- If Nina came to you for consultation on how to work with Patrick (and based on your knowledge of Patrick's practice from the previous chapters) how would you encourage her to approach assessing his needs for learning and development?
- Based on the models and approaches presented in this chapter, what factors might you encourage Nina to hold in mind?
- How would you advise Nina to proceed?

(We provide suggestions on how to approach this dilemma in Appendix 11.)

Tips for Supervisees No. 11

Providing feedback on supervision may seem a daunting task, particularly if you are receiving supervision in the context of the expert–apprentice model described above. Nonetheless, CBTS is a two-way process. Listed below are some ideas that might help you give feedback on the supervision that you are receiving that could positively impact your supervisor's learning and development:

- Holding in mind the CBT competences you want to develop and your past experiences of supervision, consider the methods that would best facilitate your learning (e.g. case discussion, formulation, playing recordings of therapy sessions, role-play, etc.). Depending on the issues you wish to explore during a particular supervision session, it might then be useful to let your supervisor know which methods you would find most helpful.
- At the end of the supervision session share your thoughts about what you found helpful and what, if anything, you would like more of. At the beginning of the next supervision session, you might like to provide a brief summary of your experience of applying some of the ideas discussed in the previous supervision session.
- Negotiate some time to review your supervision contract and learning needs. If you are on a CBT training course, this could be part of a 'mid-training review'. This gives you the opportunity to discuss what you find helpful about supervision and what, if anything, you would like more of.

- Before providing feedback ensure that you understand the context of supervision and the type of feedback that the setting encourages and discourages. For example, in the context of peer supervision or if you are more established in your career, it might feel easy and appropriate to provide feedback openly. If you are on a CBT training course or are early in your career, providing direct feedback to an experienced supervisor might seem problematic due to factors such as the power differential (Chapter 8) and the evaluative component of supervision. In these circumstances, feedback about supervision might feel easier when it is focused on your own needs (see the above points).

Conclusion

Traditionally, supervision has been seen as a role played by experienced practitioners who pass on their experience and knowledge to more junior practitioners. Today, supervision is increasingly seen as a 'whole career' activity which has implications for the way in which supervisor competence is defined, understood and nurtured.

In this chapter, we have argued that effective self-assessment of supervisory skill depends on a working knowledge of both what constitutes proficiency (i.e. domains of knowledge and specific competences) and how to adapt lists of competences to the demands of particular supervisory settings (i.e. the context in which that proficiency is delivered). We have proposed that assessing your competence as a CBT supervisor needs to entail a holistic and contextualized approach that considers stage of supervisor development as well as the different formats that CBTS might increasingly take.

In this chapter we have provided a range of models and tools to help you think about your level of competence and to enable you to invite feedback from others so that you can develop a personalized approach to the assessment and development of your proficiency. By using such feedback mechanisms you can, over time, build a robust understanding of your strengths and needs that will provide the basis for a development plan. This is the topic of our next and final chapter.

Chapter summary

- ✓ In order to self-assess supervisory skill, it is necessary to develop a robust approach.
- ✓ Self-assessment can usefully be informed by drawing on supervisor competence frameworks, stage theories of supervisor development and understanding the type of supervision offered.
- ✓ A variety of tools can help CBT supervisors evaluate their practice.
- ✓ Supervision takes place in a context which impacts on the knowledge and skills required to be effective. It is important to understand the context for your work.

TWELVE   Increase your Expertise: Developing and Looking After the Self

Learning objectives

After reading this chapter and completing the learning activities provided, you will be able to:

- Consider how you can increase your expertise while also looking after yourself.
- Reflect on how to take forward your development as a CBT supervisor, drawing on the material provided in this book.
- Prepare for the changing employment landscape that characterizes professional practice.

Introduction

The content of this book has been organized around the PURE Supervision Flower, which we have offered as a visual heuristic for assisting supervisors (and those who train them) in identifying specific areas that can inform a process of honing knowledge and skill. In this final chapter, we return to the PURE Supervision Flower to help you decide how to take forward your learning and increase your expertise.

We begin by revisiting the PURE Supervision Flower as a basis for planning your development. Recognizing that supervision is provided in complex and often stressful environments, we then explore how to establish adequate self-care in order to protect yourself against burnout. Following this, we broaden the discussion from your own journey to reflect on the way in which continuing professional development (CPD) is understood in a complex and unpredictable employment market. The world of work increasingly requires individuals to demonstrate their distinctiveness and take an active role in promoting themselves and their services. Supervisors need to be aware of this and devise an approach to professional development that befits the opportunities and challenges afforded by this climate. We conclude the book with a final word on CBT supervision and a thought for the future.

Revisiting the PURE Supervision Flower

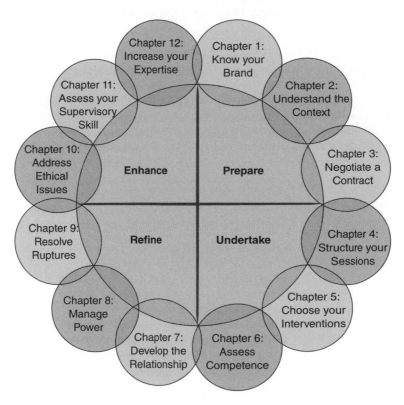

Figure 1   The PURE Supervision Flower

As we have seen, each of the 12 'petals' of the PURE Supervision Flower focuses on a specific domain of activity which CBT supervisors need to master in order to provide an optimal learning experience. These 12 domains are grouped into four classes of activity, captured in the acronym 'PURE'.

To **P**repare for CBTS you were invited to consider what needs to be in place in order to establish an appropriate, effective and ethical basis for supervision. Specifically, we asked you to:

- Understand your position within the conceptual and technical land-scape of CBT which gives rise to your personal 'brand' (Chapter 1).
- Appreciate, and be able to operate effectively within, the context in which your brand of CBTS is provided (Chapter 2).
- Use the above as a basis for negotiating a supervision contract (Chapter 3).

To **U**ndertake CBTS you identified the content and tasks of CBTS through:

- Examining how you structure your sessions and the style of relating that you bring to this structure (Chapter 4).
- Selecting interventions that optimally support the development of therapist competence (Chapter 5).
- Establishing a robust and fair approach to assessing therapist competence (Chapter 6).

To **R**efine your CBTS you explored how to hone your management of the many process issues that can arise. Specifically, we invited you to consider:

- The role of the supervisory relationship in facilitating therapist development (Chapter 7).
- The effective management of power (Chapter 8).
- How to manage and respond to resistance and ruptures in the working alliance (Chapter 9).

To **E**nhance your CBTS you thought about how to continue your process of self-development through:

- Honing your capacity to work with ethical dilemmas and focusing on your own personal ethical maturity while fostering this in others (Chapter 10).
- Assessing your level of knowledge and skill as a CBT supervisor (Chapter 11).

In this final chapter we look at how you can increase your supervisory expertise in the longer term, considering opportunities for CPD as well as effective self-care. By way of preparation, and drawing on your reflections from the preceding chapters, give some thought to your primary learning and development needs at this stage in your supervisory career, using Learning Activity 12 to guide you.

Learning Activity 12   Identifying the basis for a career development plan

What would you consider to be your primary learning and development needs at the current time? Specifically:

1. On which of the broad domains of the PURE Supervision Flower (Prepare, Undertake, Refine or Enhance) do you need to focus your efforts? Do any 'petals' require particular attention as part of your career development as a CBT supervisor?
2. Based on your responses to question 1, what objectives might you want to set yourself?
3. What is the best way to approach achieving these objectives? What sources of feedback and other forms of evidence might you need?
4. What opportunities are provided by your working context to meet these needs?
5. How will you evaluate your progress towards achieving these objectives?

How to create a development plan: Aspects to consider

There is considerable value in a process of reflection that attends to each of the domains identified in the PURE Supervision Flower. Such a process needs to include a focus on both the continuing development of specific competences and the development of the self as a route to enhancing (rather than simply maintaining) your practice. A focus on competence development is how CPD has traditionally been approached in the field of CBT. As a result, there are multiple courses that can furnish our practice with models and interventions for enhancing our expertise in the delivery of CBT and, increasingly, CBTS.

The area which is only more recently being taken seriously is the development of the 'self-as-person' and 'self-as-therapist' (Bennett-Levy and Thwaites, 2007; see also Thwaites et al., 2014). To this we would add the 'self-as-supervisor'. The stance of this book is that the relational alliance is critical to our work as CBT supervisors and, therefore, attending to our personal development is an essential part of enhancing our expertise. Without this, we would argue, it is not truly possible to address the relational elements of our practice.

If it is to prove fit for purpose, any development plan needs to start with a critical reflective process to enable us to identify ways of enhancing our strengths and addressing our limitations. Throughout this book we have attempted to provide a wide variety of models, methods and techniques to assist you in doing just this. Each of these can potentially be directed towards enhancing, rather than simply maintaining, expertise. For example, supervisee style of learning, which we examined in Chapter 4, could be applied as a tool to help you critically reflect upon your own learning preferences. Similarly, Table 3 in Chapter 6 identifies a three-stage process for conducting evaluations that can be applied to evaluating the effectiveness of your own professional development plan. If experiencing resistance to engaging in an area of development, you can also use the examples from Chapter 9 on noticing acts of resistance to identify the nature of the obstacles you are encountering.

If we have faith in the power of supervision as a vehicle for professional growth and career enhancement, then it makes sense to consider how 'supervision of supervision' can contribute to developing expertise. As

Hawkins and Shohet (2012) observe, a prerequisite for being a good supervisor is ensuring that you have access to good supervision yourself. In Chapter 11 we identified four types of supervision: the expert–apprentice, CPD, peer mentoring and process-led models. Each of these adds particular value at different points in your development. While inexperienced supervisors may, for example, appreciate having an expert guide, highly experienced practitioners may benefit more from a CPD model. The type of supervision from which you are most likely to benefit will be important to consider as you plan your professional development and make choices about who is best placed to support you in working towards your chosen objectives.

> Considering your current career development needs as a CBT supervisor, which model of supervision – expert–apprentice, CPD, peer mentoring or process-led – might be optimal? What options exist in your current service setting to be able to organize this for yourself?

As supervisors, we need to do more than reflect upon what we have learned. We must also put our learning into action. In the same way that we negotiate contracts with our supervisees, we need to formalize a contract with ourselves that commits us to delivering on our CPD and measuring the results of that activity.

Many professional bodies now provide development plans for their members that can be used as templates for this task. Where supervisors are regulated by statutory bodies they may also have to meet the CPD expectations of their registration bodies. This means that CBT supervisors may be subject to different external requirements. Underpinning the assumptions about CPD that our professional and statutory bodies impose is a belief that our approach has a clear purpose and is designed to enable effective practice. Many professional bodies have moved away from the idea that compiling lists of activities or logs of CPD 'hours' is sufficient for ensuring competence. If you are able to define the purpose of your CPD in a way that makes sense in terms of your role, takes account of your critical reflections and the feedback you receive from others, and is clearly designed to enhance practice, it is likely to meet external requirements.

In order to enhance your expertise in those areas most relevant to your current and future needs, it is essential to know how to develop a strategy that can be translated into detailed activities that can act as a guide. It is also important for any action plan to consider what will be different on completion. A development plan is not just a decision to take part in training; it is also a commitment to change. The anticipated results need to be outlined so that it is possible to establish whether they have been achieved. Finally, it is necessary to identify when the results are achieved and any possible reassessment necessary to inform future planning.

In summary, your development plan should contain elements that relate to each of the following:

- A critical reflective process to identify specific areas of development that encompass both competences, and the self-as-person and self-as-supervisor. This should include feedback from others. Out of this you determine:
- A strategy which can enhance your expertise in areas that are most relevant to your current and future needs.
- An action plan that details the activities (e.g. what, by when and by whom) which are needed to deliver on that strategy.
- A definition of results from the action plan written in such a way that it would be possible to establish whether they have been achieved.
- A process to identify when the results are achieved and any possible reassessment as a basis for further planning.

Looking after yourself as a person and as a supervisor

As we have argued, to the extent that we bring ourselves as persons to the supervisory relationship, our CPD must be concerned as much with our own well-being and level of self-knowledge as with our declarative and procedural skills.

Empathy is fundamental to successful human relationships but as a therapist and supervisor it is seen as a core competence of our work. One interesting finding is that individuals with high levels of empathy are more prone to burnout, compassion fatigue and secondary traumatic stress (Figley, 1995). Given that therapists and supervisors are exposed to distressing stories on a regular basis, the issue of secondary trauma is very real. The greater the exposure the more likely we are to experience compassion fatigue, secondary trauma and burnout. The response can be to seek distractions, or to dissociate. In both cases the quality of our work and our own well-being will be impacted.

Working in the field of trauma, Tehrani (2011a) has examined ways to manage trauma in a variety of professions. Tehrani (2011b) has specifically pointed to the potential impact of secondary traumatization for supervisors who hear distressing accounts from their supervisees but do not put in place mechanisms to manage exposure to their stories. Among the mechanisms that can be put in place are professional and peer support (Tehrani et al., 2012). Based on research with a number of professional groups, Tehrani (2011b) found that professional and peer support were positively correlated with sense of competence, learning, beliefs about 'doing a good job', and sense of fulfilment. Managerial support was also found to be related to feelings of 'doing a good job' and sense of fulfilment. Other mechanisms she reported as useful included hobbies, exercise, prayer, meditation and attention to spiritual life.

> Drawing on the work of Tehrani and her colleagues, consider: (1) what are the likely costs to you of ignoring the impact of supervision on your psychological well-being; and (2) how, as a busy supervisor, you can find ways to take better care of your own needs.

One response to the challenges of providing supervision over the longer term is to establish protective rituals. The primary purpose of such rituals is to create a partition between work and home so that we do not allow distressing scenes to 'bleed' into other aspects of life. For example, in working with police officers dealing with images of child abuse, Tehrani (2011b) recommends that officers do not have photos of their own children on their desks at work. The juxtaposition of the two images is potentially problematic.

Rituals are quick and easy to learn, focus the attention and become more impactful the more they are used. We recommend the three rituals detailed in Table 10 that Tehrani (2011b) proposes as valuable to our sense of well-being as supervisors.

Table 10 Daily rituals to support self-care

1. Protection ritual for use before the working day

Before you start work for the day ask yourself:
Why am I doing this work? (reason)
What do I want to achieve? (strategy)
What is my current goal? (task)

Now ask: 'What are my personal concerns?'

- Family health, argument, child care, etc.

Ask: 'Am I actively thinking about my personal concerns?'

- If the answer is Yes, record, then park them and/or address them.

- If the answer is No, you can safely start the day's work.

2. Protection ritual for use during the working day

Identify the work planned for the day and then ask yourself:

A. To support the development of your competence:

- Do I know what I am doing?

- What can I do to be more successful?

- How can I encourage sharing knowledge?

B. To support maintaining your boundaries:

- What can I do to prevent 'seepage' between personal and work issues?

C. To recognize and deal with physical/emotional signs of distress/fatigue:

- Remind yourself of the mechanisms you have in place to manage stress and fatigue.

- Develop some mechanisms if you have none.

- Walk out of the working area, if necessary, and compose yourself before returning.

3. Recovery ritual for use at the end of the day

There are three phases to this ritual.

Phase 1: Managing the ending. Ask yourself:

- Have I finished everything? (If not, write down what is outstanding and leave it for tomorrow. If you cannot, the day is unfinished.)

Phase 2: Closing down. Make sure you have:

- Checked yourself physically, emotionally, socially.

- Checked you are ready to move on to home and out of work mode.

Phase 3: Reconnecting. Ask yourself:

- How did my day start at home today?

- What am I hoping to do when I get back home?

CPD and critical questions for the future

Given Bennett-Levy's (2006) point that the development of our practice needs to attend to both our personal and professional selves, one of the issues for the future will be how our credentialing bodies take on board the broader issue of professional development in ways that include attention to the person of the supervisor, and their growth and well-being. Historically, other branches of psychotherapy have paid attention to this, but in CBT the issue has been either marginal or not specifically mandated.

A second issue for the future is the extent to which we look at bringing our CBT-specific supervisory expertise to fields outside CBT itself. In this book, we have explored the practice of CBTS from within a largely CBT frame. However, we have also made the point that we have to be aware of broader developments and challenges. We have assumed that to supervise

CBT practitioners we must ourselves be competent as therapists. Yet, as we saw in Chapter 11, this is not a universally accepted position.

In some fields of practice, supervision is regarded as a trans-disciplinary activity that represents an area of expertise distinct from subject matter expertise. The emphasis is on supervision as a process for enhancing practice rather than as a means of passing on subject matter expertise (Lane, 2011). While the current structures in CBTS regulation mitigate against this, some readers may wish to make supervision an area of specialism. Anecdotally, a number of CBT supervisors have reported to us that they find themselves being asked to supervise in other disciplines, such as coaching psychology, supervising internal coaches in organizations and, indeed, to therapists of other theoretical orientations. However, for most, the route to supervisor accreditation is with relevant professional bodies, in particular the BABCP (see www.babcp.com). This approach emphasizes expertise in CBT and its application to supervision. For example, BABCP specifies eight criteria that must be demonstrated to gain supervisor accreditation. These include being a dedicated and fully accredited CBT therapist with the BABCP, having experience of treating a variety of clinical presentations from a spectrum of complexity, being in receipt of regular clinical supervision from a specialist CBT supervisor, having in place appropriate 'supervision of supervision' and providing evidence of ongoing CPD in relation to both CBT and CBTS. The current process does not provide a mechanism for supervisors to specialize in process-oriented approaches to supervision.

At present it is likely that only a minority of supervisors will wish to work outside CBT therapy. However, as employment opportunities emerge in other disciplines, for which knowledge of cognitive and behavioural perspectives is sought, there may be a temptation to offer a service. Therefore, a critical issue for the future is the extent to which our CBT professional bodies want to assist members in using their expertise in fields other than therapy. (Other professional bodies are taking these steps to ensure that their members are able to operate in new fields without having to join another organization. The British Association for Counselling & Psychotherapy, for example, created a coaching section so that their therapists could work in that field without having to join a separate coaching body. Similarly, the British Psychological Society created a psychotherapy register in order that psychologists could identify themselves as specialists in psychotherapy without having to join another organization.)

An additional challenge is how we manage our learning for the future. It was once possible to obtain an initial qualification linked to professional training and be reasonably confident about remaining up-to-date in our knowledge and skill, but this is no longer the case. There is a growing recognition that our professional integrity and survival are tied to the ability to remain informed and to be able to justify our practice to our stakeholders. Globalization, the rapid pace of technological change and the growing demand for CBT require us to remain competitive. The implementation of the UK Government's 'Any Qualified Provider' (AQP) policy has also signalled the dawning of a new era. An example of this in relation to CBTS would be if a commissioning body subcontracted provision to a service that bids to offer supervision through the internet at a distance, thus significantly reducing the cost to the commissioner. We have to be alert to the importance of maintaining CPD practices in order to both benefit from changes in employment as well as lead them.

The end of the 'job for life' culture and move towards inter-industry transferable skills have, as Lane and Corrie (2006) observed, generated the need for individuals to take more responsibility for their learning, development and marketability. In consequence, we need to think about our professional development in new and more sophisticated ways. This includes developing a robust process to measure the impacts of CPD (that is, a shift away from inputs towards outputs) and understanding CPD as part of how we refine our individual brand. While personal 'branding' may seem antithetical to the values of service to which many therapists subscribe, changes in the culture of work necessitate this (Birch and Corrie, 2014).

For those who see CBTS as part of their distinct 'brand', there are likely to be many opportunities as the requirement for supervision expands alongside the development of services. Supervision is likely to become increasingly emphasized as a means of quality-controlling the delivery of CBT, yet CBTS remains a relatively under-researched activity in comparison with models of therapy. As both the demand for and expectations of CBT supervisors increase, the professional community needs to ensure that this activity is supported by a concurrent increase in scholarly activity. This activity should be directed towards identifying those components of supervision associated with enhanced therapist competence that translate into substantive benefits for clients. Creating a more fruitful dialogue between empirically-supported understanding and knowledge based on practical experience is a critical step for the future. Only then can the field look towards creating a robust and systematic approach to CBT supervisor training and credentialing.

Pulling it all together

Having read this chapter we invite you to adopt, for the final time, the role of supervision consultant for Nina and Patrick.

Case Study 12

In this book you have witnessed the supervisory dilemmas faced by Patrick and Nina, and advised them, through the case studies, on how they might develop their skills. Having got to know them, and as a prelude to planning your own CPD, we invite you to advise each of them on their CPD needs:

1. Would you see any areas where **P**reparing for CBTS needs to be a CPD priority (e.g. branding, understanding context and negotiating a supervision contract)?
2. Would you see any areas where **U**ndertaking CBTS needs to be a CPD priority (e.g. structuring and style of sessions, selecting interventions or assessing therapist competence)?
3. Would you see any areas where **R**efining their CBTS needs to be a CPD priority (e.g. developing the supervisory relationship, managing power or responding to resistance and ruptures)?
4. Would you see any areas where **E**nhancing their CBTS needs to be a CPD priority (e.g. working with ethical issues, self-assessment of competence and skill, and managing their learning and sense of well-being)?

Having reflected on these areas, now consider the five steps for creating a development plan described previously and repeated below:

1. How can you assist each of them to develop a critical reflective process to identify specific areas of development? This can include feedback from you based on your observation of their casework. Out of this, can you help them determine:
2. A strategy for enhancing their expertise in the identified areas?
3. Activities that can form part of an action plan?
4. The results from the action plan framed in such a way that it will be possible to assist Patrick and Nina in establishing whether their objectives have been achieved?
5. The changes in their behaviour that will identify that the results of the plan have been achieved?

(We provide suggestions on how to approach this in Appendix 12.)

Now repeat the process above, but this time focusing on yourself in terms of both competence and personal development. See also if you can identify a person or persons who can fulfil the role you have just taken in relation to Patrick or Nina to provide feedback to help you construct your plan.

Conclusion

CPD is not simply a list of activities you undertake; it needs to be related to your purpose as a supervisor. From time to time that purpose needs to be subject to critical examination. Throughout this book we have explored a number of approaches that can help you Prepare for, Undertake, Refine and Enhance your practice. We have brought them together in this final chapter as a way to help you structure your thinking about CPD and its role in increasing your expertise.

While CPD often takes the form of a series of activities to develop competences, increasingly it is also about our personal development so that we can engage optimally in relational processes. Additionally, we have proposed that CPD involves looking after our well-being. The work we do carries inherent dangers of secondary trauma and resulting burn-out. How we protect ourselves from this, manage our working day and maintain the boundaries between work and home are important ways to ensure well-being.

Looking after ourselves has not always been explicitly identified as a priority in CPD. As we recognize that we are present as persons as well as professionals in the encounter with our supervisees, the importance of CPD to enhance competence and well-being becomes more pressing. The work we do matters in the daily lives of our supervisees and their clients. Looking after ourselves matters for them, for ourselves and for our families.

Chapter summary

✓ Supervision is a demanding activity requiring us to pay attention to the continuing development of our expertise.
✓ As well as developing our expertise at the declarative and procedural level we need to reflect on the 'self-as-person' and 'self-as-supervisor'.
✓ Looking after the self includes protection from burnout and potentially the use of rituals to ensure a separation between our work and home lives.
✓ The world of work is changing and in the current climate, devising effective career development plans is an essential part of defining and differentiating our services.

A Final Word

Becoming an effective supervisor requires a genuine engagement with self-awareness and learning how to be a skilled trainer (Lane and Corrie, 2012). This does not occur instantaneously and entails ongoing commitment as we discover how to juggle the multiple tasks that the role bestows upon us, and how best to engage others in making sense of the complexity of the work in which they engage.

There is an inevitable tension in CBT supervision between helping therapists develop the necessary subject matter expertise and enabling them to remain open to the complexity of the phenomena that they encounter in practice. We have tried to hold this tension in the book, and at the same time present ways to respond creatively. The development and application of the PURE Supervision Flower has signposted the way to a series of activities that can assist in the preparation, undertaking, refining and enhancement of the CBTS that you provide.

At the start of this book we suggested that while the journey of supervision may start out as a requirement of your role, it can also become a vocation, affording the privilege of facilitating the development of a colleague and providing a unique perspective on the complexity of therapeutic work. Through your willingness to travel on this journey with us, we hope that you have identified some useful questions, themes, models and tools that will enable you to enhance your practice as a CBT supervisor. In the real world, practice is often challenging and the capacity to learn, and assist others in the process of learning, is an honour that can open new doors for all involved. As Corrie (2009: 301) observes:

> It is about creating possibilities for your life and facilitating transitions that might lead to new destinations. Outcomes, once achieved, give us no basis for further growth. But the learning required to get there offers an unlimited supply of opportunities for the expression of our values, our creativity, our courage and our potential.

Hopefully, we can all remember good supervisors and those who, as we progress through our careers, have been willing to invest their time, energy and commitment in the service of nurturing our development. It is these supervisors and trainers who have inspired us and who remain present with us when we work. We dedicate this book to them.

APPENDICES

APPENDICES

APPENDIX 1

Recommendations for Case Study 1

One way of conceptualizing the dilemma that Patrick and Jen are experiencing is as a scenario in which supervisor and supervisee have (apparently unacknowledged) different ideas about what effective CBT comprises and how it should be optimally delivered. Both Jen and Patrick appear to have well-formed beliefs, based on prior experience of delivering CBT in specific contexts, as to how CBT 'should' proceed from the earliest stages of assessment, formulation and intervention planning, including the amount and type of information necessary to develop an intervention plan.

Without an explicit acknowledgement of these differences, there is a risk of rupture in the working alliance. For this reason, we would recommend that Patrick raises his concerns with Jen, conveying a desire to explore this dilemma with her, and a wish to hear her perspectives on both CBT generally and supervision with him specifically. By conveying clearly his commitment to forging a positive working relationship that can support her clinical work to best advantage, Jen may feel sufficiently safe to share her concerns.

One possible way forward would be for Patrick to draw on the three-step method outlined in Chapter 1. Specifically:

Step 1:

We would recommend that if he has not done so already, Patrick spend some time clarifying his own beliefs and values about CBT as well as the 'brand' of supervision he both seeks to offer and is best-placed to offer. It will be important for him to ensure that the type of supervision he is able to provide will meet Jen's needs and also to be clear about how his approach relates to the context in which he is working. Assuming this is the case, and having clarified his own beliefs and values:

Step 2:

Patrick could spend some time talking with Jen to gain a clearer understanding of her beliefs and values, both about therapy and about CBT. How does she conceptualize this undertaking? What are her views about how CBT is best applied in contexts where clients have difficulties that could give rise to stigma and shame? In this example, Jen may have a view that 'good' CBT practice is protocol-driven and therefore looks to Patrick to ensure that she remains 'on model'. She may not, however, have fully considered how some of the essential tasks of CBT (such as assessment and formulation) need to incorporate issues that are relevant to clients living with hepatitis B.

Step 3:

By encouraging Jen to articulate her beliefs and values about CBT, Patrick can gain a clearer sense of what is driving Jen's preferred way of working. Through sharing his own beliefs and values, both parties can identify areas of similarity and difference and anticipate where differences could create disruptions in the working alliance.

Patrick may find it helpful to acknowledge the value of Jen's approach and to communicate his respect for her excellent track record as a trainee CBT therapist. However, as her supervisor, he also needs to communicate that Jen can have confidence in him to support her work and that while he is encouraging a different approach from her previous supervisor, it can be understood as just as rigorous, thoughtful and systematic. To achieve this, he might find it helpful to consider with Jen the broad field of CBT and how each tradition encompasses the expression of diverse worldviews. He could then apply this to the current context and the way in which protocols might need to be adapted to the needs of a client living with a medical condition such as hepatitis B. This way, Jen has a clear rationale for Patrick's recommendations.

In presenting his beliefs and values clearly and non-defensively, and sharing how they underpin his way of working, Patrick can invite Jen to explore with him the advantages and disadvantages of approaching therapy in a different way. Would she be willing to suspend certain assumptions she might hold about effective CBT in order to try a new approach? If she were willing to embrace this as a behavioural experiment, there is the potential to gather information about alternative ways of thinking about CBT and its delivery that may enrich her professional skills and the range of clients with whom she can work. Agreeing to revisit the outcome of her behavioural experiment at a specific future date (for example, in three months) might also reassure Jen that Patrick welcomes her feedback and is committed to working in partnership with her.

As a recently trained therapist, Jen is making a transition in identity from student to qualified professional. It would be helpful for Patrick to be aware of some of the developmental issues arising from her stage of development and to consider how he might wish to tailor his style and choice of intervention accordingly (he might benefit from some of the material we cover in Chapter 4, for example). There is an opportunity for Patrick to model an openness to diverse ways of conceptualizing and delivering CBT, and also to act as a mentor for enabling Jen to clarify her own emerging 'brand'.

APPENDIX 2

Recommendations for Case Study 2

In this scenario, it would seem that Patrick feels torn between prioritizing Ben's needs as a trainee CBT therapist and his manager's needs to enhance the image of the service.

One way of conceptualizing the dilemma that Patrick and Ben are experiencing is as a scenario in which both parties are being unduly influenced by a range of local, national and global level influences. Because he does not yet appear to have reflected upon these influences, it is difficult for Patrick, who holds ultimate responsibility for the supervisory engagement, to formulate a more helpful response.

In this context, a first step would be for Patrick to ensure that he is able to recognize, and take appropriate action to modify, any unhelpful thoughts, assumptions or beliefs about himself, Ben and his own forthcoming appraisal. He needs to be attentive to his reactions to Ben and the client which stem from cognitions about pleasing his manager or proving his worth, as these may undermine his ability to problem-solve effectively. Currently, his own anxieties about his forthcoming appraisal appear to be infecting his clarity of thinking in supporting Ben's work. It is also possible that Ben is aware of this and, carrying the unacknowledged burden of Patrick's anxiety, feels under pressure to produce results. Hence, he externalizes blame for lack of progress on to his 'resistant' client.

Having taken steps to address his own potentially unhelpful cognitions, Patrick could usefully expand his focus beyond the outcome measures in order to take a broader perspective on the extent to which the client is progressing: What are the objectives and goals of therapy? Has the client made progress in relation to these or not? How can any lack of progress be understood (for example, does the formulation need updating)? How does Ben understand what is occurring? Can the dilemma be understood by Patrick returning to his formulation of Ben's career stage and specific learning needs?

There is also evidence of local level pressures as the clinical lead seeks to 'rehabilitate' the reputation of the service in order to bring it in line with a national agenda for delivering evidence-based interventions, and retain staff. It is worth Patrick considering whether his reactions are being influenced by the anxiety of the clinical lead. It might be helpful for him to consider the pressures that this individual is facing in their more senior role, and the stakeholders who may not be immediately obvious to Patrick but who are exerting pressure. By considering these factors, Patrick would be in a better position to understand the extent of, and limits to, his responsibility and develop a clearer understanding of the actual (as opposed to the feared) expectations of him as a CBT supervisor. In relation to his appraisal, he needs to ensure what criteria are being used to evaluate his performance. (It would be unlikely, for example, that the outcome of Patrick's appraisal would be determined by the score profile of a single client of a single supervisee.)

Patrick is a relatively new supervisor and is eager to demonstrate his own competence. While he is appropriately focused on the clinical outcomes achieved by his supervisees, he is perhaps not yet sufficiently able to consider the boundaries between service development, service policy and therapist development. It would be helpful for Patrick to consider the combination of local, national and global level influences that are impacting on his reactions. (Engaging in Learning Activity 2.2 might help him identify the factors at work in this scenario.) We would also recommend that Patrick enlist the support of a more senior colleague or mentor outside the service to talk over his concerns about how he might be appraised. The guidance of a more experienced colleague would help him identify which of his concerns about Ben's performance might be reasonable and which might reflect his doubts about his own competence.

APPENDIX 3

Recommendations for Case Study 3

The dilemma that Nina and Jas have encountered can be conceptualized principally as one relating to the contracting phase of supervision. There are three principle issues arising in this scenario which we can consider in turn:

1. Confusion about what was, and was not, agreed at the outset.
2. Differences of opinion concerning Jas's readiness to apply for accreditation as a CBT therapist.
3. Jas's career progression within his service and the need to be accredited to support this.

1. Confusion about what was, and was not, agreed at the outset

Nina ensured that her work with Jas is supported by a written supervision contract. This enables both she and Jas to refer to a specific document to confirm what was explicitly agreed. Nonetheless, Jas maintains that there was tacit agreement to work towards accreditation and that he commissioned supervision on this basis.

We would recommend that Nina explains her approach to developing learning agreements and clarifies that any objectives need to be explicitly agreed to become a basis of supervision. We would also recommend that Nina suggests taking this opportunity to revisit the contract, discuss the learning agenda (inviting Jas to express any previously unarticulated hopes for supervision and his career) and develop a revised plan for moving forwards. Jas is new to both CBT and structured forms of supervision and is not familiar with the use of written contracts to formalize the aims, objectives, roles and responsibilities that will underpin the approach taken. Therefore, it may have been difficult for him to participate in this process fully when Nina introduced it. It will be helpful for Nina to recommend that she and Jas revisit, and if necessary revise, the contract periodically to ensure that it remains fit for purpose.

2. Differences of opinion concerning Jas's readiness to apply for accreditation as a CBT therapist

Nina can describe her commitment to helping Jas develop his knowledge and skill as a CBT therapist while also outlining her responsibilities as an accredited CBT therapist and supervisor. Ethically, she cannot support an application for accreditation if she does not believe that the therapist concerned has demonstrated the necessary level of competence. What she can agree to is the facilitation of a learning process that will support Jas in working towards this. Given that he is a skilled therapist, this should, with time and training, be an option for him.

Nina could suggest undertaking a skills audit of Jas's proficiency, drawing on Roth and Pilling's (2007) competence framework (see Chapter 5) as a basis for identifying priority areas. She also needs to make explicit what she would need to see evidence of (Chapter 6) in order to be comfortable about providing a reference for accreditation purposes. It will be important that Jas fully understands Nina's thinking, so that he can make an informed decision about whether he wishes to continue commissioning supervision from her.

3. Jas's career progression within his service and the need for accreditation to support this

Although there may well be outside pressures on Jas to become accredited as he indicates, the existing contractual arrangement does not involve Jas's employer and their interests are not included in the learning agreement. Nor has Jas indicated specific career objectives as part of the contract. If career progression, or the needs of the service, are to be included, a new contract should be negotiated which will require further conversations with those stakeholders who have an investment in the outcome. Specifically, Nina and Jas will need to understand what is expected by whom, how information about Nina's evaluations of Jas's competence and readiness for accreditation will be shared and with what implications.

Nina is an experienced supervisor and so has plenty of experience to draw upon and in which to have confidence. However, possibly because of this, she may have assumed that a contract developed for one supervisee will automatically generalize to another and she has been insufficiently attentive to the cognitive adjustment that Jas was having to make in contracting supervision in this new, more structured way. If working with a therapist in a similar situation to Jas in the future, it would be preferable to work towards excavating any hopes for supervision and career goals that are not automatically offered up by the supervisee.

This is likely to be a difficult conversation and Nina will need to manage the process carefully. By indicating her commitment to Jas's development and making use of the restorative function, empathizing with Jas's disappointment, she may be able to prevent a rupture in their working alliance. Through this, a clearer contract that is fit for purpose can be negotiated and a better outcome ultimately achieved for all concerned.

APPENDIX 4

Recommendations for Case Study 4

Nina is supervising a newly formed supervision group of three mid-career professionals, two of whom appear ambivalent towards Nina and/or the approach she is offering.

Because she is an experienced professional and confident in her own ability, Nina is able to maintain a curiosity about (as opposed to feeling undermined by) the situation. As a result, possible ways forward can be focused on the situation rather than the management of the supervisor's feelings. (For a less experienced supervisor it may be important to seek consultation with a colleague so that the supervisor can manage any personal material arising.)

A first step would be to formulate the dilemma occurring and each individual's contribution to it, as well as the needs that may be expressed through each member's conduct. Assuming that Nina took time at the outset to develop a formulation of each supervisee's idiosyncratic preferences, abilities and needs (see also Chapters 1 and 2), she is well placed to plan a response to this situation. If she has not done so, this would be a good place to start.

Nina might then benefit from considering the stage of therapist development relevant to each member of the group. One of the therapists is engaged in supervision and appreciates directive input. It is possible that this supervisee is at level 1 in her stage of development, motivated to learn, wanting to progress rapidly through the anxiety that comes from being relatively inexperienced in CBT and appreciating clear guidance from a position of relative dependence. As Nina is happy to provide this, it would seem that there is a match between what the supervisee needs and what Nina is providing.

For the other two therapists, it is possible that Nina is encountering a loss of confidence and ambivalence that characterizes level 2. Although the members of the group are mid-career professionals, their experience of, and skill in, delivering CBT may not yet be at the same level as their skills in other domains. For mid-career professionals it can feel exposing to have to share their practice, and the exchange of looks as well as the subtle resistance to Nina's input may indicate poorly managed anxieties about being evaluated and found wanting.

Level 2 is recognized as a turbulent stage in therapist development and Nina would do well to consider how she might adjust the style of supervision to balance structure with encouraging autonomy. This might include suggesting that supervisees take turns in setting the agenda and organizing the session, and encouraging the sharing of ideas about each other's cases (that is, fostering peer supervision). This would help the supervisees 'test out' their emerging skill within a framework that enables Nina to maintain a consistent and structured approach.

Finally, it would be worthwhile Nina reflecting on each supervisee's motivations for undertaking CBT training at postgraduate level. Are they willing participants in the process? Or is at least one individual in the group coming because they believe they have no choice in the current professional climate? The behaviour of the supervisees may reflect the felt pressure of some of the local and national level influences examined in Chapter 2 and may be important to explore further.

Nina will need to remain attentive to the emotional climate within supervision and monitor the situation carefully. If difficulties continue, it will be necessary for her to address directly with the supervisees what is occurring to ensure that supervision remains a safe and productive learning environment for all concerned.

APPENDIX 5

Recommendations for Case Study 5

In this scenario, Nina has concerns about Sandra, a newly qualified clinical psychologist who is avoiding sharing recordings of her sessions in supervision and tends to ask concrete questions such as 'What should I do?' or 'What would you do in this situation?' The uneasiness that Nina experiences is due to a perceived discrepancy between Sandra's performance in supervision and Nina's expectations of a therapist who has completed doctoral level training and previous CBT-oriented placements. Additionally, by failing to present live examples of her work, Nina is unable to form a clear impression of the quality of Sandra's work and the methods of learning that might be optimal for her development.

Nina is correct that she now needs to understand precisely what Sandra is, and is not, competent to deliver and she needs to adopt a respectful but direct approach.

As a first step, it would be helpful for Nina to share her dilemma with Sandra and explain that withholding direct access to her work is undermining her ability to evaluate Sandra's competence and support her in her learning. Nina can frame this in terms of her responsibilities as a supervisor, reminding Sandra of the normative, formative and restorative functions of supervision.

Assuming that Sandra can acknowledge Nina's position, a number of options then present themselves. Nina could ask Sandra how she experiences supervision, what enables her to learn effectively and how she self-assesses her practice currently. She can also revisit what occurred in supervision during her CBT placements and how Sandra responded to a structured learning environment in the context of clinical psychology training.

Nina can acknowledge Sandra's apparent preference for case discussion and ask her to share her understanding of the benefits and limitations of this approach. Drawing on Bennett-Levy's DPR model, as well as Padesky's

Supervision Options Grid, Nina can share her understanding of why CBTS emphasizes a multi-method approach to learning and the 'must' and 'can' interventions that follow from this. She can seek Sandra's views on this, remaining attentive to what Sandra says (and doesn't say) that may provide clues about any underlying obstacles.

If Nina senses that Sandra's reluctance to bring recordings to supervision stems from heightened anxiety, it will be helpful to enable Sandra to express this directly. Anxiety is a response with which Nina can empathize and if problematic cognitions are identified, they can consider together whether these can be appropriately addressed in supervision, modified through self-practice of CBT strategies, or need to be addressed through some other means, such as therapy. Nina could also normalize 'therapist imperfection' (particularly if Sandra is hampered by catastrophic beliefs about the consequences of imperfect performance) by sharing some of her own recordings of sessions and asking Sandra to rate these on the measure of therapist competency used by the service (such as the CTS-R).

Given that Sandra tends to ask concrete questions, Nina could encourage better preparation for supervision by asking her to generate three possible answers to her own question, derived from the client's formulation and any relevant reading, for discussion in supervision. This way, Nina can begin to enhance Sandra's capacity for autonomous decision-making and see where specific limitations lie.

Nonetheless, however facilitative Nina wishes to be, to fulfil her responsibilities as a supervisor, the situation needs to change. If Sandra's conduct in supervision contravenes what has been specified in the supervision contract, this needs to be addressed. Nina may decide to identify targets and timeframes for the presentation of recordings, formulations and intervention plans and to identify these as clearly the 'must' rather than 'can' components of supervision. If these targets are not met, then Sandra needs to understand the implications.

As Nina considers how to respond to this dilemma, it will also be necessary to consider whether she is best placed to supervise Sandra at this time. Given that she is both Sandra's CBT supervisor and line manager, there is a dual relationship in operation. This may be implicated in what is occurring and Nina will need to reflect on whether Sandra's needs, and the needs of her clients, may ultimately be better met by another supervisor.

APPENDIX 6

Recommendations for Case Study 6

In this scenario, Patrick harbours doubts about Leanne's competence despite her obvious progress, diligence in seeking feedback and now consistently passing assessments on the CTS-R. His concerns reflect the fact that any assessment of competence has a present and a future focus. Leanne is able to demonstrate competence in the present (at least with some clients, as evidenced by her scores on the CTS-R). However, Patrick harbours doubts about her ability to work with future clients based on her interpersonal skills.

In considering how to respond to this dilemma, there are two main questions to consider:

1. What should Patrick do in response to his concerns?
2. How should he prepare himself to respond to Leanne's anticipated request for a reference?

1. What should Patrick do in response to his concerns?

Given that Patrick is a relatively inexperienced supervisor, it would be useful for him to discuss this situation with a more experienced colleague. It is possible that, in the early stages of supervision with Leanne, he omitted to ensure that he had a clear operational definition of competence and has been working with an under-developed set of evaluation criteria. The benchmark criterion of whether or not he would feel comfortable referring a member of his own family to Leanne may enable him to qualify a 'hunch' but is insufficiently specified to be useful for addressing the dilemma in hand, or indeed for arriving at an impartial judgement about her overall competence.

In considering his options and in discussion with his own supervisor, it would be useful to clarify whether the service has any protocols in place for addressing such concerns. Additionally, he needs to think through whether there might be some advantage to sharing his concerns with a member of the Programme Team (Leanne is shortly due to finish her Master's degree). In sharing his doubts, Patrick needs to anticipate the potential implications – for himself, for Leanne, and for any other stakeholders with an investment in the outcome of Leanne's placement. For example, in approaching the Programme Team, is there the option for a confidential discussion, or will his doubts be shared with the Programme Director? Will Leanne be notified of the conversation and what implications might this have for their working relationship? Will sharing his concerns influence whether or not Leanne passes the course?

Patrick could also give further thought to what underpins his concerns. In elaborating his evaluation criteria, he needs to consider both which competences Leanne lacks (see Chapter 5) and whether he has used a sufficiently broad range of assessment methods to form a sound judgement. He also needs to consider Leanne's ability to apply feedback. Given that she has progressed well and is diligent in her approach, it is possible that through further exposure to supervised therapeutic practice, her current limitations will resolve.

2. How should he prepare himself to respond to Leanne's anticipated request for a reference?

Before Patrick decides how to respond, it is vital that he has thought through the points raised above. If he is to provide a clear and helpful response to Leanne's anticipated request, he needs to be able to communicate what the contents of his reference might be and what evidence this would be based upon. He would benefit from using the CORBS approach to organizing his feedback as follows:

Clear: About the feedback that needs to be given to Leanne about what a reference from him would and would not include.

Owned: Presented in a way that indicates recognition that the feedback is based on perception rather than truth (e.g. "In my opinion..." versus "You are...").

Regular: Hopefully, Patrick's feedback will resonate for Leanne based on the formative and summative feedback that she has received throughout supervision.

Balanced: Balancing positive and negative feedback so that Leanne is clear about her strengths as well as development needs.

Specific: Patrick needs to be clear about the evidence upon which he would be basing his reference, and able to supply particular instances upon which he is basing his evaluation.

Although it is important to avoid forming impressions about a therapist's competence too early in supervision (some areas of competence can only be adequately assessed over time), it is possible that Patrick failed to reflect on his concerns early enough. He may lack confidence in providing feedback, possibly falling into the common trap of providing insufficient feedback, and is now facing a dilemma as a result. Using role-plays to hone his skills in giving feedback to supervisees might, therefore, be a useful approach in his own supervision.

APPENDIX 7

Recommendations for Case Study 7

Nina is a participant in a monthly peer supervision group and is also the manager of the service. She has responsibility for the trainees who attend the group. The trainees are unable to raise questions, another individual is supporting a friend within the group and Nina experiences conflict between her role as manager and member of the peer group.

One way of conceptualizing this dilemma is that the relationships in the group are being experienced as increasingly unsafe for the participants. It is important, therefore, to explore how to establish a sense of safety. The pointers for good practice provided by Beinart (2004; see Chapter 7) might enable Nina to reflect on this issue. In particular, she would benefit from considering:

1. What steps she has taken to establish a sense of safety (a safe base) in the group.
2. How much time she devoted to establishing the relationship between members in the early stages.
3. How she has contracted to clarify responsibilities, expectations, objectives and methods of evaluation.

Through this exploration, Nina may discover that the group has evolved in a haphazard way, rendering its purpose somewhat unclear. For example, originally it may have been a vehicle to encourage staff to share their formulations so that Nina could assess the quality of their work. However, as the staff became more experienced, she may have delegated the role of chairing the meetings as a means of developing members of her team. Later, it may have been decided that the trainees would benefit from hearing how experienced therapists present their cases. Without a clearly thought through rationale, this 'organic' evolution may have contributed to the group feeling unsafe. If this is so, then it will be important for Nina to discuss with her colleagues how they set up the group and determine its functions, and how it might need to operate differently in future. One approach to this task would be to seek the group's permission to review what is, and is not, working well for each member. Sharing Beinart's principles of good practice as a means of reviewing the work, and using each of the questions as a prompt for discussion, may make it easier for members to share more openly where their concerns lie.

As part of this process of exploration, Nina could usefully introduce models that seek to understand different relationships, experiences and learning styles and to identify methods and processes of learning that might better meet the needs of trainees and experienced therapists. (It is unlikely that the needs of all the members will be adequately met by the same methods.)

Once a sense of safety has been sufficiently restored to enable collaborative decision-making, members will need to revisit the function of the supervision group and decide whether it should continue in its current form. It is important that while Nina maintains a collaborative approach to resolving this dilemma, she also accepts her role as the leader of the service in order to manage both the process of discussion and any solutions identified. If, following discussion, it emerges that Nina unwittingly allowed an 'unsafe base' to emerge, her willingness to take responsibility for her role in shaping an unhelpful learning environment will be important as a means of engendering a sense of trust.

It will be helpful for Nina to remember that supervisory relationships need to be continually renewed and that not all colleagues value, or benefit from, the same approach. Nina should also remember that in order for supervisory relationships to flourish, it is essential to create a safe learning environment which will require clear contracting between all members of the group.

APPENDIX 8

Recommendations for Case Study 8

In this scenario between Patrick and Seiko, there are a number of factors in operation. The five recommendations in Table 6 (Chapter 8) on how to make power visible provide a possible way to progress. To recap, these are:

1. Discuss power openly when you are establishing the supervision contract.
2. Discuss the different forms of power, how they might manifest in supervision and what represents the ethical use of these.
3. Anticipate ways in which the unhelpful use of power could manifest in supervision and any unhelpful reactions that could emerge from this.
4. Ensure that you have adequate time for self-reflection when maladaptive power issues begin to emerge.
5. Ensure you have consultation in place to provide you with 'supervision on your supervision' when you suspect that power issues are manifesting in unhelpful ways.

Given their past relationship, an initial consideration of role dilemmas could have usefully occurred in setting up the supervision contract. A standardized approach to contract setting would not necessarily address concerns where a previous line management relationship existed. Patrick could have drawn upon his ambivalence about becoming Seiko's supervisor to initiate a discussion with her. This would have given Seiko an opportunity to express any concerns that she harboured.

Recommendations 1–3 above would have assisted that original discussion and can now be reintroduced. Seiko's request for a change of supervisor provides an opening to revisit the contract, acknowledge their inauspicious beginning and consider how to take things forward. It will be important for Patrick to acknowledge openly that Seiko is not experiencing the supervision as helpful. He could highlight that the way the contract was set up originally failed to take account of their previous relationship and any concerns she might have had about this.

There is also the issue of Patrick's own prior perspectives. He sees Seiko as 'diligent' and 'rigid', whereas she sees staying true to the protocol as a matter of fidelity and integrity. Patrick, in questioning Seiko's approach, may be tapping into a belief about the importance of fidelity. In undermining this belief, a potential vicious cycle may come into play (fuelled by the cognition "Why is my supervisor treating me like this?"). Any perceived injustice may also be experienced by Seiko as the exercising of coercive power. Patrick needs to address this quickly before Seiko seeks remedies to correct any perceived injustice. He needs to work with Seiko to acknowledge the importance of fidelity to the model, but also to consider occasions when it operates as guidance rather than as a mandate. This step needs to precede any attempt to ask Seiko to explore the current case material differently.

Patrick could also provide examples of where he has worked within a protocol and where he has felt the need to move outside it. He needs to be sensitive, though, to cultural issues at play between him and Seiko. She may well have particular views on what a supervisor should do and what she can expect of that relationship, including what can, and cannot, be shared. Nonetheless, opening a full discussion around the role of protocols in CBT can enable a discussion about when moving away from a protocol is, and is not, helpful. To support this process, it might be useful to examine the current case from different perspectives, with Patrick adopting the role of committing to follow the protocol and Seiko the role of exploring deviations from it to discover what new perspectives might emerge.

Patrick needs to consider how he may be playing a role in setting up difficulties for Seiko through his prior perception of her as 'rigid'. Recommendations 4 and 5 above would be helpful at this point. In the same way that he might ask a trainee to consider positively connoting a client's negative behaviour, he could do the same for himself in relation to Seiko. What is positive in the challenge she is making? How might this be important feedback to him? There may also be a parallel process in operation. Specifically, Seiko may be experiencing some element of discrimination from Patrick that he is not aware of, just as Patrick views Seiko as being unaware of the client's sense of discrimination.

It will be important to explore openly the issue of the role of power in this relationship and to establish a new contract in which Seiko is given explicit permission to feed back to Patrick any concerns. Equally, it will be necessary for Seiko to acknowledge Patrick's responsibility to raise legitimate concerns and that these are designed to be helpful rather than an attack on her integrity.

APPENDIX 9

Recommendations for Case Study 9

Patrick is supervising Jason, who brings a case that is concerning him. Jason finds that his client wants to talk about his childhood experience of foster care whereas Jason believes he needs to treat the client's PTSD. Jason is angry with Patrick for not providing the supervision he believes he needs. Patrick in turn is starting to dread supervising Jason, labelling him as narcissistic.

In attempting to understand this scenario, it is clear that a pattern of resistance has been established. As this has not been addressed, a rupture in the working alliance is increasingly likely and needs to be managed before any effective client-related decision-making can occur.

At this point, we would strongly advise Patrick to draw on the support of a colleague who can provide 'supervision on his supervision'; strong reactions have been evoked within him which will hamper his ability to engage in more impartial decision-making and increase the risk of 'retaliation' against Jason's perceived attack on his supervisory skill. With this in mind, we consider how Patrick might work with his supervisor using Hersted and Gergen's (2012) approach to de-escalating the emerging animosity and restoring productive relations. This could be approached as follows.

De-construct the realities

Patrick is tending to locate the problem in Jason, labelling him as 'superior', 'entitled' and 'narcissistic'. A good starting point, therefore, may be to ask Patrick to tell the story from Jason's perspective to see what this might reveal. It is probable that Jason feels under pressure to complete the work and is 'running out' of allocated sessions. He is relatively new to therapeutic practice and encountering resistance from his client is likely to have evoked anxiety. In the context of his career stage, Jason may be looking to Patrick as a 'saviour' (see Chapter 9), expecting him to provide a solution, whereas Patrick is not really responding to the dilemma that Jason presents ('I am running out of time and getting nowhere').

De-polarize the differences

Having 'heard' the story from Jason's perspective it might be possible for Patrick to consider some potential benefits in Jason's view and acknowledge that there are different interpretations of the same event. If Patrick can do this for Jason, then it may also become possible for Jason to reflect on the story from the client's perspective ('Here is a client who was abandoned at the scene of an accident by his friends; he took the blame for them. He also describes being placed in foster care and may have experienced feelings of abandonment then which have been triggered by the current situation'). Jason is not letting his client discuss this so perhaps the client feels let down again – first his parents, then his friends and now his therapist. He may also believe that he is being blamed by Jason for his lack of progress in therapy.

Search for commonalities

Having worked through this process with his supervisor, Patrick might now be able to ask Jason to work with him in order to identify possible shared goals, values or outcomes. If this occurs, Patrick could then ask Jason to do the same with his client.

Avoid using power

If these conversations happen, exploration of the power position becomes possible. How might Jason experience Patrick? Does he believe that Patrick is using his power to determine what happens in supervision? How might Patrick be experiencing a sense of powerlessness in responding to Jason? This exploration, if successful, could open up a further conversation between Jason and his client on the issue of power.

Focus on the 'we'

Jason is new to the CBT community and part of Patrick's role is to initiate him into that culture. This includes how to manage sessions where resistance appears to be present. Helping Jason to recognize why resistance might occur could help him see its value in providing feedback that he is not fully hearing the client. This outcome is more likely where Patrick models that behaviour by ensuring Jason feels fully heard. Helping Jason to recognize when it may be necessary to re-contract both with clients and the sponsors of the intervention is an important lesson. It is possible that the service cannot help this client because it is too restrictive in its time limits. If so, understanding other referral options may be necessary and Jason can learn how to make a referral without further reinforcing the client's sense of abandonment.

APPENDIX 10

Recommendations for Case Study 10

In this scenario, Moses has completed an effective piece of work focused on his client's low mood and symptoms of depression. However, the client has raised a new issue, which is well beyond what was contracted. Surprised by this, Moses is unsure how to respond and may have been overwhelmed by the distress he witnessed. He has indicated that he will not tell the school or the client's parents about her fears, although he has made it clear that he must talk to his supervisor.

There are a number of dilemmas here that map on to the Supervision Flower. In Petal 1 we have a possible clash of values and beliefs. In Petal 2 there is the context of work, which now involves child protection issues, relationships with the client, her parents and the school, and the training programme. In Petal 3 we have the nature of the contract negotiated. This matter is beyond the original contract and it is important to consider what was negotiated about disclosures.

It is clear that there are external frameworks that would apply here – a possible forced marriage may raise child protection issues. The client's intent to run away also raises concerns of a child protection nature. Additionally, there is the matter of confidentiality. A child aged 15 would almost certainly be considered by the courts as competent to make her own decisions to seek professional help without disclosure to her parents (see Gillick competency and Fraser guidelines: Gillick v West Norfolk and Wisbech Area Health Authority, 1985). There are a number of universal principles in play relating to respect and responsibility which are owed to several parties in this case.

There is also the matter of ethical maturity. Moses is a trainee and his supervisor and training programme owe him a duty of care. His ability to negotiate the issues involved needs to be considered and some clear learning is possible once the immediate concerns are resolved. Such cases can sometimes prompt an over-reaction – a rush to turn a situation into a child protection matter (and therefore another's responsibility) rather than a response to the evidence presented (for example, how real are the threats of forced marriage or running away?).

A number of courses of action are possible here. First, we would recommend that Patrick re-examines the nature of the relationship between the training establishment and the placement setting and the requirements concerning disclosures. Using Epstein's List (see Chapter 10), he can then support Moses in thinking through the nature of the contract he has with his client.

Assuming that Moses had established a therapeutic contract that had clarified the limits of confidentiality, Patrick could direct Moses' attention to who should now be included in a wider circle of participation and what would seem right to him, ethically, in managing this. The possibility of exploring this further with the client, while also making it clear that the matter falls beyond the remit of the original contract and Moses' own area of competence, should also be considered. The purpose of any discussion would then become one of helping the client identify and approach an appropriate person in the school with whom to discuss her concerns. If Moses is prepared to attend this meeting, he is able to sensitively hand over the case to someone who has the necessary expertise. (NB: Forced marriage is illegal. In making the referral to the school all parties will need to take account of the current legislative position; see www.gov.uk/forced-marriage.)

By avoiding directing Moses to a particular stance, Patrick can avoid coming across as imposing a unilateral authority and work with Moses to arrive at a thoughtful plan which respects the client's position and his own ethical values. Moses could be encouraged to affirm the client for raising her concerns and at the same time respect his own position and his client's by stating clearly that this is not an area in which he has the necessary competence to provide support or advice.

Finally, Patrick could help Moses prepare for his next meeting with the client by role-playing the conversation and various scenarios, including helping her take the matter to someone appropriate within the school. During the meeting, it would be containing for Moses if Patrick agreed to make himself available to be called upon, if needed.

Following this, it would be important for Patrick to encourage Moses to reflect upon what he had learned from this situation. Patrick could helpfully affirm both the anxiety that this situation must have caused Moses and his ability to remain focused on the needs of his client, as well as validating the positive work that has been accomplished.

APPENDIX 11A

Recommendations for Case Study 11

This scenario brings together our two fictitious supervisors, with Patrick seeking Nina's services in order to refine and enhance his skills as a CBT supervisor. Through reading Chapters 1–11, you will have become familiar with their practice, as well as their individual strengths and needs.

Based on recent dilemmas that she has encountered (see Chapter 3), Nina would be well advised to attend carefully to contracting so that she can be clear about what Patrick needs and wants from 'supervision on his supervision'. Since she has no connection with his place of work, and this is a private arrangement for the purpose of development, she will need to explore how he sees his skills before establishing a contractual basis for any work that follows.

A good place to start would be to ask Patrick to undertake a self-assessment of his supervisory knowledge and skill, which could provide the basis for a subsequent discussion about areas of development need. One option is to introduce Patrick to models which describe the stages of supervisor development and then ask him to consider his own stage in relation to this. Nina could also ask him for specific examples from his practice that he believes are indicative of this stage of development (including examples where he has been most and least effective in his supervisory practice). She might also usefully draw on some of the exercises in Chapter 1 in order to better understand Patrick's 'brand' of CBT and CBTS.

Nina could then request some samples of his supervisory practice, clarifying any formal arrangements for recording supervision sessions in his service. Assuming this is possible, she might propose that they both rate the session according to the criteria specified by a particular measure. This will not only give Nina a sense of Patrick's work as a supervisor, but also enable her to establish his capacity for accurate self-assessment as a

basis for determining objectives for their work together. Corrie and Worrell's Supervisor Evaluation Scale (see Appendix 11B) would be a useful instrument for gaining an initial sense of Patrick's style and level of performance. Rating a specific supervision session will also enable Nina to gauge Patrick's reaction to feedback. Does he, for example, welcome this or react negatively to perceived challenges to his practice?

Based on how Patrick has conducted himself in the previous chapters, we might anticipate that he is keen to learn. We might also anticipate that he is able to identify himself as a Level 1 supervisor (see Stoltenberg and McNeill, 2010; Chapter 11), who tends to treat aspects of the task separately rather than seeing them holistically. As a result, he can be inconsistent in his judgements (his work with Seiko and Jason in Chapters 8 and 9 suggest this) and can struggle with feedback that appears hostile or challenging to his own sense of competence. As Nina becomes aware of these areas of need, she may decide that in addition to the general terms of the contract she wants to specify that the supervision process will include ongoing access to recordings of his practice. In determining learning objectives for supervision, Nina might also suggest honing their focus to one or two particular areas that could be subjected to observational analysis, such as examining samples of recordings of supervision sessions using the ORCE process. Furthermore, she might seek to include an agreement from Patrick that he will consider all feedback from her as formative for his development rather than as an attack on him. Where she senses a negative reaction, she then has permission to share what she is sensing, with Patrick agreeing in advance to step back from the emotion and explore what is giving rise to his reaction.

If these initial conversations progress well, it would be useful for Nina and Patrick to formalize their agreement, in writing, for a specified period of time, following which they agree to review their work together with the option to continue if both agree.

APPENDIX 11B

The Supervisor Evaluation Scale (Corrie and Worrell)

The Supervisor Evaluation Scale (SES) tracks the development of a supervisor's abilities as delivered in the context of a specific supervision session. It is intended as a tool for self-monitoring of professional development as well as for more formal evaluation. For this reason, it is important to use the SES on a regular basis to ensure both familiarity with the dimensions being assessed and the self-tracking of competence development.

Because CBT is now widely regarded as comprising a broad and diverse range of scientifically grounded approaches, rather than a single unified approach, CBT supervision is equally likely to include a variety of practices and approaches as a function of the type of CBT being practised and the context in which supervision is provided. For example, effective CBT supervision for a supervisee who is reasonably new to therapeutic practice and is learning CBT as part of an IAPT training would look very different from schema-focused supervision for an experienced therapist delivering their interventions in a personality disorder unit. For this reason, the SES avoids a narrow, prescriptive approach to competence in favour of a series of broad domains in which the supervisor is afforded considerable flexibility in how the competence is demonstrated.

How competence is assessed

The SES scale has incorporated Dreyfus and Dreyfus's model of skill acquisition, which is described in detail in their book *Mind over Machine* (Dreyfus and Dreyfus, 1986). The way in which this has been adapted to assess supervisor competence is outlined in the table below. Please note that the highest marks (i.e. near the 'expert' end of the continuum) are reserved for those supervisors demonstrating highly effective skills, particularly in the face of difficulties (e.g. significant process issues that are impacting on the supervision session, performance management issues, or situations where the supervisor needs to manage and repair ruptures in the supervisory alliance).

It is important to note that any score awarded is not intended as a comment on the general skills, competences or abilities of the supervisor. Rather, it is a statement about the extent to which specific skills were demonstrated within a particular session.

The pass mark is 36 or above. To account for the fact that it is possible to provide a competent and effective supervision session without securing a minimum score on each dimension, there is no minimum score required for each of the 12 dimensions assessed.

Dreyfus & Dreyfus Competence Level	Score	Translation of Competence Level into Features of Supervisor Performance
Incompetent (0–1)	0	The skill or feature is not displayed in this session.
	1	The supervisor commits significant errors and displays poor and/or unacceptable behaviour, resulting in negative consequences for the supervision session. The supervisor's performance is highly problematic, and major problems with the supervisor's style, approach or choice of intervention are evident.
Novice (1–2)	2	The supervisor displays a rigid adherence to taught rules and is unable to take account of situational factors. The session is characterized by a lack of discretionary judgement about how to adapt the content and process of the session in light of contextual factors, such as the supervisee's developmental stage and service setting. Effective use of pacing and timing, as well as the management of the session are not evident.
Advanced beginner (2–3)	3	The supervisor demonstrates evidence of competence, but this is inconsistent. The supervisor treats all aspects of the task separately and gives equal importance to each aspect, rather than prioritising. There is evidence of some degree of situational perspective and discretionary judgement but this is inconsistent and at times, the supervisor appears to be more attached to their own agenda than fostering supervisee learning.
Competent (3–4)	4	The supervisor is able to link the tasks of supervision to a specific conceptual framework. He/she makes plans within this framework and uses standardized and routinized procedures appropriately. The session demonstrates a good degree of competence despite minor fluctuations in performance.
Proficient (4–5)	5	There is evidence that the supervisor sees the supervisee's needs holistically, is able to prioritise tasks and make 'on the spot' decisions that are responsive to the supervisee's needs. The supervisor is clearly skilled and able, and demonstrates a highly effective degree of competence at a number of points during the session.
Expert (5–6)	6	The supervisor demonstrates excellent performance. He/she evidences a well-developed, tacit understanding of key issues and is able to use novel problem-solving techniques and creative interventions to facilitate supervisee learning. The skills are demonstrated consistently even in the face of difficulties (e.g. performance management issues, ruptures in the supervisory alliance, supervisee avoidance).

Domains of supervisor competence assessed by the SES

The measure assesses four broad categories, or domains, of supervisor competence. These are as follows:

A. Session Structure and Planning (three questions)
B. Facilitation of Supervisee Learning (three questions)
C. Development of CBT-Specific Competences (three questions)
D. Management of the Session (three questions)

These are described below.

Category A. Session Structure and Planning (Questions 1–3)

Session Structure and Planning is concerned with those factors that enable the supervisor to structure and plan the session in order to meet the educational and support needs of the supervisee to best advantage. The supervisor is expected to: (1) display an awareness of and sensitivity towards the context in which the supervisee is delivering their therapy; (2) negotiate appropriate session aims; (3) structure the session appropriately in light of this; and (4) plan the content of the session to facilitate the needs of the supervisee and their client/s.

Category B. Facilitation of Supervisee Learning (Questions 4–6)

Facilitation of Supervisee Learning examines the supervisor's ability to accommodate the generic learning needs of the supervisee as an adult learner at a particular stage of their career development. The questions in category B are concerned with the 'goodness of fit' between the style and content of supervision and the supervisee's development needs. As such, this category taps into the supervisor's ability to formulate their supervisee's competence level and learning needs, and to adapt their approach accordingly. For example, attempting to use guided discovery to instruct the therapist in a skill of which they do not have prior knowledge and where direct instruction would be considered an example of poor competence on this category. A balance between guided discovery, direct instruction and supervisor 'modelling' of specific CBT competences needs to be demonstrated here, as does the use of supervisee feedback (direct and indirect) to modify the approach taken. The supervisor's use of any specific CBT models of supervision to inform choice of supervision strategy (such as Padesky's Road Map or Bennett-Levy's Declarative-Procedural-Reflective model) is also assessed in questions 4–6.

Category C. Development of CBT-Specific Competences (Questions 7–9)

Development of CBT-Specific Competences is the skill with which specific supervision interventions are delivered that would be recognizable as CBT-informed (e.g. the supervisor's use of questioning techniques that encompass the Socratic style of questioning, use of particular interventions such as setting up a behavioural experiment, setting homework, etc.). Unlike Category B which is concerned with demonstrating generic supervisor competences, Category C is concerned with the extent to which the learning opportunities provided in the session are consistent with the style of CBT being supervised (i.e. fidelity to the model), the use of specific methods of change to foster specific CBT competences and the methods used to foster reflective practice.

Category D. Management of the Session (Questions 10–12)

Management of the Session examines the skill with which the supervisor manages process issues arising in the session and adapts the pacing, structure or content of the session in light of this. As such, the supervisor creates the potential for any process issues to become valuable sources of learning and development. The supervisor's effectiveness in providing feedback, appropriate use of humour to aid learning, interpersonal effectiveness and management of any ruptures, as well as management of the pacing and timing of the session, are considered under this category.

SES Item	Examples of this in the supervision session	Score	Comments
A1. Context Did the supervisor demonstrate awareness of the service context in which the supervisee is providing therapeutic work and factors that have shaped the supervision contract? Did the supervisor demonstrate an ability to adapt the style, content and approach taken according to the organizational context in which the supervisee is working (e.g. IAPT, secondary mental health care, specialist CBT services, etc.)	Example: The supervisor provides an opportunity for the supervisee to update on general issues and concerns before agreeing the agenda for the session. The supervisor asks for an update on any main events that have occurred in the supervisee's place of work, or other areas of their life, since the last meeting that could impact on use of the supervision session. Any adjustments are made in light of pressures or concerns facing the supervisee (e.g. if the supervisee is a trainee CBT therapist, the supervisor skilfully accommodates gaps in knowledge arising from when the supervisee encounters clinical issues before formal teaching on that topic has been provided; how the supervisor balances the normative, formative and restorative functions of supervision in light of approaching coursework deadlines).		
A2. Supervision aims Were the aims of the session negotiated effectively? Did the session begin with an agenda to which both supervisor and supervisee contributed items? Were the aims of the session clear before supervision began and, if so, were they realistic and manageable in the time available?	Example: At the start of the session, time was spent in ensuring that the session had a clear aim and focus (however tightly or loosely organized around a formal 'agenda'). The supervisor explicitly encouraged the supervisee to contribute to deciding on the aims of the supervision session and demonstrated a genuine respect for and interest in the supervisee's stated needs and preferences.		

© Corrie and Worrell, 2012

SES Item	Examples of this in the supervision session	Score	Comments
A3. Structure Was the session sufficiently well structured to ensure effective pacing and time management in the session? Did the supervision session have clear beginning, middle and end phases (see also item D12)?	Example: The supervisor works with the supervisee in an explicit way to develop a realistic and helpful agenda which provides a useful framework for the session that follows. This may include the setting of a formal agenda at the start of the session, or a more fluid and flexible framework. However, the important point to note is that priorities are clearly established and renegotiated in the session if necessary.		
B4. Use of educational principles Did the supervisor effectively accommodate the supervisee's learning style and needs in order to facilitate learning? Were the supervisor's style and interventions appropriate to the supervisee's stage of development? (For example, was there a greater level of didactic instruction and direction if the supervisee was more junior, and greater guided discovery if the supervisee was more senior? Was there an appropriate balance between the roles of teacher, consultant, therapist, educator?) Was there evidence of the supervisor working with an implicit formulation of the supervisee's learning needs and level of competence that served to guide their style and approach?	Example: The supervisor introduces explicitly, or draws on more implicitly (but in a way that is still evident), educational principles and concepts from the discipline of adult learning to support a supervisee in achieving optimal learning in supervision. The supervisor draws upon an established CBT model of supervision (such as Padesky's Supervisory Options Grid) to inform choice of intervention. The supervisor demonstrates a good balance between the normative, formative and restorative components of the session.		

© Corrie and Worrell, 2012

(Continued)

SES Item	Examples of this in the supervision session	Score	Comments
B5. Developing CBT competences Does the supervisor use appropriate methods for facilitating the supervisee's ability to present clinical information to best advantage? Does the supervisor encourage the supervisee to draw upon CBT methods of intervention typically used with clients, to support the supervisee's own well-being needs (see also C7)?	Example: The supervisor supports the supervisee in developing a clear supervision question or area of focus for a specific client enquiry. The supervisor sensitively 'shapes up' the supervisee's ability to select and present relevant clinical information to best advantage (e.g. selecting a specific segment of a recording to play in supervision; presenting a formulation; helping the supervisee identify a specific competence area with which they need help). The supervisor draws on interventions consistent with the type of CBT being supervised. Where specific learning and development needs are identified, the supervisor encourages the application of CBT methods for self-reflection, self-practice and self-care. The supervisor provides multiple opportunities for the supervisee to ask about and practise specific CBT skills.		
B6. Soliciting and using Supervisee feedback Did the supervisor elicit feedback from the supervisee on the previous supervision session? Were any areas of confusion appropriately identified and addressed? Was the supervisor able to respond to feedback in a non-defensive manner? Was the supervisor able to work in such a way that there was evidence of a goodness of fit between the style and content of supervision and the supervisee's learning needs?	Example: The supervisor actively seeks feedback from the supervisee on what was most helpful about the previous supervision session, and anything that felt unhelpful or confusing, and adjusts their approach accordingly. Feedback is sought throughout the session. The supervisor conveys genuine interest and curiosity and is able to adjust their style and approach in light of supervisee response. Feedback is sought at the end of the supervision session to discover what was most helpful for the supervisee and what, if anything, did not go so well. Examples of this category may also include asking supervisees to complete a supervision satisfaction inventory and using the data from these to inform the approach taken.		

SES Item	Examples of this in the supervision session	Score	Comments
C7. Fidelity to the model Is the style of supervision provided consistent with, and obviously recognizable as, CBT-focused? Did the supervisor's use of intervention methods relate to the type of CBT they practise? (For example, if the therapy being supervised is first, second or third generation CBT, is the approach to supervision consistent with this?) Was there a consistency between the style of supervision provided and the style of therapy in which the therapist is being supervised?	Example: The supervisor models explicitly an aspect of intervention that the supervisee will be using with clients (such as setting an agenda, eliciting supervisee emotions, cognitions and behaviours as they relate to a specific supervisory dilemma, use of guided discovery).		
C8. Application of change methods Did the supervisor employ a suitably broad range of methods to respond effectively to the supervisee's question/dilemma and to gauge the supervisee's performance and level of competence?	Example: The supervisor goes beyond case discussion in order to incorporate a balance of learning methods in the session – such as presenting a formulation, playing a recording, experiential skills practice and/or role-play. Where appropriate, the supervisor explains CBT-related concepts and provides opportunities to practise this in order to facilitate theory-practice integration. Observational methods (recording, video, role-play) are used to facilitate supervisee learning.		

© Corrie and Worrell, 2012

(Continued)

SES Item	Examples of this in the supervision session	Score	Comments
C9. Reflective practice	Example:		
Does the supervisor use interventions that actively encourage the development of reflective practice?	The supervisor's ability to facilitate reflective practice will be embedded in all items on the SES. As such, the intention to facilitate reflective practitioner skills may take any number of forms in the session, including (but not restricted to) the following:		
	The supervisor elicits feedback from the supervisee on reading or homework tasks, self-assessed competence on the CTS-R or other forms of self-evaluation; reflection on experiential skills practice is encouraged.		
	The supervisor seeks to elicit the supervisee's own reactions – to the client, therapy or the supervision session – and works with the supervisee to consider how these reactions might provide valuable clinical information; the supervisee's own experience of therapy and how this relates specifically to client material is identified as important and worthy of exploration.		
D10. Giving feedback	Example:		
Did the supervisor provide an effective balance of positive feedback as well as constructive criticism?	The supervisor works with the supervisee to rate segments of a particular session on the CTS-R.		
Was feedback given with tact and sensitivity? Did feedback demonstrate responsiveness to diversity?	The supervisor provides feedback on an entire therapy session (live or a recording) using the CTS-R or some other rating of competence.		
Did the supervisor offer specific suggestions as to what the supervisee might have done differently?	The supervisor facilitates experiential skills practice of a new technique in the session and then combines positive and constructively critical feedback, with specific recommendations on how practice could be improved.		
Was the balance of positive and critical feedback, as well as any suggestions for improvement, appropriate to the developmental stage of the supervisee?			

SES Item	Examples of this in the supervision session	Score	Comments
D11. Relationship Was there evidence that a good supervisory relationship had been established? Are the 'core conditions' in evidence in the supervisor's manner of relating? Are any interpersonal issues, including ruptures in the therapeutic relationship, effectively managed? Is the supervisor able to adjust their method of intervention and style of relating to accommodate the supervisee's own style, approach to learning and use of supervision?	Example: The supervisor was able to collaborate with the supervisee to reflect on the supervisory relationship and how their experience of this may shed light on the supervision question, provide novel challenges or open up new avenues of exploration. The supervisor uses humour appropriately to lighten supervisee anxiety. Supervisee cognitions, emotions and behaviours are elicited and used effectively to explore a dilemma in supervision or in the work with the client. The supervisor models 'good enough' practice (for example, through demonstrating a specific intervention and being open to constructive criticism from the supervisee).		
D12. Pacing and timing Does the supervisor manage the session well to ensure that the aims of the session are adequately met? Or, if this is not possible, is a plan of action put in place to ensure that key items are reviewed at a later date? Is the ending well managed such that there is a natural, logical conclusion to the supervision session?	Example: The session is well managed in terms of overall pacing. The supervision session allows for pauses in conversation to accommodate reflection on what is being discussed. This might be evidenced in the supervisor recommending a pause to consider what is being discussed, use of capsule summaries to review new learning or to capitalize on emerging insights, or other interventions that lend an unhurried 'feel' to the supervision session. Any interventions used are appropriate to the overall aims of the session and are well timed. Total score:		

Assessor's comments:

General:

_____
_____
_____
_____
_____
_____

Areas of specific strength demonstrated in the session:

_____
_____
_____
_____
_____

Areas for potential development based on the session:

_____
_____
_____
_____
_____
_____

If the submission did not achieve a pass mark, were there any challenges in this session that would appear to warrant particular note and which may have contributed to a lower grade being awarded?   Y   N

If yes, what were these?

_____

_____

_____

_____

_____

APPENDIX 12

Recommendations for Case Study 12

In this case study the primary purpose was to help you to think about your own CPD and we have suggested ways to do so. We also asked you to consider how you might advise Patrick and Nina based on knowledge of their casework.

Patrick's needs

Throughout the book, we have seen examples of Patrick being keen to do the right thing but at times becoming defensive when challenged. In this situation he tends to take a stand on his own position rather than explore the other's point of view. On several occasions we have seen a need for him to collaborate more. A mentor to support him at this stage of his development has been suggested.

Looking at his casework we might help him reflect upon:

1. How he 'Prepares'

For example, in case study 1 with Jen, the issue 'is he best placed to support?' was raised. He needed to have spent more time in the Preparation stage thinking about how to set up the working alliance. We saw Patrick's tendency to become defensive when challenged rather than seeing Jen's reactions as valuable feedback. This could come across as failing to value the other's position.

These issues were further elaborated in case study 2 with Ben. Patrick clearly wanted to support Ben and the service in which he operates, but had not sufficiently thought through the context for the work.

2. How he 'Undertakes'

An issue arose in case study 6 with Leanne where there was insufficient clarity on the definition of competence. Patrick also appeared to lack confidence in giving feedback. Greater familiarity with both competence models and methods for giving feedback would be helpful to him. Possibilities might be to spend more time using the range of competence tools available (referenced in the text). He perhaps could also spend some time setting up opportunities to create 'safe to fail' experiments on giving feedback using tools such as CORBS.

3. How he 'Refines'

The work Patrick undertook with Seiko raised issues about how he had set up the contract initially – there were clearly gaps that, based on their past relationship, should have been addressed. Each came with assumptions which were neither explored nor tested. However, we also saw in Patrick a tendency to blame Seiko when things started to go wrong, with his attributing the cause to her 'rigidity'. He struggled with the issue of power and needed to consider his own role in setting up difficulties. A similar issue was raised in his work with Jason where he quickly labelled Jason's resistance as 'narcissistic' rather than seeing it as feedback. A mentor was suggested to help him deal with his own reactions and de-escalate the potential rupture. There is perhaps an opportunity for Patrick to begin to use tools such as OCRE to explore specific reactions in his case work and build into his CPD plan opportunities to get feedback on specific patterns in his behaviour.

4. How he 'Enhances'

Case study 10, working with Moses, encapsulates the range of difficulties that can emerge if the Preparation, Undertaking and Refinement of the work are not attended to fully. Patrick was faced with a dilemma of how to support Moses without directing him to a solution at the same time as dealing with his responsibilities to the client, Moses and the service setting. Reflection on this case would enable Patrick to enhance his practice on each of these issues and to be sure he pays attention to his own needs as part of his CPD Plan.

Nina's needs

We have seen examples of Nina getting into some bad habits. She has shown that she can deal with complex material and is dedicated to supervision. Nonetheless, her experience has led her on several occasions to be less than careful with the basics in terms of how she sets up supervision contracts.

Looking at her casework, we might help her reflect upon:

1. How she 'Prepares'

An issue arose in case study 3 with Jas where there was insufficient clarity on the definition of what was included in the contract. Assumptions were made by Nina that did not sufficiently take account of the fact that Jas was new to this process; his assumptions needed to be fully explored. A similar issue arose in case study 7 in the supervision group, where matters were allowed to drift to the point where supervision became unsafe. Helping her to reflect on the basics of brand, context and contract might be difficult given Nina's experience. Nonetheless, with experience come shortcuts. Since she is committed to supervision, recognizing when her shortcuts need to be challenged would be helpful.

2. How she 'Undertakes'

In case study 4 we saw how Nina needed to pay attention to the ongoing relationships. Issues of sensitivity to the emotional climate in the group and how to monitor the ongoing psychological safety of the supervisees were raised. This issue was also featured in case study 5 with Sandra. The dual relationship was not sufficiently explored in the preparation and attention to how she assessed Sandra's work and the development of the ongoing relationship became problematic.

3. How she 'Refines'

Case studies 4 and 5 raised questions about how Nina seeks to refine the work as it progresses. Issues of power in case study 5 and resistance and potential rupture in case study 7 were important points for reflection.

4. How she 'Enhances'

Case study 11 with Patrick encapsulates Nina's need to be really clear about how she contracts with her supervisees. Setting this work up carefully would be central to ensuring an effective arrangement for the future.

A useful approach for Nina across all the cases would be to set up opportunities to undertake a STAR analysis of her casework. In particular, she could usefully pay attention to *how* issues emerge, not just *what* emerges. It seems that problems can emerge in her work because she is not sufficiently prepared and it would be important for Nina to understand this tendency in order to avoid drift. This might enable her to enhance her practice as well as ensure appropriate self-care and the care of her supervisees.

References

Abeles, N. and Ettenhofer, M. (2008) 'Supervising novice geropsychologists', in A.K. Hess, K.D. Hess and T.H. Hess (eds), *Psychotherapy Supervision: Theory, Research and Practice*. Hoboken, NJ: Wiley. pp. 299–312.

Anderson, H. and Goolishian, H. (1992) 'The client is the expert: A not-knowing approach to therapy', in S. McNamee and K.J. Gergen (eds), *Constructing Therapy: Social Construction and the Therapeutic Process*. London: Sage. pp. 25–39.

Arcinue, F. (2002) The Development and Validation of the Group Supervision Scale. Unpublished dissertation. University of South California.

Barber, J.P., Liese, B.S. and Abrams, M.J. (2003) 'Development of the cognitive therapy adherence and competence scale', *Psychotherapy Research*, 13(2): 205–21.

Barnes, K.L. (2002) Development and Initial Validation of a Measure of Counselor Supervisor Self-Efficacy. Unpublished dissertation. Syracuse University.

Barnett, J.E., Cornish, J.A.E., Goodyear, R.K. and Lichtenberg, J.W. (2007) 'Commentaries on the ethical and effective practice of clinical supervision', *Professional Psychology: Research & Practice*, 38: 268–75.

Beinart, H. (2004) 'Models of supervision and the supervisory relationship', in I. Fleming and L. Steen (eds), *Supervision and Clinical Psychology*. Hove, East Sussex: Brunner-Routledge. pp. 47–62.

Bennett-Levy, J. (2006) 'Therapist skills: A cognitive model of their acquisition and refinement', *Behavioural and Cognitive Psychotherapy*, 34: 57–78.

Bennett-Levy, J. and Beedie, A. (2007) 'The ups and downs of cognitive therapy training: What happens to trainees' perception of their competence during a cognitive therapy training course?', *Behavioural and Cognitive Psychotherapy*, 35: 61–75. DOI:10.1017/S1352465806003110.

Bennett-Levy, J. and Thwaites, R. (2007) 'Self and self-reflection in the therapeutic relationship', in P. Gilbert and R.L. Leahy (eds), *The Therapeutic Relationship in the Cognitive Behavioral Psychotherapies*. Hove, East Sussex: Routledge, pp. 255–81.

Bennett-Levy, J., Thwaites, R., Chaddock, A. and Davis, M. (2009) 'Reflective practice in cognitive behavioural therapy: The engine of lifelong learning', in J. Stedmon and R. Dallos (eds), *Reflective Practice in Psychotherapy and Counselling*. Maidenhead, Berkshire: Open University Press. pp. 115–35.

Bentovim, A. (1992) *Trauma-Organized Systems: Physical and Sexual Abuse in Families*. London: Karnac Books.

Bernard, J.N. and Goodyear, R.K. (2014) *Fundamentals of Clinical Supervision* (5th edn). Upper Saddle River, NJ: Pearson.

Beutler, L.E. and Bergan, J. (1991) 'Value change in counselling and psychotherapy: A search for scientific credibility', *Journal of Counseling Psychology*, 38: 16–24.

Birch, J. and Corrie, S. (2014) 'Standing out from the crowd: What's your USP?', *Coaching Today*, 10: 6–11.

Blackburn, I.M., James, I.A., Milne, D.L., Baker, C., Standart, S., Garland, A. and Reichelt, K. (2001) 'The revised cognitive therapy scale (CTS-R): Psychometric properties', *Behavioural and Cognitive Psychotherapy*, 29: 431–46.

Bloom, S.L. (2011) 'Trauma-organised systems and parallel process', in N. Tehrani (ed.), *Managing Trauma in the Workplace*. Hove, East Sussex: London: Routledge. pp. 139–53.

Bolitho v City and Hackney Health Authority (1997) 4 All ER 771 [1997] 3 WLR 1151 ('Bolitho') (www.publications.parliament.uk/pa/ld199798/ldjudgmt/jd971113/boli01.htm).

Bordin, E.S. (1979) 'The generalizability of the psychodynamic concept of the working alliance', *Psychotherapy: Theory, Research, and Practice*, 16: 252–60.

Bordin, E.S. (1983) 'A working alliance model of supervision', *The Counseling Psychologist*, 11: 35–42.

Bradford, M. and Aquino, K. (1999) 'The effects of blame attributions and offender likableness on forgiveness and revenge in the workplace', *Journal of Management*, 25: 607–31.

British Association for Behavioural & Cognitive Psychotherapies (2010) Standards of Conduct Performance and Ethics (www.babcp.com/files/About/BABCP-Standards-of-Conduct-Performance-and-Ethics.pdf).

Brown, B. and Brooks, L. (1991) *Career Counseling Techniques*. Needham Heights, MA: Allyn & Bacon.

Bryant, A. and Kazan, A. (2013) *Self-Leadership: How to Become a More Successful, Efficient and Effective Leader from the Inside Out*. New York: McGraw-Hill.

Buckman, J.R. and Barker, C. (2010) 'Therapeutic orientation preference in trainee clinical psychologists: Personality or training?', *Psychotherapy Research*, 20: 247–58.

Burke, W., Goodyear, R.K. and Guzzardo, C. (1998) 'A multiple-case study of weakenings and repairs in supervisory alliances', *American Journal of Psychotherapy*, 52: 450-62.

Careers Advisory Service, University of Bath (2013) Interview and Assessment Centres Guide (www.bath.ac.uk/careers/development/interviewsassesscentres.pdf).

Carroll, M. (1996) *Counselling Supervision: Theories, Skills and Practice*. London: Cassell.

Carroll, M. and Shaw, E. (2012) *Ethical Maturity in the Helping Professions: Making Difficult Life and Work Decisions*. London: Jessica Kingsley.

Ciarrochi, J.V. and Bailey, A. (2008) *A CBT Practitioner's Guide to ACT*. Oakland, CA: New Harbinger.

Cohen, B. (1987) 'The ethics of social work supervision revisited', *Social Work*, 32(3): 194–6.

Copeland, S. (1998) 'Counselling supervision in organisational contexts', *British Journal of Guidance and Counselling*, 26(3): 377–86.

Copeland, S. (2006) 'Counselling supervision in organisations: Are you ready to expand your horizons?', *Counselling at Work*, 51: 2–4.

Corrie, S. (2003) 'Keynote Paper: Information, innovation and the quest for legitimate knowledge', *Counselling Psychology Review*, 18(3): 5–13.

Corrie, S. (2009) *The Art of Inspired Living: Coach Yourself with Positive Psychology*. London: Karnac.

Corrie, S. and Lane, D.A. (eds) (2010) *Constructing Stories, Telling Tales: A Guide to Formulation in Applied Psychology*. London: Karnac.

Corrie, S. and Worrell, M. (2012) The Supervisor Evaluation Scale. Unpublished instrument. Available from sarah.corrie@nhs.net.

Davidson, K., Scott, J., Schmidt, U., Tata, P., Thornton, S. and Tyrer, P. (2004) 'Therapist competence and clinical outcome in the Prevention of Parasuicide by Manual Assisted Cognitive Behaviour Therapy Trial: The POPMACT study', *Psychological Medicine: A Journal of Research in Psychiatry and the Allied Sciences*, 34(5): 855–63.

Department of Health (2008) *IAPT Implementation Plan: National Guidelines for Regional Delivery*. London: Department of Health (www.iapt.nhs.uk).

Department of Health (2011) *No Health without Mental Health: A Cross-Government Mental Health Outcomes Strategy for People of All Ages*. London: Department of Health.

Doehrman, M. (1976) 'Parallel processes in supervision and psychotherapy', *Bulletin of the Menninger Clinic*, 40: 3–104.

Drake, D.B. (2008) 'Finding our way home: Coaching's search for identity in a new era', *Coaching: An International Journal of Theory, Research and Practice*, 1(1): 15–26.

Drake, D.B. (2009) 'Evidence is a verb: A relational approach to knowledge and mastery in coaching', *International Journal of Evidence Based Coaching and Mentoring*, 7(1): 1–12.

Drake, D.B. (2011) 'What do coaches need to know? Using the Mastery Window to assess and develop expertise', *Coaching: An International Journal of Theory, Research and Practice*, 4(2): 138–55.

Dreyfus, H.L. and Dreyfus, S.E. (1986) *Mind over Machine*. New York: Free Press.

Dryden, W. and Feltham, C. (1992) *Psychotherapy and its Discontents*. Buckingham: Open University Press.

Dudley, R. and Kuyken, W. (2014) 'Case formulation in cognitive behavioural therapy: A principle-driven approach', in L. Johnson and R. Dallos (eds), *Formulation in Psychology and Psychotherapy: Making Sense of Peoples Problems*. Hove, East Sussex: Routledge. pp. 18–44.

Efstation, J.F., Patton, M.J. and Kardash, C.M. (1990) 'Measuring the working alliance in counselor supervision', *Journal of Counseling Psychology*, 37: 322–9.

Epstein, R.M. (2006) 'Mindful practice and the tacit ethics of the moment', in N. Kenny and W. Shelton (eds), *Lost Virtue: Professional Character Development and Medical Education*. Oxford: Elsevier. pp. 115–44.

Falender, C.A., Cornish, J.A., Goodyear, R., Hatcher, R., Kaslow, N.J., Leventhal, G., Shafranske, E., Sigmon, S.T., Stoltenberg, C. and Grus, C. (2004) 'Defining competencies in psychology supervision: A consensus statement', *Journal of Clinical Psychology*, 60(7): 771–85.

Falender, C.A. and Shafranske, E.P. (2004) *Clinical Supervision: A Competency-Based Approach*. Washington, DC: American Psychological Association.

Falender, C.A. and Shafranske, E.P. (2012) 'The importance of competency-based clinical supervision and training in the twenty-first century: Why bother?', *Journal of Contemporary Psychotherapy*, 42: 129–37.

Figley, C.F. (1995) 'Compassion fatigue as secondary traumatic stress disorder: An overview', in C.F. Figley (ed.), *Compassion Fatigue: Coping with Secondary Traumatic Stress Disorder in Those Who Treat the Traumatized*. New York: Brunner/Mazel. pp. 1–20.

Freeston, M., Armstrong, P., Twaddle, V. et al. (2003) Supervision: Integrating Practical Skills with a Conceptual Framework. Unpublished document. Newcastle upon Tyne: Newcastle Cognitive and Behavioural Therapies Centre.

Freiheit, S.R. and Overholser, J.C. (1997) 'Training issues in cognitive-behavioral psychotherapy', *Journal of Behavior Therapy and Experimental Psychiatry*, 28: 79–86.

French, J.R.P. and Raven, B. (1959) 'The bases of social power', in D. Cartwright (ed.), *Studies in Social Power*. Ann Arbor, MI: Institute for Social Research. pp. 150–67.

Friedberg, R.D., Gorman, A.A. and Beidel, D.C. (2009) 'Training psychologists for Cognitive-behavioral therapy in the raw world', *Behavior Modification*, 33(1): 104–23.

Friedlander, M., Keller, K.E., Peca-Baker, T.A. and Olk, M.E. (1986) 'The effects of role conflicts on counsellor trainees' self-statements, anxiety levels and performance', *Journal of Counselling Psychology*, 33: 73–7.

Friedlander, M.L. and Ward, L.G. (1984) 'Development and validation of the Supervisory Styles Inventory', *Journal of Counseling Psychology*, 31(4): 541–57.

Gale, C. and Shröder, T. (2014) 'Experiences of self-practice/self-reflection in cognitive behavioural therapy: A meta-synthesis of qualitative studies', *Psychology and Psychotherapy: Theory, Research and Practice.* DOI:10.1111/papt.12026.

Gambrill, E. (2005) *Critical Thinking in Clinical Practice* (2nd edn). Hoboken, NJ: Wiley.

Gambrill, E. (2007) 'Transparency as the route to evidence-informed professional education', *Research on Social Work Practice*, 17(5): 553–60.

Garrett, M.T., Borders, L.D., Crutchfield, L.B., Torres-Rivera, E., Brotherton, D. and Curtis, R. (2001) 'Multicultural supervision: A paradigm of cultural responsiveness for supervisors', *Journal of Multicultural Counseling and Development*, 29(2): 147–58.

Geller, J.D., Farber, B.A. and Schaffer, C.E. (2010) 'Representations of the supervisory dialogue and the development of psychotherapists', *Psychotherapy: Theory, Research, & Practice*, 47: 211–20.

Gergen, K.J. (2001) 'Relational process for ethical outcomes', *Journal of Systemic Therapies*, 20(4): 7–10.

Gilbert, M. and Evans, K. (2000) *Psychotherapy Supervision: An Integrative-Relational Approach.* Maidenhead, Berkshire: Open University Press.

Gilbert, P. (2007) 'Evolved minds and compassion in the therapeutic relationship', in P. Gilbert and R.L. Leahy (eds), *The Therapeutic Relationship in the Cognitive Behavioural Psychotherapies.* Hove, East Sussex: Routledge. pp. 106–42.

Gilbert, P. and Leahy, R.L. (eds) (2007) *The Therapeutic Relationship in the Cognitive Behavioural Psychotherapies.* Hove, East Sussex: Routledge.

Gillick v West Norfolk and Wisbech Area Health Authority (1985) *Gillick Competency and Fraser Guidelines* (www.nspcc.org.uk/Inform/research/briefings/gillick_wda101615.html).

Glover, G., Webb, M. and Evison, F. (2010) Improving Access to Psychological Therapies: A Review of the Progress made by Sites in the First Roll-Out Year (www.iapt.nhs.uk/silo/files/iapt-a-review-of-the-progress-made-by-sites-in-the-first-roll8208-out-year.pdf).

Goldfried, M.R. and Davison, G.C. (1994) *Clinical Behavior Therapy.* Hoboken, NJ: Wiley.

Gordon, P.K. (2012) 'Ten steps to cognitive behavioural supervision', *The Cognitive Behaviour Therapist*, 1–12.

Gosling, P. (2010) 'Every child does matter: Preventing school exclusion through the Common Assessment Framework', in S. Corrie and D.A. Lane (eds), *Constructing Stories Telling Tales: A Guide to Formulation in Applied Psychology.* London: Karnac. pp. 173–98.

Gray, D. and Jackson, P. (2011) 'Coaching supervision in the historical context of psychotherapeutic and counselling models: A meta-model', in T. Bachkirova, P. Jackson and D. Clutterbuck (eds), *Coaching and Mentoring Supervision: Theory and Practice.* Maidenhead, Berkshire: Open University Press, pp. 15–27.

Greenberger, D. and Padesky, C.A. (1995) *Mind over Mood*. New York: Guilford Press.

Greenwald, M. and Young, J. (1998) 'Schema-focused therapy: An integrative approach to psychotherapy supervision', *Journal of Cognitive Psychotherapy*, 12: 109–26.

Griffiths, S., Foster, J., Steen, S. and Pietroni, P. (2013) *Centre for Psychological Therapies in Primary Care Report No. 1 – Mental Health's Market Experiment: Commissioning Psychological Therapies Through Any Qualified Provider*. Chester: University of Chester.

Guest, G. (2000) 'Coaching and mentoring in learning organizations', Conference Paper TEND United Arab Emirates, 8–10 April.

Haddock, G., Devane, S., Bradshaw, T., McGovern, J., Tarrier, N., Kinderman, P., Baguley, I., Lancashire, S. and Harris, N. (2001) 'An investigation into the psychometric properties of the Cognitive Therapy Scale for Psychosis (CTS-Psy)', *Behavioural and Cognitive Psychotherapy*, 29(2): 221–33.

Hammersley, M. (1996) 'The relationship between quantitative and qualitative research: Paradigm loyalty versus methodological eclecticism', in J.T.E. Richardson (ed.), *Handbook of Qualitative Research Methods for Psychology and the Social Sciences*. Leicester: British Psychological Society. pp. 159–74.

Harper, G. and Chitty, C. (2005) *The Impact of Corrections on Re-Offending: A Review of 'What Works'*,. Home Office Research Study 291. London: Home Office Research Development and Statistics Directorate.

Hatcher, R.L. and Lassiter, K.D. (2007) 'Initial training in professional psychology: The practicum competencies outline', *Training & Education in Professional Psychology*, 1: 49–63.

Hawkins, P. and Shohet, R. (2012) *Supervision in the Helping Professions* (4th edn). Maidenhead, Berkshire: Open University Press.

Hawkins, P. and Smith, N. (2006) *Coaching, Mentoring and Organizational Consultancy: Supervision and Development*. Maidenhead, Berkshire: Open University Press.

Hayes, S.C. (2004) 'Acceptance and commitment therapy, relational frame theory, and the third wave of behavioral and cognitive therapies', *Behavior Therapy*, 35: 639–65.

Hayes, S.C., Strosahl, K.D. and Wilson, K.G. (1999) *Acceptance and Commitment Therapy: An Experiential Approach to Behaviour Change*. New York: Guilford Press.

Hayes, W.A. (1991) 'Radical Black Psychology', in R.L. Jones (ed.), *Black Psychology* (3rd edn). New York: Harper Row. pp. 65–78.

Heid, L. (1997) 'Supervisor development across the professional lifespan', *The Clinical Supervisor*, 16: 139–52.

Hersted, L. and Gergen, K.J. (2012) *Relational Leading: Practices for Dialogically Based Collaboration*. Chagrin Falls, OH: Taos Institute.

Hess, A.K. (2008) 'Psychotherapy supervision: A conceptual review', in A.K. Hess, K.D. Hess and T.H. Hess (eds), *Psychotherapy Supervision: Theory, Research and Practice*. Hoboken, NJ: Wiley. pp. 3–22.

Hess, A.K., Hess, C.E. and Hess, J.E. (2008) 'Interpersonal approaches to psychotherapy supervision: A Vygotskiian perspective', in A.K. Hess, K.D. Hess and T.H. Hess (eds), *Psychotherapy Supervision: Theory, Research, and Practice* (2nd edn). Hoboken, NJ: Wiley. pp. 157–76.

Hess, S.A., Knox, S., Schultz, J.M., Hill, C.E., Sloan, L., Brandt, S., Kelley, F. and Hoffman, M.A. (2008) 'Predoctoral interns' nondisclosure in supervision', *Psychotherapy Research*, 18: 400–11.

Hinderliter, A.C. (2010) 'Defining paraphilia: Excluding exclusion', *Open Access Journal of Forensic Psychology*, 2: 241–72.

Hobson, A.J. (2012) 'Fostering face-to-face mentoring and coaching', in S. Fletcher and C. Mullen (eds), *The SAGE Handbook of Mentoring and Coaching in Education*. London: Sage. pp. 59–73.

Hoffman, M.A., Hill, C.E., Holmes, S.E. and Freitas, G.F. (2005) 'Supervisor perspective on the process and outcome of giving easy, difficult, or no feedback to supervisees', *Journal of Counseling Psychology*, 52: 3–13.

Holloway, E.L. (1995) *Clinical Supervision: A Systems Approach*. Thousand Oaks, CA: Sage.

Holloway, E.L. and Neufeldt, S.A. (1995) 'Supervision: Its contributions to treatment efficacy', *Journal of Consulting and Clinical Psychology*, 63: 207–13.

International Union of Psychological Science (2008) Universal Declaration of Ethical Principles for Psychologists (www.am.org/iupsys/resources/ethics/univdecl2008.pdf).

Jackson, C.G. (1977) 'The emergence of a black perspective in counseling', *Journal of Negro Education*, 46: 230–53.

James, I.A., Blackburn, I.M., Milne, D. and Freeston, M. (2004) Supervision Training and Assessment Rating Scale for Cognitive Therapy (STARS-CT). Unpublished dissertation. University of Newcastle upon Tyne.

James, I.J., Milne, D., Blackburn, I.M. and Armstrong, P. (2006) 'Conducting successful supervision: Novel elements towards an integrative approach', *Behavioural and Cognitive Psychotherapy*, 35: 191–200.

Jaworski, A. and Coupland, N. (1999) *The Discourse Reader*. New York: Routledge.

Kadushin, A. (1992) *Supervision in Social Work* (3rd edn). New York: Columbia University Press.

Kagan, C.M. and Duggan, K. (2011) 'Creating community cohesion: The power of using innovative methods to facilitate engagement and genuine partnership', *Social Policy and Society*, 10(3): 393–404.

Katzow, A.W. and Safran, J.D. (2007) 'Recognizing and resolving ruptures in the therapeutic alliance', in P. Gilbert and R.L. Leahy (eds), *The Therapeutic Relationship in the Cognitive Behavioural Psychotherapies*. Hove, East Sussex: Routledge. pp. 90–105.

Kelly, S. (2006) 'Cognitive-behavioral therapy with African Americans', in P.A. Hays and G.Y. Iwamasa (eds), *Culturally Responsive Cognitive-Behavioral Therapy: Assessment, Practice, and Supervision*. Washington, DC: American Psychological Association. pp. 97–116.

Kennerley, H. and Clohessy, S. (2010) 'Becoming a supervisor', in M. Mueller, H. Kennerley, F. McManus and D. Westbrook (eds), *The Oxford Guide to Surviving as a CBT Therapist*. Oxford: Oxford University Press. pp. 323–70.

Kimmerling, R.E., Zeiss, A.M. and Zeiss, R.A. (2000) 'Therapist emotional responses to patients: Building a learning-based language', *Cognitive and Behavioral Practice*, 7: 312–21.

Kline, N. (1999) *Time to Think: Listening to Ignite the Human Mind*. London: Ward Lock, Cassell Illustrated.

Kolb, D.A. (1984) *Experiential Learning*. Englewood Cliffs, NJ: Prentice-Hall.

Korinek, A.W. and Kimball, T.G. (2003) 'Managing and resolving conflict in the supervisory system', *Contemporary Family Therapy*, 25: 295–310.

Kozlowska, K., Nunn, K. and Cousins, P. (1997) 'Adverse experiences in psychiatric training. Part II', *Australian & New Zealand Journal of Psychiatry*, 31: 641–52.

Krasner, L. and Ullmann, L.P. (1973) *Behavior Influence and Personality: The Social Matrix of Human Action.* New York: Holt, Rinehart and Winston.

Kuyken, W. and Tsivrikos, D. (2009) 'Therapist competence, comorbidity and cognitive-behavioural therapy for depression', *Psychotherapy and Psychosomatics,* 78(1): 42–8.

Ladany, N., Ellis, M.V. and Friedlander, M.L. (1999) 'The supervisory working alliance, trainee self-efficacy, and satisfaction', *Journal of Counseling & Development,* 77: 447–55.

Ladany, N., Hill, C.E., Corbett, M.M. and Nutt, E.A. (1996) 'Nature, extent, and importance of what psychotherapy trainees do not disclose to their supervisors', *Journal of Counseling Psychology,* 43: 10–24.

Ladany, N., Lehrman-Waterman, D., Molinaro, M. and Wolgast, B. (1999) 'Psychotherapy supervisor ethical practices: Adherence to guidelines, the supervisory working alliance, and supervisee satisfaction', *The Counseling Psychologist,* 27(3): 443–75.

Ladany, N., Constantine, M.G., Miller, K., Erickson, C.D. and Muse-Burke, J.L. (2000) 'Supervisor countertransference: A qualitative investigation into its identification and description', *Journal of Counseling Psychology,* 47: 102–15.

Lambert, M.J. and Ogles, B.M. (1997) 'The effectiveness of psychotherapy supervision', in C.E. Watkins (ed.), *Handbook of Psychotherapy Supervision.* New York: Wiley. pp. 421–46.

Lambeth Commission (2004) The Windsor Report (http://anglicancommunion.org/windsor2004/index.cfm).

Lane, D.A. (1983) *Models for Analysis of Uncertainty.* London: Professional Development Foundation.

Lane, D.A. (1990) *The Impossible Child.* Stoke-on-Trent, Staffordshire: Trentham.

Lane, D.A. (1994) *Professional Development Relationships: A Benchmarking Study.* London: Professional Development Foundation and Accenture.

Lane, D.A. (2011) 'Ethics and professional standards in supervision', in T. Bachkirova, P. Jackson and D. Clutterbuck (eds), *Coaching and Mentoring Supervision: Theory and Practice.* Maidenhead, Berkshire: Open University Press. pp. 91–104.

Lane, D.A. and Corrie, S. (2006) *The Modern Scientist-Practitioner: A Guide to Practice in Psychology.* Hove, East Sussex: Routledge.

Lane, D.A. and Corrie, S. (2012) *Making Successful Decisions in Counselling and Psychotherapy: A Practical Guide.* Maidenhead, Berkshire: Open University Press.

Lane, D.A., Stelter, R. and Stout Rostron, S. (2010) 'The future of coaching as a profession', in E. Cox, T. Bachkirova and D. Clutterbuck (eds), *The Complete Handbook of Coaching.* London: Sage. pp. 357–68.

Larson, L.M. (1998) 'The social cognitive model of counsellor training', *The Counseling Psychology,* 26: 219–73.

Leahy, R.L. (2001) *Overcoming Resistance in Cognitive Therapy.* New York: Guilford Press.

Leahy, R.L. (2007) 'Schematic mismatch in the therapeutic relationship: A social-cognitive model', in P. Gilbert and R.L. Leahy (eds), *The Therapeutic Relationship in the Cognitive Behavioural Psychotherapies.* Hove, East Sussex: Routledge. pp. 229–54.

Lehrman-Waterman, D. and Ladany, D. (2001) 'Development and validation of the evaluation process within supervision inventory', *Journal of Counseling Psychology,* 48(2): 168–77.

Lesser, R.M. (1983) 'Supervision: Illusions, anxieties, and questions', *Contemporary Psychoanalysis,* 19: 120–29.

Lewis, K. (2012) 'Is there a profession of CBT therapists?', *CBT Today, Accreditation Supplement, October 2012*. Bury, Lancashire: British Association for Behavioural & Cognitive Psychotherapies.

Liese, B.S. and Beck, J.S. (1997) 'Cognitive therapy supervision', in C.E. Watkins (ed.), *Handbook of Psychotherapy Supervision*. New York: Wiley. pp. 114–33.

Liu, J., Kwan, H.K., Wu, L.-Z. and Wu, W. (2010) 'Abusive supervision and subordinate supervisor-directed deviance: The moderating role of traditional values and the mediating role of revenge cognitions', *Journal of Occupational and Organizational Psychology*, 83: 835–56.

Lo, M.-C.M. (2005) 'Professions: Prodigal daughter of modernity', in J. Adams, E.S. Clemens and A.S. Orloff (eds), *Remaking Modernity: Politics, Processes and History in Sociology*. Durham, NC: Duke University Press. pp. 381–406.

Loganbill, C., Hardy, E. and Delworth, U. (1982) 'Supervision: A conceptual model', *The Counseling Psychologist*, 10: 3–42.

Long, K. (2011) 'The self in supervision', in T. Bachkirova, P. Jackson and D. Clutterbuck (eds), *Coaching and Mentoring Supervision: Theory and Practice*. Maidenhead, Berkshire: Open University Press, pp. 78–90.

Lower, R.B. (1972) 'Countertransference resistances in the supervisory relationship', *American Journal of Psychiatry*, 129: 156–60.

Luepker, E.T. (2003) *Record Keeping in Psychotherapy and Counseling: Protecting Confidentiality and the Professional Relationship*. Hove, East Sussex: Brunner-Routledge.

Lunt, I. (2006) 'Foreword', in D.A. Lane and S. Corrie (eds), *The Modern Scientist-Practitioner: A Guide to Practice in Psychology*. Hove, East Sussex: Routledge. pp. xiii–xiv.

MacIntyre, A.C. (1998) *A Short History of Ethics: A History of Moral Philosophy from the Homeric Age to the Twentieth Century* (2nd edn). Notre Dame, IN: University of Notre Dame Press.

Martell, C.R., Addis, M.E. and Jacobson, N.S. (2001) *Depression in Context: Strategies for Guided Action*. New York: W.W. Norton.

Martin, I. and Levey, A.B. (1987) 'Knowledge, action and control', in H.J. Eysenck and I. Martin (eds), *Theoretical Foundations of Behavior Therapy*. London: Plenum. pp. 133–51.

McCarthy Veach, P., Yoon, E., Miranda, C., MacFarlane, I.M., Ergun, D. and Tuicomepee, A. (2012) 'Clinical supervisor value conflicts: Low-frequency, but high-impact events', *The Clinical Supervisor*, 31: 203–27.

McClelland, L. (2014) 'Reformulating the impact of social inequalities: Power and social justice', in L. Johnstone and R. Dallos (eds), *Formulation in Psychology and Psychotherapy: Making Sense of People's Problems*. London: Routledge. pp. 121–44.

McHugh, R.K. and Barlow, D.H. (2010) 'The dissemination and implementation of evidence-based psychological treatments: A review of current efforts', *American Psychologist*, 65(2): 73–84.

McNab, S. (2011) 'One disaster after another: Building resilience in the trauma therapist and the role of supervision', in N. Tehrani (ed.), *Managing Trauma in the Workplace*. London: Routledge. pp. 282–97.

McNicoll, A. (2008) The Power of Peer Coaching (http://nzli.co.nz/file/Conference/Presentations/the-power-of-peer-coaching-tools-for-effective-leadership-coaching-groups.pdf).

Mead, D.E. (1990) *Effective Supervision: A Task-Oriented Model for the Mental Health Professions*. New York: Brunner/Mazel.

Mehr, K.E., Ladany, N. and Caskie, G.I.L. (2010) 'Trainee nondisclosure in supervision: What are they not telling you?', *Counselling and Psychotherapy Research*, 10: 103–13.

Meichenbaum, D. (1977) *Cognitive-Behavior Modification*. New York: Plenum Press.

Milioni, D. (2007) 'Oh, Jo! You can't see that real life is not like riding a horse!': Clients' constructions of power and metaphor in therapy', *Radical Psychology*, 6(1). (www.radicalpsychology.org/vol6-1/milioni.htm).

Miller, G.E. (1990) 'The assessment of clinical skills/competence/perfor mance', *Academic Medicine, September Supplement: Invited Reviews*, 65(9): S63–7.

Milne, D. (2009) *Evidence-Based Clinical Supervision: Principles and Practice*. Chichester, West Sussex: BPS Blackwell.

Milne, D.L. and James, I.A. (2002) 'The observed impact of training on competence in clinical supervision', *British Journal of Clinical Psychology*, 41(1): 55–72.

Milne, D.L., Reiser, R.P. and Raine, R. (2011) 'SAGE: Preliminary evaluation of an instrument for observing competence in CBT supervision', *The Cognitive Behaviour Therapist*, 4: 123–38. DOI:10.1017/S1754470X11000079.

Miranda, R. and Andersen, S.M. (2007) 'The therapeutic relationship: Implications from social cognition and transference', in P. Gilbert and R.L. Leahy (eds), *The Therapeutic Relationship in the Cognitive Behavioural Psychotherapies*. Hove, East Sussex: Routledge. pp. 63–89.

Mohan, J. (1996) 'Accounts of the NHS reforms: Macro-, meso- and micro-level perspectives', *Sociology of Health and Illness*, 18: 675–98.

Moskowitz, D.S. (2009) 'Coming full circle: Conceptualizing the study of interpersonal behaviour', *Canadian Psychology*, 50: 33–41.

Mpofu, M. (2014) Change2Choose. Summary Report on the Pilot Programme on Undiagnosed Posttraumatic Stress Distress in Inner City Youth Exposed to Street and Domestic Violence in Birmingham, England 2014. Unpublished document.

Murphy, M.J. and Wright, D.W. (2005) 'Supervisees' perspectives of power use in supervision', *Journal of Marital and Family Therapy*, 31(3): 283–95.

Muse, K. and McManus, F. (2013) 'A systematic review of methods for assessing competence in cognitive-behavioural therapy', *Clinical Psychology Review*, 33: 484–99.

Muse-Burke, J. and Tyson, A. (2010) Supervisee Needs Index. Unpublished instrument.

Nadelson, C. and Notman, M. (1977) 'Psychotherapy supervision: The problem of conflicting values', *American Journal of Psychotherapy*, 31: 275–83.

Nelson, M.L., Barnes, K.L., Evans, A.L. and Triggiano, P.J. (2008) 'Working with conflict in clinical supervision: Wise supervisors' perspectives', *Journal of Counseling Psychology*, 55: 172–84.

Nelson, M.L. and Friedlander, M.L. (2001) 'A close look at conflictual supervisory relationships: The trainee's perspective', *Journal of Counseling Psychology*, 48: 384–95.

Nelson, M.L., Gray, L.A., Friedlander, M.L., Ladany, N. and Walker, J.A. (2001) 'Toward relationship-centered supervision. Reply to Veach (2001) and Ellis (2001)', *Journal of Counseling Psychology*, 48: 407–9.

Olatunji, B.O., Deacon, B.J. and Abramowitz, J.S. (2009) 'The cruelest cure? Ethical issues in the implementation of exposure-based treatments', *Cognitive and Behavioral Practice*, 16: 172–80.

Olk, M. and Friedlander, M.L. (1992) 'Trainees' experiences of role conflict and role ambiguity in supervisory relationships', *Journal of Counseling Psychology*, 39: 389–97.

Osborn, C.J. and Davis, T.E. (1996) 'The supervision contract: Making it perfectly clear', *The Clinical Supervisor*, 14(2): 121–34.

Padesky, C.A. (1996) 'Developing cognitive therapist competency: Teaching and supervision models', in P.M. Salkovskis (ed.), *Frontiers of Cognitive Therapy*. New York: Guilford Press. pp. 266–92.

Patton, M.J. and Kivlighan, D.M. (1997) 'Relevance of the supervisory alliance to the counseling alliance and to treatment adherence in counselor training', *Journal of Counseling Psychology*, 44: 108–15.

Pope, K.S. and Vasquez, M.J.T. (2011) *Ethics in Psychotherapy and Counselling: A Practical Guide*. Hoboken, NJ: Wiley.

Porter, N. and Vasquez, M. (1997) 'Covision: Feminist supervision, process, and collaboration', in J. Worell and N.G. Johnson (eds), *Shaping the Future of Feminist Psychology*. Washington, DC: American Psychological Association. pp. 155–71.

Prasko, J. and Vyskocilova, J. (2010) 'Countertransference during supervision in cognitive behavioral therapy', *Activitas Nervosa Superior Rediviva*, 52(4): 253–62.

Proctor, B. (1988) 'A cooperative exercise in accountability', in M. Marken and M. Payne (eds), *Enabling and Ensuring*. Leicester: Leicester National Youth Bureau and Council for Education and Training in Youth and Community Work. pp. 21–34.

Proctor, B. and Inskipp, F. (1988) *Skills for Supervising and Being Supervised*. Sussex: Alexia Publications.

Proctor, B. and Inskipp, F. (2001) 'Group supervision', in J. Scaife (ed.), *Supervision in the Mental Health Professions: A Practitioner's Guide*. Hove, East Sussex: Brunner-Routledge. pp. 99–121.

Proctor, G. (2008) 'CBT: The obscuring of power in the name of science', *European Journal of Psychotherapy and Counselling*, 10(3): 231–45.

Psychological Testing Centre (2012) Design Implementation and Evaluation of Assessment and Development Centres: Best Practice Guidelines Leicester: British Psychological Society (www1.lsbu.ac.uk/osdt/materials/BPSGuidelines.pdf).

Quarto, C.J. (2002) 'Supervisors' and supervisees' perceptions of control and conflict in counselling supervision', *The Clinical Supervisor*, 21: 21–37.

Rachlin, H. (1976) *Behavior and Learning*. San Francisco: W.H. Freeman.

Rajan, A., Eupen, P. van, Chapple, K. and Lane, D.A. (2000) *Employability: Bridging the Gap between Rhetoric and Reality: First Report: Employers' Perspective*. Tonbridge: Create/PDF/CIPD.

Reiser, R.P. and Milne, D. (2012) 'Supervising cognitive-behavioral psychotherapy: Pressing needs, impressing possibilities', *Journal of Contemporary Psychotherapy*, 42: 161–71.

Robertson, I. (2012) *The Winner Effect: How Power Affects Your Brain*. London: Bloomsbury.

Robiner, W.N., Fuhrman, M. and Ristevedt, S. (1993) 'Evaluation difficulties in supervising psychology interns', *The Clinical Psychologist*, 46: 3–13.

Rokeach, M. (1973) *The Nature of Human Values*. New York: Free Press.

Ross, L.E., Doctor, F., Dimito, A., Kueli, D. and Armstrong, M.S. (2008) 'Can talking about oppression reduce depression?', *Journal of Gay & Lesbian Social Services*, 19(1): 1–15.

Ross, M.W. and Rosser, B.R. (1996) 'Measurement and correlates of internalized homophobia: A factor analytic study', *Journal of Clinical Psychology*, 52: 15–21.

Roth, A.D. and Pilling, S. (2007) *The Competences Required to Deliver Effective Cognitive and Behavioural Therapy for People with Depression and with Anxiety Disorders*. London: Department of Health (www.ucl.ac.uk/CORE).

Roth, A.D. and Pilling, S. (2008a) The Competence Framework for Supervision. (www.ucl.ac.uk/clinical-psychology/CORE/supervision_framework.htm).

Roth, A.D. and Pilling, S. (2008b) 'Using an evidence-based methodology to identify the competences required to deliver effective cognitive and behavioural therapy for depression and anxiety disorders', *Behavioural and Cognitive Psychotherapy*, 36(2): 129–47.

Rudd, M.D. and Joiner, T. (1997) 'Countertransference and the therapeutic relationship: A cognitive perspective', *Journal of Cognitive Psychotherapy: An International Quarterly*, 11(4): 231–51.

Russell, R.K. and Petrie, T. (1994) 'Issues in training effective supervisors', *Applied & Preventive Psychology*, 3: 27–42.

Safran, J.D. (1990a) 'Towards a refinement of cognitive therapy in the light of interpersonal theory: I. Theory', *Clinical Psychology Review*, 10: 87–105.

Safran, J.D. (1990b) 'Towards a refinement of cognitive therapy in the light of interpersonal theory: II. Practice', *Clinical Psychology Review*, 10: 107–21.

Safran, J.D. and Muran, J.C. (2000) *Negotiating the Therapeutic Alliance: A Relational Treatment Guide*. New York: Guilford Press.

Scaife, J. (2001) *Supervising the Reflective Practitioner: An Essential Guide to Theory and Practice*. Hove, East Sussex: Routledge.

Schein, E.H. (1997) The Concept of Client from a Process Consultation Perspective: A Guide for Change Agents (http://dspace.mit.edu/bitstream/handle/1721.1/2647/SWP-3946-36987393.pdf?sequence = 1).

Schön, D. (1983) *The Reflective Practitioner: How Professionals Think in Action*. San Francisco: Jossey-Bass.

Schwartz, S.H. (1992) 'Universals in the content and structure of values: Theoretical advances and empirical tests in 20 countries', *Advances in Experimental Social Psychology*, 25: 1–65.

Seegers, J.L.L. (1989) 'Assessment centres for identifying long-term potential for self-development', in P. Heriot (ed.), *Assessment and Selection in Organisations: Methods and Practice for Recruitment and Appraisal*. Chichester, West Sussex: Wiley. pp. 745–71.

Shohet, R. (2012) 'Listening to resistance', in D. Owen and R. Shohet (eds), *Clinical Supervision in the Medical Profession*. Maidenhead: Open University Press. pp. 143–56.

Stern, E., Lane, D.A. and McDevitt, C. (1994) *Europe in Change: The Contribution of Counselling*. Rugby: European Association for Counselling.

Stober, D.R. and Grant, A.M. (2006) 'Introduction', in D.R. Stober and A.M. Grant (eds), *Evidence-Based Coaching Handbook*. New York: Wiley. pp. 1–14.

Stoltenberg, C. (1981) 'Approaching supervision from a developmental perspective: The counsellor-complexity model', *Journal of Counseling Psychology*, 28: 59–65.

Stoltenberg, C. and Delworth, U. (1987) *Supervising Counselors and Therapists*. San Francisco: Jossey-Bass.

Stoltenberg, C.D. and McNeill, B. (2010) *IDM supervision: An Integrative Developmental Model for Supervising Counsellors and Therapists*. New York: Routledge.

Stoltenberg, C.D., McNeill, B.W. and Delworth, U. (1998) *IDM Supervision: An Integrative Developmental Model for Supervising Counselors & Therapists* (3rd edn). New York: Routledge.

Strunk, D.R., Brotman, M.A., DeRubeis, R.J. and Hollon, S.D. (2010) 'Therapist competence in cognitive therapy for depression: Predicting subsequent symptom change', *Journal of Consulting and Clinical Psychology*, 78(3): 429–37.

Sutter, E., McPherson, R.H. and Geeseman, R. (2002) 'Contracting for supervision', *Professional Psychology: Research and Practice*, 33(5): 495–8.

Talen, M.R. and Schindler, N. (1993) 'Goal-directed supervision plans: A model for trainee supervision and evaluation', *Clinical Supervisor*, 11(2): 77–88.

Tannenbaum, R. and Schmidt, W.H. (1973) 'How to choose a leadership pattern', *Harvard Business Review*, May–June: 3–12.

Tehrani, N. (2011a) *Managing Trauma in the Workplace*. Hove, East Sussex: Routledge.

Tehrani, N. (2011b) Dancing with the Devil. Presentation for Metropolitan Police Covert Internet Investigators, 27 September.

Tehrani, N., Osborne, D. and Lane, D.A. (2012) 'Restoring meaning and wholeness: The role for coaching after a trauma', *International Coaching Psychology Review*, 7(2): 239–46.

Tharp, R. and Gallimore, R. (2002) 'Teaching as the assistance of performance', in A. Pollard (ed.), *Readings for Reflective Teaching*. London: Continuum, pp. 256–9.

Thomas, J.T. (2007) 'Informed consent through contracting for supervision: Minimizing risks, enhancing benefits', *Professional Psychology: Research and Practice*, 38: 221–31.

Thwaites, R., Bennett-Levy, J., Davis, M. and Chaddock, A. (2014) 'Using self-practice and self-reflection (SP/SR) to enhance CBT competence and metacompetence', in A. Whittington and N. Grey (eds), *How to Become a More Effective CBT Therapist: Mastering Metacompetence in Clinical Practice*. London: Wiley-Blackwell. pp. 241–54.

Townend, M., Iannetta, L.E. and Freeston, M. (2002) 'Clinical supervision in practice: A survey of UK cognitive behavioural psychotherapists accredited by BABCP', *Behavioural and Cognitive Psychotherapy*, 30: 485–500.

Tracey, T.J., Ellickson, J.L. and Sherry, P. (1989) 'Reactance in relation to different supervisory environments and counsellor development', *Journal of Counseling Psychology*, 36: 336–44.

Undrill, G. (2012) 'Incidental supervision', in D. Owen and R. Shohet (eds), *Clinical Supervision in the Medical Profession*. Maidenhead, Berkshire: Open University Press. pp. 62–72.

Vinten, G. and Lane, D.A. (2003) 'Integrating survivors in redundancies', *Euro Asia Journal of Management*, 13(1): 41–54.

Voigt, C. (2008) The Role of General Principles of International Law and their Relationship to Treaty Law (www.retfaerd.org/gamle_pdf/2008/2/Retfaerd_121_2008_2_s3_25.pdf).

Vygotsky, L.S. (1978) 'Interaction between learning and development', in M. Cole, V. John-Steiner, S. Scribner and E. Souberman (eds), *Mind in Society: The Development of Higher Psychological Processes*. Cambridge, MA: Harvard University Press. pp. 79–91.

Watts, R.J. (2004) 'Integrating social justice and psychology', *The Counseling Psychologist*, 32(6): 855–65. DOI:10.1177/0011000004269274.

Watzalwick, P. and Beavin, J. (1976) 'Some formal aspects of communication', in P. Watzalwick and J.H. Weakland (eds), *The Interactional View*. New York: W.W. Norton. pp. 56–67.

Westbrook, D., Kennerley, H. and Kirk, J. (2012) *An Introduction to Cognitive Behaviour Therapy: Skills and Applications* (2nd edn). London: Sage.

Wheelahan, L. (2007) 'How competency-based training locks the working class out of powerful knowledge: A modified Bernsteinian analysis', *British Journal of Sociology of Education*, 28(5): 637–51.

Williams, A. (1995) *Visual and Active Supervision: Roles, Focus, Technique*. New York: W.W. Norton.

Worthen, V. and McNeill, B.W. (1996) 'A phenomenological investigation of 'good' supervision events', *Journal of Counseling Psychology*, 43: 25–34.

Wulf, J. and Nelson, M.L. (2000) 'Experienced psychologists' recollections of internship supervision and its contributions to their development', *The Clinical Supervisor*, 19: 123–45.

Index

Tables and Figures are indicated by page numbers in **bold**.